T0113144

"With its vivid and riveting 'thick' description of the social, spiritual, and creative genius of Ballroom culture, Tucker's book is an essential read for those who want to gain deeper knowledge and appreciation for these Black and Latinx LGBTQ communities."

—MARLON M. BAILEY, author of *Butch Queens Up in Pumps: Gender, Performance, and Ballroom Culture in Detroit*

"A powerful debut that captures the soul of New York's vogue, house, and Ballroom community while serving as a historical archive of the Black queer and trans narrative in the United States. An instant classic that deftly champions and solidifies vogue, house, and ball culture as radical activism, art, freedom, and refuge for Black trans women and others. Tucker enlightens with sharp critical analysis and a vulnerability that is compelling and full of love. This is a must-read of the utmost urgency."

—KEISHA BUSH, author of *No Heaven for Good Boys*

"*And the Category Is . . .* is a deep dive into the beauty of Ballroom culture and a chronicle of Ricky Tucker's life as a queer North Carolina native. It's that last part that makes this book so wonderful. Tucker's observations are reverent and always careful. He shows us the many ways in which ball culture is a space of care and healing, of mutual aid and familial bonds. He's dazzled by the glamor of Ballroom but willing to explore the politics and difficulties that come with creating art in a highly gendered and racialized space. Tucker helps us understand the work that goes into producing balls and protecting ball culture, as well as the performances of race, class, gender, and sexuality that hold the scene together. This is a beautiful celebration of embodiment and an original, timely contribution to the study of one of NYC's most vibrant queer scenes."

—DIANA CAGE, author of the Lambda Award–winning *Lesbian Sex Bible*

"This book honors the legacy of Ballroom culture and its members without deifying either; yet the reader gets remarkable insight into the real-life struggles of Black and brown queer folk who undergird the fierce and extravagant beauty that is Ballroom—where a Ballroom member can symbolically and literally snatch their freedom. Through prose that pops, dips, and kicks off the page and with an analysis that reads the children for filth who commodify queerness and Blackness, Ricky Tucker's *And the Category Is . . .* is snatched for the gods! Tens across the board!"

—E. PATRICK JOHNSON, author of *Honeypot: Black Southern Women Who Love Women*

"The Reading Room is open, *And the Category Is . . .* is a must-read for anyone interested in pop culture. Ricky Tucker explores how Ballroom's language, fashion, and family structure have permeated pop culture for decades. He takes us beyond the watered-down, sanitized version we see in corporate ad campaigns and on TV shows to give us *the* history, the Black, queer, often marginalized origins of our culture. From the 1930s Harlem Ballroom scenes, with prizes less than $50, to the international balls of today, held across the globe with thousands of dollars at stake, this is the definitive book on Ballroom's legacy. Once you read this, the category is *closed.*"

—BEVY SMITH, media personality and author of *Bevelations: Lessons from a Mutha, Auntie, Bestie*

"*And the Category Is . . .* is an electrifying book about ball culture. Through interviews, archival research, personal narration, and cultural criticism, Tucker offers another glimpse into a well-known but often misunderstood community. Readers will come away with a sense of the amazing lives, which are led even under considerable constraint, as the ball reveals itself to be a space to make relationships, politics, and freedom in performance. In *And the Category Is . . .* , Tucker shows us how the ball can teach us how to live more fabulous Black, brown, queer, and trans lives!"

—C. RILEY SNORTON, author of *Black on Both Sides: A Racial History of Trans Identity*

"With mainstream interest in Ballroom culture at an all-time high, Ricky Tucker's *And the Category Is . . .* is a treasure trove of insider perspective—deeply respectful, full of critique and celebration, oral history and personal narrative. A little bit academic, a lot of wisdom, and glamour, yes, of course, and context. This work is, like Ballroom itself, a crucial piece of queer history and contemporary queer culture."

—MICHELLE TEA, author of *Against Memoir* and *Black Wave*

"A long overdue exploration of a community that reveals the humanity, challenges, and significance of a scene that has been both marginalized and mainstreamed throughout history but never included in our libraries. Our histories are worth remembering, and this is an important read for the preservation of our culture and the legacy of those who paved the way. I give this book my tens for capturing the spirit of Ballroom and keeping it grounded with love as the message."

—EMANUEL XAVIER, activist and author of *Christ Like*

AND
THE
CATEGORY
IS...

AND THE CATEGORY IS...

INSIDE NEW YORK'S VOGUE, HOUSE, AND BALLROOM COMMUNITY

RICKY TUCKER

BEACON PRESS
BOSTON

BEACON PRESS
Boston, Massachusetts
www.beacon.org

Beacon Press books
are published under the auspices of
the Unitarian Universalist Association of Congregations.

25 24 23 22   8 7 6 5 4 3 2 1

This book is printed on acid-free paper that meets the uncoated paper
ANSI/NISO specifications for permanence as revised in 1992.

Text design and composition by Kim Arney

Some names and identifying characteristics of people mentioned
in this work have been changed to protect their identities.

Library of Congress Cataloging-in-Publication Data

Name: Tucker, Ricky, author.
Title: And the category is . . . : inside New York's vogue, house, and ballroom
    community / Ricky Tucker.
Description: Boston : Beacon Press, 2021. | Includes bibliographical references.
Identifiers: LCCN 2021019362 (print) | LCCN 2021019363 (ebook) |
    ISBN 9780807007327 (paperback) | ISBN 9780807003497 (ebook)
Subjects: LCSH: Drag balls—New York (State)—New York—History. |
    New York (N.Y.)—Social life and customs.
Classification: LCC GV1749.5 .T83 2021 (print) | LCC GV1749.5 (ebook) |
    DDC 793.3/8097471—dc23
LC record available at https://lccn.loc.gov/2021019362
LC ebook record available at https://lccn.loc.gov/2021019363

For those pushed to the margins
who delight in the pushback.

. . . .

And to Heidi. Told you so.

CONTENTS

EQUAL PARTS SUGAR AND SHADE

As far back as I can remember, Ballroom has been in my periphery. Without even having to really search for it, its cultural touchpoints lay out before me over the years like a giant constellation, waiting for me to play connect the dots. It's been one of my greatest joys.

From the moment Madonna's hit song "Vogue" was released, to the wig-snatching revelation of *Paris Is Burning*, to the world-changing finality of that mouse click that registered me for the first Vogue'ology course taught at the New School, I was academically, personally, and professionally bolstered by every engagement with this smart, innovative, loving, and *funny* community and century-old culture that today is still, to me, like no other in the world.

After our course had ended in fall 2011, I kept up with my newfound Ballroom family, which now included an array of some of our country's most agile and fierce dancers, activists, scholars, mothers, fathers, sons, and daughters, united under one cause: freedom. Unfortunately, only being an amateur dancer, whose most prominent talents are writing and teaching, I had never been quite sure how to contribute to the community that nurtured me for the greater part of a decade. At thirty years old, when I came into contact with Ballroom, I was a little over the hill to start walking balls. I'd never even joined a house, though I may have been able to vie for honorary membership by way of our co-instructor Michael Roberson, then father of the House of Garçon. I could even argue that my cohort of fellow students that made up the first Vogue'ology class are our own house of co-conspirators dedicated to upholding the fidelity of this rich arts community. In fact, I am arguing that. We are a family.

Still, after attending a decade of balls, workshops, and protocols on ball culture, showing up to every lecture, panel, and exhibition I could, and even teaching a few voguing workshops myself, I continued to be at a loss as to how such a great debt could ever be paid. It was an awkward waltz I performed in my mind over and over again, praying I wasn't appropriating the culture, and not shallowly leaning on my being the right demographic—Black and gay—as an automatic ticket to entry. In spite of those doubts, I continued to show up with only the greatest of intentions, to be of service wherever and in whatever way I could.

Then, in 2016, along with my beloved Vogue'ology instructors Robert Sember and Michael Roberson, I joined 400 Years of Inequality, a crack team of activist scholars working all over the globe, many based at the New School, all dedicated to dismantling America's centuries-old ecology of inequality. I was senior writer for the New School's in-house ad firm at the time, so my capacity at 400 Years was to sit on the organizing committee and help get the word out about this worthwhile, radically progressive initiative. I'd say we accomplished this in our time there, but more than anything, our coalition became a family, checking in, eating together, announcing and applauding each other's personal and professional achievements. I felt so fortunate to be a part of two collectives where freedom was the mandate. Then, on October 25, 2018, Michael sent out the following email to our family:

Michael Roberson
Oct 25, 2018, 12:32 PM

GOD morning Great Ones

How are you all? I hope this email finds you all well and in the Greatest Spirits. I wish I could be there. I am co-curating with the Icon Pony Zion part of BRIC's 40th anniversary Gala (https://www.bricartsmedia.org). I will also include Icons such as Jose Xtravaganza (Madonna dancer), Icon Jack Mizrahi, Icon Sinia Braxton, Icon Dawan Milan, Icon Prince Miyake-Mugler, and the one and only Icon Tyra A. Ross aka Dominique Jackson (Elecktra Abundance on Pose). Event is at the Brooklyn Navy Yard. Also, Robert, Dean Yvette Wilson-Barnes (Union Theological Seminary) and I are co-organizing the event for Reimagine, Thursday November 1st at Union

Theological Seminary, 7pm-9pm. It's entitled "Ballroom has something to say about Death and Dying." It's free of course and it would be lovely to have you all there. The link is below.

Remain A Blessing
Michael[1]

I didn't miss a beat, replying only three minutes later:

Ricky
Oct 25, 2018, 12:35 PM

Yessss. So many amazing events. I'm marking my calendar![2]

To which he replied:

Michael Roberson
Oct 25, 2018, 12:37 PM

OMG!!!! Is this my Beloved Ricky Tucker that is sending this email out!!!!!!
HEYYYYYYY U!!!![3]

Then:

Ricky
Oct 25, 2018, 12:38 PM

Yes, it is, Father—all day. Love ya tons![4]

And finally, about two weeks later, from Roísín Davis, another friend, 400YOI colleague, and literary agent to me:

Roísín Davis
Nov 6, 2018, 5:53 PM

Was just looking at this thread. I would love to help publish a book on the House/ Ballroom scene and politics—if you or Robert have any ideas, I'm in![5]

And there it was, my chance to give back to Ballroom, a community that had given me so much.

I was over the moon about the opportunity. It felt like kismet, evidenced by the fact that it had come together so organically, that from the beginning all I'd ever done was follow and express my love for ball culture and the people in it. This occurred independent of any professional ambition and had everything to do with an ongoing adoration and curiosity. Frankly, the way it unfolded was a bit of a relief, knowing that instead of a navel-gazing collection of essays about my upbringing or love for weirdo art, my first book would be an act of service. A love letter.

Once I got the "okay to proceed" from my two greatest mentors in the community, house father and theological scholar Michael Roberson, and artist, professor, and public health scholar Robert Sember, I needed some rules for engaging my readers and the Ballroom community, the latter audience being the one I cared about most. I needed to know explicitly what the service I was providing was going to be.

Some of that road map I wrote along the way, often ambling my way across Ballroom's rugged, artistically rich terrain, only to then be halted for months at a time at a new categorical shoreline, not knowing exactly how I was meant to proceed intellectually, desperately awaiting the next life raft in the form of a cultural practice I'd overlooked, a work of art, or an interview providing a fresh lens through which to view the community. Talking to Robert and Michael intermittently knocked my line of inquiry back into focus as they practically reside on the front lines of all things Ballroom. Pretty soon, I had guidelines for what this book was going to be, much of that dictated by what I knew it sure as hell wasn't going to be.

So. First off, this book is not the end-all-be-all historical bible on all things Ballroom. With its unencumbering word count, and my being a normal human at the mercy of time itself, there's no way that this book, or any book for that matter, could ever claim to be the *law* on Ballroom, a paradoxical, mind-altering subculture. No. Instead, this book is a compendium of voices, personal narratives, and critiques, a cobbled-together pastiche of prose used to paint an impressionistic view of Ballroom in its current incarnation, which is always in flux. It does, however, stand out from previous books on the matter, I hope, in its core use of art criticism as proof point, its narrative baseline, and its intimacy with its subjects, including myself. To that end, the gracious folks who allowed me to interview them within these pages were part of my ball culture friends-and-family network, and therefore are all of a particular range of ages and personal experiences that could never be considered *the* definition of Ballroom. They are activists, artists, Black and brown, men and women, professionals, and loved ones bound by a global culture, particularly here in New York City, where Ballroom was founded. Because of these specificities, this book cannot be everything to everyone. Luckily, I would dare never make an attempt to write such a book.

This book is not an ethnography, and I am not an anthropologist or a journalist. A lifelong love of art and oral history drives my work in all genres, and it was important to me in this space to both get out of the way of the illuminating narratives of the folks who make up the house-ball system, letting them speak for themselves and only stepping in to provide context—and to heavily implicate myself. Trust is earned, and being the vessel through which a story about Ballroom is told alone isn't enough of an offering to warrant trust. Perhaps my decade of showing up as a friend of the community was a start, but I felt I still needed to risk something myself. An offering. So, as you will see ahead, though I play archivist throughout the book, as if answering the question I've asked every "subject" over these last few years, "How did you find Ballroom?," my journey to and through this subculture is very much notated here.

Despite the name and flashy cover, I am sad to inform you that this book isn't some confectionary morsel of entertainment, like a glad rag or an episode of *Behind the Music* that claims to voyeuristically "pull back the curtain" on Ballroom, one of the world's most unique and precious cultural resources. Nor is it investigative journalism. There are no big reveals or gotchas, only a blueprint for the marginalized to find artistic, personal, and professional grounding in a groundless world. It is an observance of struggle and an offering of freedom.

So, then what is *And the Category Is . . . ?*

Well, once the ink dried on the book contract, Robert Sember came to me with two mandates with which I concurred. The first was that the book be unapologetically Black, to which I replied, how dare you—and no problem. The second was that it be an indictment of capitalism, a system at the root of American slavery and the only seeable justification for the centuries of marginalization of the LGBTQ BIPOC lives that make up ball culture. Not only did I accept Robert's terms, but I internalized them, making them the driving force behind the book, that last term aligning me with a sense of purpose, regularly sending an affirming cold blue bolt of lightning down my spine every time I felt like I'd even come close to the vicinity of achieving it. That being said, this book is a radical act.

But I've also been referring to it as the spoonful of sugar that helps the medicine go down. I teach writing, and in every workshop I've ever facilitated, I've outwardly maintained that if you as a writer are bored, then your audience will be bored. With that in mind, I followed every fantastical and mentally enriching path that laid before me, and because of that, this book was a joy to write, and consequently, I hope it will be a joy to read. At the same time, central to that joy lies the process of learning something substantial about a culture and arts collective that you maybe only knew a trifling bit of information about, a family that has influenced other cultures far and wide, both high and low art, queer and straight people, men and women, young and old for over a century until this very day. Ballroom is every paradox, and I hope that you take delight in diving into the following conundrums and find answers to some of your own within. To this last point about paradoxes, it is my wish that my love letter to Ballroom also provides a thought-provoking space where it is okay to question Ballroom, where the community gets it right as a family, as a subculture, and where there is room to love more and own more of its own story in the wake of mass marginalization and capitalist motives. Like Baldwin said of America, I criticize her because I love her. And so, if I do so within, it is only with the love and affection of a family member who uses inquiry to push our tribe out of finding the will to survive and into a realm where we dare to thrive. So, there you go. Equal parts sugar and shade. Bon appétit.

CHAPTER 1

WERK

w/the Legendary Pony Zion and Benji Hart (Benji Ninja)

*Paris Is Burning, America's Best Dance Crew, Pose,
and Madonna and the art of appropriation*

To know that identity is a construct means being able to find freedom within constraint. It draws back the curtain on our systems of oppression and provides a back door to escape the seemingly indestructible house of white patriarchal hegemony.

And ancient houses are meant to be toppled.

In house-ball culture, we encounter a freedom, a fearlessness, in walking a category: in deconstructing and reinventing oneself in front of a crowd, in running the risk of being chopped, receiving a low score from a panel of shrewd judges, or being told that your dream of a new or even truer identity is half-baked, even daring to lower the reputation and retail value of your house and subsequently answer to your "house mother." Or worse still, of being shamed and "shaded" into oblivion.

The Ballroom community is unabashedly radical in its awareness of the ability to use identity as creatively as a makeup brush, whilst liberated from the gravity of greater social norms and the consequences of defying them: some so heavy—like transphobia—that they could be fatal. This is only one of many paradoxes that Ballroom as a subculture so gorgeously embodies. And for over a century, it has advanced a concept that the mainstream is still grappling with: all things can be many things at once.

A flurry of ostrich feathers fills the frame. They lift, revealing black-and-white, old-Hollywood opulence refreshed for the year 1990.

Synthesized strings suggest that something fabulous this way comes: a very fine Black man in a very fine white suit lifts his right hand and pristine face to the sky. He holds them there, frozen in place, bathing in *all* of the spotlight. To his left sits an easel displaying a Renaissance-like portrait of a voluptuous white woman playing a mandolin. She's looking down and off to the side, as if lamenting the mundanity of her ever-static, two-dimensional existence. If only she could move, then maybe she could strike a chord on her ne'er-used mandolin. Then maybe her music would be worth anyone lending an ear to it.

A stark comparison is struck between the finely suited man and the mandolin lady. Like the painting, the man is motionless, but his current state is filled with potential energy, the kind that at any moment could spring him into kinetic life—and you get the sense it would be magnificent. The painting of the woman, on the other hand, could be worth billions of dollars and end up spending its days gathering dust above a mantle somewhere, or losing relevance yet somehow gaining value in the stark halls of the Museum of Blah Blah Blah.

As the camera pans right, the dichotomies continue.

A young Asian American man strikes a pose, mimicking a form comparable to Eve receiving the apple of knowledge from the snake. A Grecian marble statue of a white woman looms stiffly in the back.

Pan left.

That same ominous statue now photobombs a young, gorgeously suited Latinx man, his impeccable finger-waved hair shimmering in the light.

Dissolve.

A powdered-faced, handsome woman extends an arm forward, her hands casually open like that image of the red-nailed hand holding a rose that is superimposed onto the window of every New York City nail salon. Like the others, the dancer is positioned next to a painting of a doe-eyed Josephine Baker in her prime—short haired and sumptuous, but for some reason reimagined as white. It's crystal clear now that every person who could be qualified as "exotic" or "other" in this tableau is only allowed to exist next to a white woman's body.

A finger snaps. At once, the static but now living "others" spring into action. They ease us into the art of dance with sharp poses that ironically have nothing to do with white Renaissance paintings and more closely resemble both the future and the majestic hieroglyphic angles of ancient Egyptians, an innovative people with a stylistic sensibility centuries ahead of their time.

A dress seemingly made of diamonds drapes down a white woman's back. It's now clear that the bold lighting in this black-and-white music video is meant to enhance her milky complexion. It blows her face out to the point that it's glowing. Blonde ringlets frame her neck. A bored-to-tears Asian American man dressed as a butler dusts off a Roman column. The white woman undulates her back from side-to-side like a python.

The woman is Madonna. The video is "Vogue."

∞

What is Ballroom? First, let's be clear about what it *isn't*. Ballroom is not a single song, movie, catchphrase, TV show, pop star, or "scene." Ballroom, ball culture, or the house-vogue system is part of a thriving arts-based culture founded over a century ago by LGBTQ African American and Latinx people of Harlem.

Rooted deeply in beauty pageants and pageantry—obligatory shade aside—queer, trans, and cis men and women of color compete for trophies, cash prizes, and adoration (victories that elude them in the outside world) at events known as balls. Balls are to be "walked." The categories for walking are varied, but they often bend gender, class, and physical makeup, requiring participants to assume an identity other than that dictated to them by mainstream culture. If identity is a construct, and the world a stage, then Ballroom is the world's Met Gala.

Categories walked at balls include "fem realness" (who is most convincingly female), "butch realness" (most ostensibly heterosexual and male), "voguing" (a feminine dance-based art form and bodily interpretation of life), and "executive realness" (business attire and swagger). The very idea of *realness*, in particular, subverts the collective "reality" we all assume. Balls allow the poor to be rich, the masc to be fem (and celebrated), and the outcast to perform center stage. And whether or not these transformations are fully realized, the stage is always set for liberation.

MTVABDCS04E01

Vogue Evolution's first appearance on MTV's *America's Best Dance Crew* in 2009 portrayed its five members, Dashaun, Devon (aka the legendary

Pony Zion), Malechi, Leiomy, and Jorel, as green and rambunctious—which they were.[1] Years of being chopped and trophied at New York City balls and in their day-to-day lives as LGBTQ people of color propped the dance team up to be fierce contenders for the title of "best dance crew." Yet watching them on this first episode, you get the feeling that nothing could have prepared them, or anyone for that matter, for the juggernaut of a corporate wringer MTV was about to put them through.

But the first reel shows our New York crew in context, on a brownstone stoop on the Chelsea Piers, fingers snapping, limbs stretching and angling like some scene out of *West Side Story*. Their signature color is a royal audacious purple, and they dazzle in it.

Their first words:
> *"Who are we? VOGUE EVOLUTION!"*

Cut to a shot of the dance troupe on the piers, chorus lined up and tipping imaginary hats to the camera.
> *"And where are we from? New York City!"*

Dizzying MTV B-roll from Times Square flashes through the frame.
> *"And what do we do? VOGUE!"*

From the stoop, their heads, hands, and eyes elegantly angle upward to find the light. Pony lays out for us the definition of voguing.
> *"Voguing is made up of different elements. There's hands, spins, dips, and there's duckwalks."*

The music and mood shift to a sentimental tone. Pony says:
> *"We're gay, ya know. We wanna show you that that doesn't matter. We're here to break barriers. We're here to [make] change."*

Malechi follows that thought from the stoop:
> *"We get to show people we're comfortable in our own skin, and also, this is the life that we live."*

Cut to a contemplative shot of Leiomy on the piers:
> *"I'm a transgender woman. I realized I wasn't living a happy life just being the person that society saw me being. I just had to change and the change is actually keeping me happy."*

Ballroom footage begins. Leiomy continues:

> *"We participate in the Ballroom scene. A ball is an underground competition."*

Dashaun's voiceover plays against silhouettes voguing at night:

> *"Categories like runway, then voguing. We gather with different groups and we all compete."*

Pony, confidently:

> *"It's time that America's Best Dance Crew receives something special."*

Prince, sassily:

> *"And something new."*

Prince shakes his shoulders fancifully. The troupe laughs—cut to *ABDC*'s soundstage where the host, an unusually uncomfortable Mario Lopez, introduces Vogue Evolution:

> *"Hu-ho! They got a style alllll their own—but will the judges think they're fabulous? Performing to their own master mix featuring 'Took the Night' by Chelley, here is Vogue Evolution . . ."*

The crowd isn't prepared for Vogue Evolution's breakout performance. Prince cartwheels into the frame, kicking the choreography into motion. Hands are the entrée of the day with every member serving up sharp angles and donning white gloves that draw the eye like a beeline to their hands as they swirl and twirl mini-hurricanes across the stage. From the floor, Leiomy is putting in some werk—her vixen game is crazy. It's plain to see that springing from splits into high jumps is nothing for her and this entire crew. A flagrant mix of hard air-drumming paired with impossibly high kicks convey to the crowd, judges—and other dance troupes—that they'd better find some range in the coming weeks, cuz Vogue Evolution embodies both male and female ends of the spectrum and every nuance in between. An onslaught of sudden deep back dips across the stage reconfigure into duckwalks. The transition—so fresh, so clean. They strike poses on their way into a military Janet Jackson–style lineup of crisp right angles. They all fall back, except for Leiomy, who comes forward to unleash a fierce firestorm of handwork all around her face. They all spin around into simultaneous dips. Shablam! The crowd goes insane. Leiomy flicks her hair flirtatiously.

Someone from the crowd screams, "Work, honey!" They all strike playful and triumphant poses. If they didn't know before, now they know what the fuck voguing is. The last minute was everything—a safe space and time carved out by the Ballroom community on the world's most visible stage.

Enter Mario Lopez:

> "You know what? I like me some Vogue Evolution. Y'all are fearless!"

The crowd still buzzes. Enter the first judge, the ever thirsty Lil Mama, declaring:

> "Tens. Tens! Across the board. When I step out, they all applaud."

The members of Vogue Evolution laugh anxiously and wait for her to finish her try-hard display:

> "You guys are perfect as far as when it comes to a ball. I'm so excited about the ball right now, cuz I'm having my own ball—10/10 [October 10]."

Lil Mama sniffs awkwardly as the crowd is dead silent, then continues:

> "I think you guys are bringing a new element to the show. It's new, it's hot, it's fun. It's interesting, you know what I mean? It's daring, and when I say daring—I dare you to go, I dare you to make it, I dare you to win every-thing . . . because no one would expect a group like yours to be America's Best Dance Crew. Which makes it even harder, but I'm telling you HO-NEY, you gotta bring it!"

The final judge and full-time choreographer Shane Sparks wraps up the comments:

> "Yo, I don't know how I feel right now. . . . I don't know how I feel, cuz y'all just ripped the stage, but I didn't know what to expect."

All of this is code for "y'all are queer and I am not." He then tries to clean it up:

> "Y'all are so committed to what y'all do, and it's about time for this style to be exposed. It's been underground for so long. I was in New York a while ago, and they kept talking about the House of Ninjas, they keep talking about all these styles, and they kept telling me, 'Shane, y'all need to get something like this.' Thank you, y'all here."

∞

I was of a very impressionable age—around twenty-two—when I first watched the 1990 documentary *Paris Is Burning*. Many circumstances conspired, I believe, to bring Jennie Livingston's breakthrough film into my line of vision: Leaving the South for Boston and meeting my first boyfriend, who was also my first art school boyfriend. A liberal exploration of drugs that unlatched years of internal homophobia followed. And then there was the opening of Video Underground in 2004, a Jamaica Plain safe haven for progressive ideas cinematically captured for critical consumption.

It's an understatement to say that *Paris Is Burning* was *everything* to me. Seeing it finally put a name on what I had somehow known existed perhaps through family conversations, run-ins in the city, and pop cultural dots connected over a couple decades of life—BALLROOM. I was finally able to say, "There it is!"

My takeaways from that cult classic are numerous: The dulcet tones of Pepper LaBeija, draped in silk in a lamplit corner, chain-smoking and unravelling the yarn of how she became the next mother of the very first house in Ballroom, the House of LaBeija. The soft-faced, sharp-tongued Venus Xtravaganza, laying out the fine details of how to read someone to filth. Though seemingly made of porcelain, she was actually Teflon, only underscoring the tragedy of her later being found strangled under a bed at the Duchess Hotel in New York City on Christmas Day, 1988. The thrill of learning the categories walked. What it must have been like to have been in those rooms then.

For me, the greatest takeaway came from just being able to listen to Dorian Corey lay out the history of ball culture in such a profoundly elegant way. She was a beauty, an enigma, a force, a historian, a grand dame, and a poet. Hearing her say things like, "You don't have to bend the world. I think it's better just to enjoy it. Pay your dues and enjoy it. If you shoot an arrow and it goes real high, hooray for you,"[2] told me that contrasts like order and chaos and failure and success aren't paradoxical or conflicting; they're one and the same and all around us.

And of course, finding out that the entire time they were filming *Paris Is Burning* there was a vinyl-wrapped, mummified body hidden in Dorian's closet was simply revelatory. Evidently, an intruder, perhaps a former lover, broke into Dorian's home and became violent with her, causing her in turn to shoot him and stuff him into a chest in her closet, adding another captivating level to her narrative. The consequences of homicide for a trans woman would have been, and still are, dire. But also, like a symbol for all of us on the margins of society, what it must have been like to live with that weight. Every. Day. And to still get up and wade through daily routines and major performances, all while looking fabulous? Like I said, she was an enigma, if not a genius at life.

∞

She wears a lot of faces: many of them Black, sometimes Kabuki or Latinx, but rarely her own. For better or worse, her singles are at the very least derivatives of authentic Black music, which nowadays, is deemed good enough to download.

I remember when "Vogue" first came out. I was eight years old, and my mother was in the wood-paneled bathroom of my great-grandmother's North Carolinia home, getting ready to go out with her best friend, Reggie, a gay man. They both had roots in New York and in the South, and were known for being way too fabulous for their immediate podunk surroundings.

We were listening to 102 JAMZ, the Piedmont Triad's local "urban" radio station, when Shep Pettibone's irresistible synths and snaps began to slowly trickle in across the airwaves. Madonna comes in, robotically demanding that we strike poses, followed by that whispered, goosebump-inducing word, "vogue." Mommy and Reggie, at first staring into the brightly lit mirror above the sink, respectively teasing and scrutinizing themselves, turned at once to face each other—now struck with incredulity. They listened intently as I watched on blankly.

"Can you believe this, Trix?" Reg asked. He always called her Trixie. "Do you see what this woman is doing?!" My mom didn't miss a beat. "Yes, honey," she said. "I guess she thinks she's one of the children now."

I tried to remain small, sitting on the corner of the tub as they went on clutching their pearls about how that leech Madonna went and lifted brown gay life right out of the club and plopped it onto the pop charts. I got the feeling from their conversation that maybe most of America didn't exactly deserve or couldn't even comprehend such a gift.

Ultimately, I gleaned the fact that secret, precious events go down in the club during those times when I was at home asleep, never able to see the payoff for Mommy and Reggie's pregame show. As an adult, I later learned that clubs and balls were just as viable a way to come to Jesus as church was. I also figured out that queer Blackness, when fully unleashed, is some kind of mystical, magical commodity sparked from having to constantly laugh in the face of death in the name of life, a rebirth that can never actually be impersonated, like a pigeon that paints itself red and throws on a sandwich board reading "I'm a phoenix. You *must* believe me." Girl, sit down.

Two decades later, in New York City, with *Paris Is Burning* on my mind and in my heart, I registered for the part dance instruction, part theory-focused course "Vogue'ology"—a cerebral and aerobic space that would change my life. There, I was introduced to co-instructors Robert Sember (artist, public health advocate, and cofounder of the Vogue'ology collective), Michael Roberson (theologist, then father of the House of Garçon, and current father of the House of Margiela), the choreographer the legendary Pony Zion (lead member of Vogue Evolution), and vogue instructor Derrick Xtravaganza.

In the course, we learned both vogue technique and ball history, but most importantly, we became a family, something like our own house. We were welcomed into the Ballroom community as allies, joining the fold with a critical/theoretical perspective and an understanding that we should proceed with respect and appreciation for the community—not a desire for appropriation. Trust and mindfulness were front of mind that term, and as Robert Sember once told me in regard to gaining the trust of the Ballroom community: "You have to keep showing up." So, that's exactly what I did.

In that first week, we were required only to absorb a lot of information. Source texts, like Marlon Bailey's rare and stand-alone cultural analysis of Detroit's Ballroom culture, *Butch Queen Up in Pumps*, and the late and powerful José Munoz's breakthrough insight into gender identity and disruption, *Disidentifications: Queers of Color and the Performance of Politics,* stripped away for us any false curtains of gender and class normativity, exposing our cohort to a spectrum of queer experiences. Documentaries like *Paris Is Burning, The Queen* (1968), and other footage from Ballroom performances magnified for us the value of Ballroom and the subsequent marginalization and commodification of its population—including Madonna's live performance of "Vogue," during the 1990 MTV Video Music Awards.

We watched that performance with both rapture and horror as she took the slave/madam of the manor metaphor from the music video and amplified it into a full-on Marie Antoinette scenario, ripe with misdirected class and race cultural codes. It was both aesthetically gorgeous and conceptually horrible. A common prop at balls is folding fans, used to either stoke or keep asunder the flames of fierceness, and Madonna and her two longest-running backup singers, Donna De Lory and Niki Harris (also figures in the music video) use them—and human beings—as props too. The dancer José Xtravaganza is again a focus. He bends down trying to tend to "Madame X" as she lifts her hoop skirt sensually, only to kick his head away. The opulence is stunning, but just like the crass disparities we live with every day, the highs of the rich and privileged only further accentuate the lows of the marginalized majority. Madonna begins the performance by pointing her fan at each of her dancers while demandingly saying "Vogue," again tapping them out of a frozen state into campy, couture animation—as if she is the arbiter of dance.

This pivotal moment in her career wouldn't be the first or the last time Madonna shook one hand with Black culture only to pickpocket it with the other. In videos like "Secret," "Like a Prayer," "Music," and "Human Nature," she mines and plucks from Black culture, commodifying gospel music, pimp paraphernalia, cornrows (and to this day, grills she never seems to put away)—all tropes and symbols meant to couch her in the cutting-edge credibility of Blackness.

That day in class, in the fall of 2011, after watching this performance, Robert and Michael asked us, "What did you see and what did you hear?" We now saw and heard so much: pomp and circumstance, posturing, beauty, commodification, social hierarchy, ambition, an illusion. The contradictions went on and on. That friction continues to burn, and it becomes more and more clear that there is a false narrative of ownership created around ball culture.

∞

To praise a marginalized community like Ballroom for surviving systemic oppression without acknowledging its singular power, through one butch-queen vogue or high-fashion glamour performance, to dismantle gender binaries and class disparity is foolish, or maybe just ignorant. Conversely, to marvel at the wild freedom of voguers like Pony Zion and Leiomy Maldonado for crushing their competition by spinning in slow motion up from the floor to standing and dipping back down again, like real life Neos dodging the matrix bullets, without delving into the hard work, training, self-awareness, and everyday emotional fortitude it takes to do so, reads as a necessarily vapid interpretation. But if anyone could make such a shallow assumption, it would be Karen.

MTVABDCSO4EO2

Beyoncé endorses Vogue Evolution's second performance on *America's Best Dance Crew*, and our team is elated.[3] Through a television monitor wheeled in to their practice space, the Ballroom ambassadors convene with the queen of cool, jumping around and jittering like any group of young people coming "face-to-face" with destiny('s child). She says their name, Vogue Evolution, and it sends bolts of electricity from Beyoncé's screen to their eyes and ears, and then through the computer screen and straight to the heart. It's a stolen, utterly Black moment captured by the corporate media machine but captured nonetheless. Even a broken clock gets it right twice a day. It's a thrilling glimpse of freedom under impossible constraints.

Our queen Bey speaks:

> *"Hello, Vooogue Evolution. Your challenge is to take us all back to the roots of dance and bust a little African flavor."*

You wonder here if Beyoncé understands the ancestry of vogue, if she's aware of the influences already infused into our hopeful Vogue Evolution members by way of the mother continent lineage supreme, Africa; how Nefertiti, Shaka Zulu, Josephine Baker, and Alvin Ailey are lining up on the astral plane as spiritual reinforcement, how they all may as well be on the receiving end of her message—or if she just hopes that all of that would come true. Honestly, she could just be reading a cue card. Beyoncé's awareness can be hard to read at times. Either way, her virtual presence is a vote of confidence for our dance crew, and if any team is able to pull this off, they can.

We leave Beyoncé in the dance space for the soundstage and another one of Mario Lopez's corny intros:

> *"Can they add some African spice to their voguing? Performing to 'Déjà Vu' by Beyoncé, here's Vogue Evolution!"*

Leiomy fucking shines as Sasha Fierce.

In fact, looking at Vogue Evolution's performance, with Leiomy's hair whips, arm circles, sharp angles, and spins while falling back onto a throne made of her dance mates, makes it seem like she's the living embodiment of Beyoncé's alter ego, like the best crack team of MTV scientists finally figured out how to extract the spirit from the #1 pop star and transplant it into another person, Leiomy. You know they would if they could. All this is to say—she slayed. But Vogue Evolution has always been rich in fierceness.

Like an inkblot test, this second round of commentary from the judges begins to really reveal their individual inner workings. JC Chasez tells Leiomy she's a queen and praises Prince's high kicks and the entire group for their democratic use of the stage. It's a fervent declaration of affection for Vogue Evolution's queerness and a stellar demonstration of masculine self-awareness and security. Conversely, Lil Mama's backhanded compliments are demonstrative of her fragile femininity and always fledgling popstar status. Shane Sparks isn't much better. His comment seems to be a postcard mailed in from afar saying, "As a straight Black male choreographer in this world, I like y'all and all, just not *that way*."

Lil Mama:

> *"Y'all brought the energy the show needed tonight, and it took a transgender woman to bring out the femininity in Beyoncé—are you crazy? Leiomy, again, I want to commend you for swinging that hair and not being fearful—you were fearless tonight with that hair, swung it all over the stage. You brought the queen out of me tonight, so I'm wit' it."*

Shane Sparks:

> *"Ever since the show aired, every day someone has said your name. They been like, 'I can't believe she's on the show.' They trippin,' cuz you're like a god in New York or the underworld or wherever you're from. They like love you. And I'm trippin' cuz now I see why. You ripped the stage tonight."*

THE UNDERWORLD OR WHEREVER YOU'RE FROM

So, what did we hear? Well, we heard that transgender femininity should be so qualified as "other" that it's shocking when it is quintessentially female. We learned that Lil Mama assumes or unconsciously infers that trans women can't have long hair, and if they do, it's brave that they even dare twirl it. In any event, it always comes back to herself. And Shane Sparks can't seem to find the words "goddess" or "Ballroom," but instead, favors calling a woman a "god" who came from the "underworld or wherever."

These remarks are called "microaggressions," because they float under the radar. But the detectability of a microaggression is in direct correlation to the wokeness of both the culture at the time and the people in the room.

Take Al Jolson performing blackface on stage in the context of the 1920s. This was considered fine entertainment for a room full of white folks having dinner and doing whatever it was white folks did back then, but put Jolson in the same getup on a stage today at the Apollo, and you can just throw the "micro" part out the window and say with certainty that it was in fact an act of *macro*-aggression—if not a suicide attempt.

∞

Since day one, Madonna has enlisted geniuses of color to help shroud her in edgy otherness. It's always been her calling card. From the very beginning, brown producers like Reggie Lucas, John "Jellybean" Benitez, and Stephen Bray co-signed her co-ethnicity with dazzling music production that targeted Black radio and audiences—mostly by Madonna's design. A 2013 *Rolling Stone* article highlights the corporate whitewashing that marked Madonna's debut.[4] In it, Lucas, the main producer of Madonna's self-titled debut album, is fairly forthcoming about this process of appropriation. He says, "At Warner Brothers, when they first met her—Mo Ostin, Michael Ostin, Lenny Waronker—they said, 'She wants to sing black music, so just have her go promote her singles at the black radio stations.' Which is what she did. But they didn't have a vision of, 'Oh my god, she's going to be an enormous pop star.' Because she expressed an interest in black music, they said, 'Oh! Go sell it to the black people, then.' That's how she was visualized."

Michael Rosenblatt, the executive known for signing seminal acts like Madonna and the B-52's, is a little more candid in his admission of their marketing goals at the time, saying, "You had this girl coming out of the new wave scene doing dance music. I thought if we were able to do it right, we'd be able to capture a lot of audiences. We'd get the new wave kids, we'd get the pop people, and the dance community. We'd be able to get everybody. I didn't want her picture on the cover of the 'Everybody' single, because I thought I could get a lot of R&B play on that record, because a lot of people thought she was black."

∞

I spent the winter evening of December 10, 2016, at the house of the *Paris Is Burning* director, Jennie Livingston, in Brooklyn. I was invited by my friend Shannon, a happy-go-lucky southern girl with that obligatory dark streak running through anyone who spends enough time below the Mason-Dixon. I have it myself. My roommate, Andrew, and Shannon had been finishing up their master's together at the School of Visual Arts in Chelsea, and Shannon had nabbed a gig doing archival and everything-but-the-kitchen-sink kind of work for Livingston. Through a series of drunken vogue showcases I'd lapsed into at some of our parties, a video homework assignment that Andrew had recorded of me doing my morning rooftop routine of modern dance, and voguing, Shannon knew I had at least a toe dipped into ball culture. So when the time came to invite folks to a gathering at her boss's house in the Kensington neighborhood, I immediately came to mind.

Livingston had billed the gathering as a fundraiser/holiday party. For the life of me, I can't remember where these raised funds were meant to go, but basically, I didn't need details to know I definitely needed to be there. I was a poor student and never really intended on buying anything anyway.

But when that winter evening finally arrived, I was feeling a little anxious. It wasn't that I thought I'd be starstruck, though, even for a stone-faced New Yorker, there was an element of that to my reticence. It was more that, just like in the case of Madonna, I felt I'd learned too much in Vogueology about the fallout in the years following the release of *Paris Is Burning*, how Pepper LaBeija, Dorian Corey, Paris Dupree, and the ball community, despite their obvious postproduction canonization, had feelings of abandonment and of being exploited, and experienced a lack of compensation for and ownership of their contributions. What began as Livingston's New York University MA thesis had transformed into a cult sensation, and to the community, that changed everything. And I was especially conflicted because my poker face is complete garbage. If I felt some sort of way while talking to Livingston, it was going to show.

Shannon and I met at her place, not too far from Livingston's home. She and her friend Sally, who also worked for Livingston, were bright and bubbly, having downed some rosé before I arrived. They were nibbling on crackers and hummus, and there was that air of excitement that you only get on winter nights laddering up to the holidays. I tried not to kill it.

"So . . . what's she like?" I asked, because little had been seen or heard from her since the promotional tour for *Paris Is Burning*.

"Jennie? She's nice to work for, but it's a ton of work, and it's random stuff. Archiving film, cleaning, setting up for tonight, stuff like that," Shannon said.

"Cool, cool . . . Who do you think will be there?"

"A few of her friends, neighbors, us." She pointed to the three of us in the room.

"Anyone from Ballroom, you think?"

"No, I don't think so."

That was my in. I did my best to ease us into a conversation about the feelings the houses had about being used, couching it all in the discussions we'd had in class and less in my own personal feelings, though the two had become less of a Venn diagram and more just a circle by that point. I tried to be opaque and rhetorical, praying I wouldn't say anything that would make Shannon or Sally want to retract my invitation.

I figured out that I was on my own, having gathered that they felt the community should be first and foremost grateful for the exposure Livingston had bestowed upon them. Having worked for her in the past few months and been in her home, Shannon and Sally had gleaned that she really hadn't gotten any substantial financial compensation herself for the release of a movie that had up until then only garnered a noteworthy cult following. I suppose the fact that her holiday party was also a low-key (hi-key, really) yard sale was a confirmation of that fact. Anyway, I left that conversation feeling my lone queer Blackness and aware of the duality of all truths and how their contrast can sometimes literally be split into black and white.

I wish I can say I had a profound discourse about the corporate beast with Jennie Livingston that night, but I didn't. Instead, I told her that her little film that could, *did*. I told her that it changed my life, which is true. And I came away with these facts:

1. I don't think she sold many personal items that night.
2. Her look had drastically changed. A once urbane and youthful bob was now a very butch crew cut setting off the severity of her signature cat-eye frames.
3. It was like she was hiding.
4. She makes vegetarian holiday dishes so fulfilling it dawns upon you the next day that you had virtually no meat all night—and you *love* meat.

5. Her friends were a bunch of randos, but whose aren't in New York City?

6. I do in fact think the corporate machine chewed her up a bit. She seemed affected. But that doesn't necessarily mean Ballroom was not adversely (and positively) affected by her film. It's very complicated.

∞

As a nod to the glitz and gold of old Hollywood, Madonna uses the bridge of her song "Vogue" as a parenthetical opportunity to resurrect by name sixteen major stars of yesteryear. It's a compelling roster of original influencers that perfectly paints the image of opulence and austerity she'd intended. Super effective. The only problem is, these people have absolutely nothing to do with vogue, Ballroom, or the Black and Latinx urban experience. A literal whitewash. She starts with a high-watt, high-white list of celebs—Greta Garbo, Marilyn Monroe, Marlene Dietrich, Joe DiMaggio, Marlon Brando, and more—all before claiming there is nothing to doing a gorgeous and acclaimed dance form such as vogue.

Now, in knowing the cultural implications of a list like this, how the use of white names and sensibilities are used as lube for the ears and sensibility of white audiences dying to be penetrated by the Black experience, and knowing that two words paired together are endlessly generative, I could easily be here for all of eternity explaining to you precisely why this list is fucked-up in the context of vogue. But some of this list's infractions are worse than others, and I'd like to point some of them out.

While, yes, Marilyn Monroe is likely one of the most drag-inspiring pop icons out there, with men, women, and Madonna alike platinum-blonding themselves to death and never leaving the house without an eyeline pencil to self-induce a beauty mark above their top lips, Monroe is not Ballroom. Although here, Madonna mistakenly got it sort of right, as drag balls sparked ball culture, and the reverence for Monroe is there. She was busty, ambitious, and died of a melodramatic pill overdose—the girls live for her. To that end, the cross-dressing, original dyke Greta Garbo scratches that same itch. Yet, where Madonna starts to get me wholly fucked-up is her mention a few names later: Joe DiMaggio, a baseball player with no connection to queerness, or Blackness, or dance, or anything. Not even run-of-the-mill glamour. Dropping DiMaggio's name also inserts straight, white, privileged love into the very top of what should be a brown queer list. He and Monroe were married at the peak of their respective careers.

I don't know how privy America was in 1990 to the longstanding rumors about Marlon Brando and James Baldwin's romantic dynamic in the 1960s and '70s, or the corroborated stories of James Dean and Dennis Hopper's intimate moments while roommates during the filming of *Rebel Without a Cause*, but other than these exploits, what in the hell do they have to do with voguing?

It goes on and on. Along with literally propping up two-dimensional white female figures next to fantastically animated, brown queer bodies like those in her music video, Madonna chose to fabricate white hetero connections with vogue and Ballroom, instead of using this section of her single to give homage to the people the artform actually belongs to.

The second season of the TV series *Pose*, a fictional Ballroom narrative very parallel to *Paris Is Burning*, takes place in 1990, the year Madonna lifted vogue from New York's house-Ballroom culture and landed it in Middle America's living room.

To his credit, *Pose* co-creator Ryan Murphy, as well as a host of writers from within the contemporary Ballroom community, decided to take the Madonna contradiction head-on this season, even if the aim of a show like *Pose* is so broad it would be damn near absurd to expect it to hit the crux of the matter squarely on its head. And that's fine. The acclaimed program knows its lane, being one of a few entertainment vehicles to spotlight Ballroom, and grant unprecedented representation to Black and Latinx LGBTQ talent both behind the scenes and in front of the camera. If nothing else, you come away from *Pose* understanding that brown and trans and queer is beautiful. That's huge.

But back to Madonna. It's hard to swallow lines like "Madonna is shining a bright spotlight on us. . . . Everything is changing,"[5] spoken by "House of Evangelista" Mother Blanca, arguably the show's main plot-driving character in its season premiere. First of all, whether that does or does not shake out by the finale, I know the sound of famous last words when I hear them. Call me a pessimist, but I see a shadow to every spotlight. Spoiler: the bottom drops out in the finale, so the writing is a little didactic if not basic at times.

In real life, Madonna plucked several fairer-skinned Latinx men from Ballroom, like the legendary José Xtravaganza, to be dancers for her "Vogue" video, tour, and *Truth or Dare* documentary, a casting choice that pinged the discords of colorism and favoritism across the houses of Ballroom. Some of those same dancers later sued her for invasion of privacy and financial compensation; yet, today they hold no ill will toward the pop icon. They actually seem to miss her, as seen in the *Truth or Dare* follow-up documentary, *Strike a Pose*. In both documentaries, you can tell that they were a family (the House of Blonde Ambition?),´and that even Madonna, a woman who built her career on commodifying Black and brown bodies and culture, was likely well-intended in her role as a major cog in the capitalist machine. I also know that it doesn't matter.

More important than resolving these contradictions are the critical questions raised by Madonna's complex relationship to vogue and Murphy's popularization of Ballroom *poses* (pun intended): How does someone vogue when the dance is rooted in a particular struggle? When have you crossed the line from appreciation to appropriation? And how does the community continue being spotlighted without catching a burn? Again, there are no straightforward answers, but there are directions we can take on our path to awareness—and they should come from *within* the Ballroom community.

Vogue'ology taught us that vogue is not about an external imitation; it's about performing your internal liberation. Pony taught us to think of it as personal storytelling. He put it to me this way: "Voguing is a temple, a space where freedom occupies. *You* author what it is—it's your penmanship, your script. You need not win or lose [at a ball] to know how."[6]

Pose, along with Madonna's "Vogue," elevated the exposure of Ballroom. With that has come an influx of folks who want to either live or absorb that life—and the line between the two is blurry. In a conversation I had with legendary artist and vogue/Ballroom pedagogue Benji Hart, he carved it down to a profoundly fine point, saying, "You can't vogue properly if you can't hold Black, poor, trans, and queer folks in regard. Everybody loves us when we're creating these beautiful, powerful, visceral pieces of art, but what about when we're being harassed on the street? We're fighting for our freedom."

It seems that in the face of this long-awaited mainstream popularity, the community is also calling for a heightened awareness both from its spectators and itself. In order to have a fair exchange, both parties require a new pedagogy. As Robert Sember, educator and my Dumbledore (mainly because he likely has no idea who that is), says, "We see this a lot outside of the Ballroom scene. 'I can give you this if you grace my particular moment with your fabulousness'—that process of co-optation and exploitation. Pedagogy is about building a greater awareness of that complexity. It enables folks to really understand what's happening and how to make decisions at those crucial moments." Awareness is key.

In a 1997 video, *Cultural Criticism & Transformation*, theorist and activist bell hooks suggests that appropriation and misrepresentation in mass media are indeed conscious efforts on the part of those who create said media. For hooks, "Part of the power of cultural criticism and cultural studies has been its sort of political intervention as a force in American society to say, there really is a conscious manipulation of representations and it's not about magical thinking, it's not about like pure imagination, creativity. It's about people consciously knowing what kinds of images will produce a certain kind of impact."[7] She then calls for a new kind of awareness, for new "enlightened witnesses" to these misrepresentations, and says, "The issue is not freeing ourselves from representation. It's really about being enlightened witnesses when we watch representations, which means we are able to be critically vigilant about both what is being told to us and how we respond to what is being told." It seems that on both macro and micro levels, in American society at large and in Ballroom culture in particular, what's required of audiences or "witnesses" moving forward is an awareness of the possibly dire implications of being represented by, caught up in, and spat out of the corporate machine.

MTVABDCS04E04

The time has come for Leiomy, Vogue Evolution's crown and jewel, to be dismantled from her throne. Episode four of *America's Best Dance Crew* is MTV basically dictating that plotline.[8]

Mario Lopez's voiceover sets it up:
"Last week, after repeatedly missing dance practice, Leiomy walked out during dress rehearsal."

Cut to Pony:
"This is our final rehearsal before showtime, and she didn't do the dance. She walked off. We didn't know what happened."

A montage of clips show the team in various states of disappointment and in shades of sepia for seriousness.

Enter Leiomy:

> *"My heart really wants to be here, but in a way, I'm not happy. I miss just being home. But the fact that I have fans out there, you know—I'm the only face of transgender. That's what's actually keeping me on the show—that's what keeps me motivated."*

The screen flashes and fades into the practice space once more where our voguers are told by a placid-looking Indian woman that their challenge this week is the Bollywood style of Rajasthan, a form of Indian scarf dancing that when performed by experts has the power to stop time—and to go on forever when performed by novices. Props have the potential to be slapstick, and the audio and visual evidence of Vogue Evolution's inadequacy plays out in a final montage before their Rajasthani-style performance.

Dashaun:

> *"You can't have no sloppiness whatsoever. If one person messes it up, they mess it up for everyone . . ."*

Leiomy:

> *"These (scarves) hurt my arms."*

Pony:

> *"With Leiomy, every single day its worse than eggshells, like, we're walking on glass. We showed America that we were one, and if Leiomy leaves, I feel like it's not the truth anymore."*

Enter ol' morose Mario:

> *"Uh-oh. Can the voguers rock the Rajasthani without falling apart? Performing to a master mix of 'Calabria 2008,' by Enur, here is Vogue Evolution."*

The group comes out and does its best, their scarves playing a minor role, leaving room for more traditional Bollywood moves that in execution are comparable to Voguing, stark angles dovetailed with waves of androgyny. Watching it, you feel the decline of Vogue Evolution's standing because it seems they sense it too, likely based on the behavior of the judges and production team. It becomes hard to tell whether VE's somewhat staid performance lies in MTV's negative edit (along with Mario's undying weirdness), the awkwardness of scarves as a dance prop, or Leiomy's reticence to move forward, or if everybody is just tired and ready to go home. The answer is probably yes.

Vogue Evolution was eliminated shortly thereafter. The crux of their turbulent journey and arrival on this corporate, Orwellian platform is brutally summed up by the ever-thirsty, loud, and wrong Lil Mama:

> *"Leiomy, c'mon. Your behavior is unacceptable. I just feel that you always have to remember your truth: you were born a man, and you're becoming a woman. And if you're gonna become a woman, act like a lady. Don't be a bird. Like, 'Oh my god, I'm not doing this.' It gets too crazy, and it gets confusing. You're doing this for America."*

Does someone's gender have anything to do with their mediocre performance, if that was even the case? How could being transgender be both Leiomy's advantage and demise?

∞

As I said earlier, there is a shadow to every spotlight. One rarely exists without the other. And even though she's the catalyst of many a shadow cast, "granting" people of color a moment to shine while simultaneously sucking them dry, Madonna had at least one thing right: beauty is where you find it.

In so many ways, house-Ballroom culture is the living embodiment of this notion, the invisible creating visibility for themselves. The economically marginalized reinventing the very definition of wealth. Men of color seen by society as physical specimens of masculinity and sources of capital through labor transforming their destinies by drawing out of them a literal wealth of femininity, using Vogue to circumvent the pain of being sucked into the prison-industrial complex or to wholly circumvent shitty options like joining the NFL, NBA, and other acronyms for contemporary slavery. It's just stunning.

But like all of us—you, me, Madonna, everybody—we sometimes sidestep the capitalist machine only to unconsciously get sucked back into it. That is why awareness is so critical. We have to be aware of what we are doing and whom we are glorifying. We have to be enlightened witnesses.

Michael Roberson has a saying: We speak your name. He says the names of ball legends, including the late Hector Xtravaganza and Pepper LaBeija, but also those trans and POC pioneers who weren't featured in high-profile music videos, hit TV shows, and films, like Stonewall heroine Marsha P. Johnson and NYC Black Pride founder Lee Soulja. It is an evocation and acknowledgment of un-canonized icons. In an effort to once again brownwash what is theirs, I have reconfigured the bridge to the song "Vogue." We speak your name.

(to the melody of "Vogue")
Crystal LaBeija, Ms. Corey
Rich and Larry Ebony

Willi Ninja, Paris Dupree
All visions of a Legacy

Andre Mizrahi, Marsha P.
Picture of a trans queen

Twiggy's catwalk, Leiomy's hair
In love and war, all shade is fair

They had style, they had grace,
Kia and Venus give good face

Angie, Hector, José too
Pony Zion, we love you

MCs with an attitude
Icons get our gratitude

Big ups to Harlem
Where they grew it

Respect our lives
Or girl, don't do it.
Vogue.

THE INTERVIEW

w/Pony Zion and Benji Hart (Benji Ninja)

On April 19, 2019, I was privileged to participate in a conversation with some of Ballroom's community leaders and allies: the artist and legendary voguer Pony Zion, artist and educator Benji Hart, New School professor Robert Sember, and NYU professor Pato Hebert to discuss the many contradictions at the core of Ballroom and who's allowed to vogue.[9]

ROBERT SEMBER: When did you each come to your political awareness around the frictions within Ballroom?

PONY ZION: I don't remember a moment where there wasn't friction, when I didn't live with resistance, being raised by my uncle who was very homophobic and abusive. For me, it was more about, What am I going to do with this friction?

BENJI HART (BENJI NINJA): This conversation is going to get me. I can already tell.

ROBERT: Pony is one of like the three teachers that I have in my life— we've been friends many, many years—and every time we meet, I leave changed.

PONY ZION: Thank you.

BENJI NINJA: My upbringing and my road to Vogue was a very different one. I grew up middle class and living in the suburbs. I was lucky to receive a lot of support and a lot of affirmation that I think helped in my political analysis, like actually having access to teachers, social programs, and after-school programs that were carving and channeling my political analysis. But at the same time, as a Black person and a queer person, as a gender-nonconforming person, I think my femininity was the first thing that taught me I was in friction with the world. It was the first thing in my life that people told me was wrong about me, or that needed to be corrected—that I move like a girl, that I talk like a girl. I felt that something was off there and that I was in friction, but also didn't see a problem with who I was. The first time I was arrested was when I was eighteen years old. I was visiting friends in the Bronx and got arrested—attacked by four police officers who I looked suspicious to. As a middle-class person who grew up outside of the hood, that

was like a huge eye-opening moment for me. That first violent inter-
action with the police was, I think, an early time of being like, Oh,
there are systems and power dynamics that I can't even see that I am
in friction with. And what does that mean for my safety? What does
that mean for my resistance? All of the above.

ROBERT: Pony, you've taught me over and over that the definition of
vogue is telling your own story. And so this process of telling your
story is a way of building consciousness, of looking back, of turning
experience into knowledge, and then knowledge building analysis.
Out of that comes the possibility of having a vision of a world that's
different. A world of justice and a world of emancipation. This is a
very, very different conception of creative work from the dominant
conception that exists in the most visible and elevated and honored
parts of the world.

PONY ZION: Yes, yes. Absolutely.

PATO HEBERT: To Robert's point, can you all talk a little about how
vogue and Ballroom help you to imagine and shape freedom?

BENJI NINJA: These deep questions—I feel like we could talk about
that for three hours! One of my favorite quotes is by [Ballroom
legend and trans activist] Jonovia Chase, who I look up to so much.
She says, "Ballroom is not fantasy; it's the real world reimagined." As
young Black, brown, trans, queer people, just by being who we are,
we're already existing outside of the confines and the expectations
of what is supposed to be possible in terms of identity, movement,
how you live, how you support yourself, how you survive—how you
create family. Out of necessity, Ballroom is actively challenging how
you can exist in the world. That in and of itself is a radical act that
I think is often not appreciated by outsiders or by folks who aren't
fighting for their survival in the same way. Folks who describe balls
as these "lavish productions," where people live in this fantasy world
and for one night get to be whoever they want to be—that's not
wrong or inaccurate, but that's the vision of someone who doesn't
see a community asserting themselves both on the Ballroom floor
and off of it. It's a practice of asserting your right to exist.

RICKY TUCKER: That idea of personal emancipation through Vogue, of
bumping up against the system through your personal movement,
it's so rich. So, in terms of your pedagogical practice, how do you
even begin to teach that?

BENJI NINJA: I just want to say I admire Pony's Vogue so much, but I also really admire Pony's teaching.

RICKY: Oh, for sure. Having been one of his students, I can say he's just wonderful.

BENJI NINJA: Your pedagogy, Pony—I think even just from clips, and the ways that I've been a witness from afar, I am so in admiration of your teaching skills, not just your voguing skills. But I think for me, as with teaching anything, teaching Vogue doesn't always work. One of the exercises I do regularly is have folks do a daily, everyday motion, like brushing their teeth or tying their shoes. Then, through a series of activities, we turn that into a phrase of Vogue. Part of the reason I do that is to show folks how they are already moving in a liberated way.

PONY ZION: Absolutely.

BENJI NINJA: You already have your own vocabulary and your own way of moving through the world. It's about investing in that with power and with purpose, cultivating that into something that can actually be a source of empowerment for you. One summer, one of the young folks that I worked with was a young trans man—this amazing young trans masculine person who just saw folks voguing and was like, "I want to do that. I want to learn how to do that." They were religious in coming to the workshops. Seeing a trans masculine person vogue and take back their femininity, being brought into the space in this incredibly powerful way, was one of my fondest memories of all the years of doing those workshops. So, it's about creating the space where we can input together, and imagine liberation together.

PONY ZION: And to me that's what voguing is. It's a temple that freedom occupies. Vogue has always been a performance. You don't need to know how to dance to perform. Every spirit, every soul has a performance. I think, then, that's the duty of a teacher, to pass it on. It's funny you said the word "vocabulary." I have a column I write for *DBQ*, my brother's magazine. It's called "Vogue-cabulary."

RICKY: Yeah, your personal vocabulary—your Vogue-cab?

PONY ZION: Yes, yes. It tells a story that needs to be expressed. You author what Vogue is—it's your penmanship. It's your script. You need not win or lose to know how to Vogue—Vogue is a part of the Ballroom story, but it has its own conversation in and of itself.

ROBERT: I was thinking of a statement by Leanne Simpson, a First Nations Canadian, who writes about the wisdom within. She says, "My very existence is my resistance." Existing is itself a kind of contradiction with the world. Benji, when you were talking about this reconciling with yourself when you started voguing, it made me think of the deep labor of reclaiming who you are, reconnecting with a long lineage of existing as resisting. Can we think together a little bit about the tension between American individualism, which is so capitalist in its formation, and then the notion of a self, of growing and learning and developing who I can possibly be here in this world, which is not a project of this kind of isolating individualism.

PATO: Buddhism teaches me that self is not singular, and it's not fixed, right? What have you learned about caring for self and caring for others? Which, to your point Robert, is really a false division.

PONY ZION: As far back I could remember, there was something inside of me that said, "In order for me to do this Vogue, I have to do this for people." Whether it was teaching dance, you know, starting out in the House of Latex or the POCC [People of Color in Crisis] or teaching peer education—it's been hand in hand.

BENJI NINJA: I think what's coming up for me are all the ways that we love what Black people, and what queer and trans Black people, create that doesn't translate into actually caring about them, the *creators*. That's a huge part of my practice as a Vogue instructor, setting that expectation, because you're learning part of a tradition that goes back. It's actually about making a commitment to a community, and specifically making a commitment to the people that are passing this tradition on to you.

PONY ZION: Absolutely.

BENJI NINJA: This is an important value for me as an educator. You can't Vogue properly if you can't hold Black, poor, trans, and queer folks in regard. Everybody loves Black and queer folks when we're voguing, when we're creating these beautiful, powerful, visceral pieces of art, but what about when we're being harassed on the street? What about when we're homeless? What about when we're locked up and you can't see us voguing, but we're still voguing? Our lives exist outside of the ball, and we're fighting for our freedom. You can create these moments of emancipation when you're voguing, but that's actually not enough.

PONY ZION: Right. Freedom is just an idea.

BENJI NINJA: It's just an idea.

PATO: I do feel in responding to care, you both are exploding capitalism's notion of the consuming individual that exists by what you do. Pony, as your prominence and people's love and respect for you as a legend and icon grew, how did you navigate the caring for others?

PONY ZION: It made me crazy.

RICKY: It made you crazy?

PONY ZION: It absolutely drove me crazy. I lost my mind make-believing, making people believe this idea of "Pony Zion." It's a practice to appreciate, to pretend that I believe that idea. Even now, I'm going through some kind of "What am I, who am I, where am I" confusion because of that idea. My identity in this world is something that I've lost. I'm being put together as I go, and literally, when I look around me, I can hear and see what I am to people. Alone, I don't feel like those things. I don't see those things.

ROBERT: A couple of things. One is, for many people, the promise of emancipation, the promise of a kind of liberation from the sense of suffering or incompleteness, looks like the capitalist's fantasy. Wealth and fame. "If I can have those things, then I will be relieved of everything else." Ballroom partakes of that very violent fantasy. This has hurt many, many people. It reminds me of something that Barbara Smith, who is this great Black feminist elder and one of the founders of the Combahee River Collective, says. "I don't want to be your black queen. I demand to be ordinary, to live as I am." Part of what it means to be deeply loved is to know that you are seen, and it can be terribly painful to be seen. So a lot of folk shut it down. It's too hard to be loved. Give me the fame, give me the fortune, allow me the drug. Allow me to disappear from the truth of my life through the spectacle that you were talking about earlier.

PATO: What has Ballroom taught us about love? Radical love?

PONY ZION: It's so all together: the celebration, the suffering. If you change one of the ingredients, do you not change what it is? If I take the suffering out of my life, would I still know how to vogue? Would I be here today?

RICKY: You may never know. You're already what you are—a walking paradox. No matter how much notoriety you get, that's never going to be taken away from you. It's impossible.

PONY ZION: Absolutely. That's the joyride of all of this.

BENJI NINJA: I think I hear the notion of folks reading things onto Ballroom without necessarily sitting with the actual nuances and the complexities of it, which can mean reading freedom onto the Ballroom scene where it's more complicated than that, but also reading suffering, or oppression, or sadness and desolation that also isn't there.

PONY ZION: Yes.

BENJI NINJA: I think for me the hardest thing about the Ballroom scene is how complicated and often contradictory it is. I feel like some of the greatest moments of love that I've felt in my life have been in the Ballroom scene, and then some of the moments where I felt the most fucked-up—

PONY ZION: Yes, it's like there are two ends.

BENJI NINJA: This contradiction around Ballroom and how capitalism has infiltrated the scene is *huge*. Someone might be coming down the runway in Chanel from head to toe, and one person is like, "Wow, it's so sad that they need to be wearing Chanel to think they matter, to think they're beautiful." Then someone else is like, "It's a gag that she stole all of that last night. She's proving you don't have to have wealth to look sickening. It's an anti-capitalist act." I think a lot of times it's actually both.

PONY ZION: Yes. It's a simultaneous kind of reality. Absolutely.

BENJI NINJA: In some ways we're subscribing to capitalism and attaching our wealth to it. Does the system accept me? Does the system say that I'm valuable? Does the system say that I'm beautiful, I'm worthwhile, passing, whatever it is? And in other ways, people are completely rejecting what anyone has to say about them.

PONY ZION: I think seeing it from every point of view allows us to see the whole picture. My point of view will be the conditions that I believe.

ROBERT: Pedagogy is about really building a greater and rare awareness of that complexity, so that there can be the capacity to make decisions at crucial moments. We see this a lot outside of the Ballroom scene: "I can give you this if you come and grace my particular moment with your fabulousness." That process of co-optation and exploitation. Pedagogy enables folks to really understand and read what's happening in that moment.

PONY ZION: But what's a performance without applause?

RICKY: If a crowd claps in the woods . . . You know, in literature there's reader-response theory. As a writer, you anticipate what sort of thing you want to say when you write it down, how someone's going to receive it on the page. But sometimes, the person who is writing that statement doesn't know how it's going to be received; they're just acting unconsciously, right? That particular person wearing Chanel down the runway, the fact that they even stirred up that question is point A, and point B is the fact that they're using the tools of capitalism to inadvertently indict it—who's to say how someone is going to receive that? Yeah. There's a kind of complexity to Ballroom that there isn't elsewhere.

PONY ZION: I agree with that.

PATO: To your point, Robert, I would suggest that that's one of the things that Ballroom does for me—is that it is a kind of conscious-ness that can hold that complexity, right?

BENJI NINJA: And the contradiction. While you were talking about living for the applause, I was thinking about whose applause. I think being seen is so important, and being appreciated is actually so important. And voguing as an opportunity to actually create that for each other. To be seen and to be celebrated is so beautiful. But it's so different being celebrated at an art museum than it is being celebrated at a ball. I hear you describing a more fleeting setting of someone being like, "Oh, we want you to be in this video, and then after that we don't even want to hear from you anymore." So often, vogue isn't seen as valuable until it's taken outside of Ballroom, which really means until it's taken away from poor, homeless, queer, trans, Black, and brown people. I think we as voguers even reinforce that a lot. You'll hear voguers say all the time, "Wait, you gon' see me in a video. You gon' see me on TV. I'm going places, I'm doing big things." It's not that I'm shading anybody's dreams, but why don't we see ourselves as doing big things right where we are? Why don't we see the folks who are applauding for us right here? That applause is just as affirming as applause coming from rich white folks. Or the fashion industry. Or applause from a pop artist or whoever.

PATO: And the awareness to decode all of that, too.

PONY ZION: For me, it's not an either-or; it's a both-and. I'm the kind of person that will go down and teach vogue at P.S. 198 for free, and then be on television the very next day. I don't think one takes away from the other. One's a blunt; one's a vape. It does the same mother-fucking thing, like choosing which way you want to get high. I don't pick my audience—my audience picks me.

ROBERT: I really connected with something that Benji said in the very beginning, which is this awareness of frictions early on in life, these mundane moments where you come up against the school, against family restrictions. You have a kind of *Matrix* moment, realizing there is actually a world of historical structures, you know? Anti-Blackness is what so much of history is organized around.

BENJI NINJA: I was really moved with what you were saying before, about how difficult love actually is. And actually how scary and difficult it is to be seen. And that fame can be a surrogate for that. I think consumption can be a surrogate for that, and it all ties back to this. I think as voguers, as artists, as Black queer people, we are consumed all the time without actually being seen.

ROBERT: It's almost slavery.

BENJI NINJA: Right! Exactly. We want all these things from Black folks without wanting Black people.

ROBERT: It's extraction of labor—

BENJI NINJA: Exactly.

ROBERT: —without the investment of love.

RICKY: Extracting your lexicon, your vogue'cabulary. To circle back to contradictions, I think maybe that's why people feel a philosophical breakthrough when they see Ballroom and voguing, because again with these paradoxes—male, female; life and death—Ballroom gets right at the major paradoxes we're all here to address. It answers the great philosophical questions through movement. That lack of fear. Not being afraid of death is where most people are trying to get to, not even knowing that they're on that trajectory. They see it in you all, and they're like, "Holy shit." You know? They just don't have the tools to explain it. But *you* do.

CHAPTER 2

MEMORY

w/Lee Soulja

Hidden figures and the history of having a ball

LANGSTON

Because I've been there and have it committed to memory, I can imagine how alien Langston Hughes must have felt walking into his first ball.

He probably paused in the foyer.

Hands in his pockets.

Brow a lil sweaty.

Ears perked up to the music.

Heart thumping.

He steps forward.

The sounds rushing out of the place somewhere between that of a church and a brothel. Chattering. Glasses clinking. Way more perfume in the air than there were women in the room. I bet he was put off and turned on by the spectrum of fem and masculine realness that scattered that Ballroom. Long eyelashes met with both feigned and neglected five o'clock stubble. Top hats and tiaras where they usually aren't. Not being able to tell who's who. Maybe the 1926 Irving Kaufman hit song, "Masculine Women, Feminine Men," providing a subtlety-free musical accompaniment:

Masculine Women Feminine Men
Which is the rooster which is the hen
It's hard to tell 'em apart today

I'm sure every eye in the room landed on Langston as he walked through the door, each pair scanning him from top to bottom, searching their internal and communal Rolodexes for some semblance of facial recognition, perhaps finally registering Langston as his own up-and-coming Black literati self, or another drag spectator, or a new pre-drag queen, or the type of timeless, curious "down low" Harlem trade that visits such lavish events only under the auspices of being "looped into this," woodenly and cravenly linked arm-in-arm with whatever depraved debutante "it girl" reigned supreme that day.

I'd bet on everything he was the "looped-in" type. During the explosive newness of the Harlem Renaissance, an era that would ignite the flames of experimentation across art, race, gender, and sexuality, Langston Hughes (if the rumors were true) was able to fly just under the radar, reading less as a friend of Dorothy and more just another voyeuristic pal to A'Lelia Walker, daughter of haircare mogul Madame C. J. Walker and arguably the first Black socialite to make an indelible impression on the art scene, first there in Harlem and then spanning out to the rest of the United States and parts of Europe.[1] A'Lelia was rich, excitable, queer-friendly, and dead set on building a legacy. Hanging out with artsy types such as Hughes only lent her credence in her contribution to this mecca of Black excellence.

However, despite having A'Lelia as his escort into this "subterranean" world, I'm sure Hughes still felt conspicuous entering that ballroom, maybe even seen for the first time, like the *strictly* hetero façade he'd been maintaining all of his artsy Black life was suddenly awkward, ill-fitting, woolen—an itchy sham next to the breathable tweed, satin-drenched gender-bending men and sometimes women competing for prizes during the Hamilton Club Lodge Ball, an annual event held by the men of lodge No. 710 since 1869.[2] This fraternity of Harlemite "Odd Fellows" created the grandmother of all balls. First gaining the right to even create the all-Black lodge, which was sanctioned by white lodgers in England, this group of Black men (and presumably pre-trans trans women) quickly parlayed their annual gala for men into the gender-dismantling ball Hughes documented in his autobiography *Big Sea*.

Whatever his orientation, Hughes was there to savor the camp of it all—why be there otherwise, if not to drown in the sea of feather boas, eau de toilette, and stray hands grazing your awkward person on their way in and out of the changing areas? I know his eyes were as wide as saucers.

But I honestly don't have to read between the lines to know how Hughes felt at that ball, when I can simply read it in his own words. In *Big Sea*, he lays out for us three scant yet heavily codified (almost Freudian) paragraphs that detail his own complicated feelings, his reservations, his intrigue—his sheer arousal—from the colorful spectacle that was the annual drag ball at Hamilton Club Lodge in Harlem.

He starts:

> Strangest and gaudiest of all Harlem spectacles in the '20's, and still the strangest and gaudiest, is the annual Hamilton Club Lodge Ball at Rockland Palace Casino. I once attended as a guest of A'Lelia Walker. It is the ball where men dress as women and women dress as men. During the height of the New Negro era and the tourist invasion of Harlem, it was fashionable for the intelligentsia and social leaders of both Harlem and the downtown area to occupy boxes at this ball and look down from above at the queerly assorted throng on the dancing floor, males in flowing gowns and feathered headdresses and females in tuxedoes and box-back suits.[3]

For all the fences he's straddling in this opening paragraph, Hughes knows what he is writing, and there's a lot of information here. I've read this section of *Big Sea* perhaps a hundred times over and somehow never noticed until recently a crucial admission—he likely attended more than one drag ball in Harlem. This can be deduced by his very first sentence (emphasis added):

> Strangest and gaudiest of all Harlem spectacles in the '20's, *and still the strangest and gaudiest*, is the annual Hamilton Club Lodge Ball at Rockland Palace Casino.

Big Sea was published in 1940, so chances are there was a significant gap of time between Hughes's attending the aforementioned drag ball in the 1920s and writing these reflections on them. Yet, the assertion of the line ". . . *and still the strangest and gaudiest . . .*" infers that he kept up with drag balls in one fashion or another up until the point in which he is speaking, circa a period closer to 1940. He likely could not have assumed the Hamilton Club Lodge Ball, a once-a-year event, was still strange and gaudy almost two decades later, and subsequently he would not have made such a declarative statement about the event without firsthand information. This choice of words, though ambiguous, is again a conscious one. Chances are, Hughes was a reluctant but regular friend of the burgeoning Ballroom scene.

But outside the obvious context of men dressed as women/women dressed as men, this section of *Big Sea* is filled with paradoxes commensurate with its intentionally oblique author. Langston Hughes has often been debated as straight, bi, asexual, or gay in scholarly circles since forever, as there is substantial evidence in any of those directions. From his ongoing correspondence with the Black gay Harlem intellectual Alain Locke (one that constantly skirted on flirtation) to his somewhat romantically ambiguous poems and casual entries about an array of women from Harlem to Paris, any Google search for a black-and-white answer about Langston Hughes's sexuality turns up gray.

But I know for a fact how he felt about balls because his reception of them in *Big Sea* is blatantly mixed. In it, he vacillates between awe and disdain, or rather, shade so shady you'd think he was the emcee of said ball as opposed to an innocent bystander:

> For the men, there is a fashion parade. Prizes are given to the most gorgeously gowned of the whites and Negroes who, powdered, wigged, and rouged, mingle and compete for the awards. From the boxes these men look for all the world like very pretty chorus girls parading across the raised platform in the center of the floor. But close up, most of them look as if they need a shave, and some of their evening gowns, cut too low, show hair on the chest.
>
> The pathetic touch about the show is given by the presence there of many former "queens" of the ball, prize winners of years gone by, for this dance has been going on a long time, and it is very famous among the male masqueraders of the eastern seaboard, who come from Boston and Philadelphia, Pittsburgh and Atlantic City to attend. These former queens of the ball, some of them aged men, still wearing the costumes that won for them a fleeting fame in years gone by, stand on the sidelines now in their same old clothes—wide picture hats with plumes, and out-of-style dresses with sweeping velvet trains. And nobody pays them any mind—for the spotlights are focused on the stage, where today's younger competitors, in their smart creations, bid for applause.[4]

Let's tally up Hughes's impression of the "spectacle."

In Awe
1. Gorgeously gowned.
2. Pretty chorus girls.
3. In their smart creations.

Throwing Shade
1. Most of them look as if they need a shave.
2. And some of their evening gowns, cut too low, show hair on the chest.
3. "Queens" of the ball, prize winners of years gone by.
4. Fleeting fame.
5. *Nobody pays them any mind.*

Except for the fact that Hughes seems to be paying these queens a lot of mind, or at least enough to add them to the book about his life story.

Anyhow, his shade takes the lead, but if you look past the shady quantity and check out its quality, it sounds as if Langston Hughes is a young queen today reading an old queen, going straight for the jugular. He comments on their lack of binary realness, their dusty old gowns, their old age, and subsequently their dwindling relevance. In short, he seems to read them like he's one of the children . . . though, here is not the time nor the space to start dredging up Hughes's sexuality. No, it's not about who he desires. What I more so want to point out here is that his *aesthetic* is timelessly queer. And through such an aesthetic lens, we can view Hughes as classically self-hating in his straddling implementation of reverence and queerphobia when describing his ball. Independent of his proximity to queer life, in a lot of ways, Hughes's sentiment was that of the times.

Not able to resist attending and covering Harlem's Odd Fellows drag balls in the early twentieth century, newspapers and other publications of the day struck a similar balance of fascination and disdain in tone, ensuring they never glorified too much this "spectacle," which, in that pre-Stonewall moment, was very much illegal. The *New York Age*, an influential Black newspaper at the time, published an article in 1926 covering that year's Hamilton Lodge Ball (aka, "the faggots' ball"). The description is so comparable to Hughes's own assessment of balls in its on-the-fence wording and tone that it drives me to believe they were referring to the same ball:

HAMILTON LODGE BALL: AN UNUSUAL SPECTACLE

It seems that many of the class known as "fairies," and many Bohemians from the Greenwich Village section, took the occasion to mask as women for this affair. They appeared to make up at least 50% of the 1,500 people. . . . Many of the people who attended dances generally declare that the masquerade and civic ball was the most unusual spectacle they ever witnessed.

The prize winners were Harry Walter, 963 Columbus avenue (white), first prize; George Jackson, 108 134th street (colored), second prize.[5]

A "spectacle." And it's used twice here. Both Hughes and this *New York Age* article refer to balls put on by Hamilton Lodge, No. 710, as such. The article takes other liberties in description, pejoratively naming the attendees as "fairies" similar to Hughes's "Queens." Yet, if neither nomenclature came from a standpoint from within the burgeoning LGBTQ community, they could definitely be seen as on the lighter end of hate speech for the times.

It's worth mentioning that the *NYA*'s observation about the mixed crowd of local and bohemian contestants (aka whites from Greenwich Village) is innocent enough and points to Ballroom's timeless commitment to inclusivity. The over 1,500 mixed attendees suggests that, like *Paris Is Burning*, Madonna's "Vogue," and countless resurgences after it, this ball in Harlem 1926 was well-integrated and indicative of an upswing in Ballroom's popularity. This type of public interest in the spectacle comes and goes and plays into the feeding habits of capitalism, a ravenous creature that thrives on the life, death, and consumption of subcultures like Ballroom.

What is explicitly menacing however is the final paragraph in the article. At a time in America when wearing the clothing of the opposite gender assignment was illegal and punishable, printing the full names and addresses of the winners of a drag ball was a malicious act, shrouded under the guise of a little fun, yet a frowned-upon poke at the community. In a contemporary context, this part of the article feels like a "Karen" 911 call, a bullshit citizen's report that often ends in the arrest and/or death of an innocent "other." Except this article was likely written by a Black person. Personally, I would even go so far as to say I detect an element of queer self-hatred in the chosen execution, but that's neither here nor there, I suppose.

At any rate, the *New York Age* articles in years to come doubled down on this 1926 piece's alternately reverential and offensive language, becoming increasingly discriminatory and on a trajectory parallel with the aforementioned pendulum swing of tentative capitalistic enthrallment. They seem to be intrinsically linked. In later copy of the 1930s, groups of drag contestants would be described as "Frail and Freakish Gangs."[6] Arrests at drag balls were described in graphic detail in newspapers, one in particular that resulted in a young woman being pushed down a flight of stairs and lacerating her head against a radiator.[7]

Another cruel *NYA* clip from a column titled "Double Feature," written by the duo Alfred A. Duckett and Thelma Staples (if only I could find their addresses and print them into the past . . .), serves as a sort of *Birth of a Nation* for transgender citizens, setting up a foundation of transphobia and general ignorance that projects hysteria into the future and wrongfully substantiates heterosexual violence against trans folks, something akin to the gay/trans panic defense:

DOUBLE FEATURE:

Here's a very Grimm Fairy Tale—Jimmy Springer attended the Hamilton Lodge Ball. Jim started out by taking a lady home, but the lady wasn't a lady. Jim was really surprised to discover "You can't tell a man by his clothes or a woman either for that matter."[8]

Personally, I think this clip falls flat in terms of conveying any pertinent or thrilling information, no matter the historical context. It implies that, in 1937, people were fearful they wouldn't be able to judge a person by their clothing or gender. How tragic. The most notable "feature" of this article is its only ostensible objective: injecting fear into specifically Black audiences in and around New York City, the city where drag balls were held. The effects of such sensationalism can be seen all around us today in the form of the countless acts of violence against Black fem trans lives that have occurred over the twentieth century up until today. However murderous in consequence, the tone this clip takes is that of bewilderment and intrigue, like at the end it should say, "A man dressed as a lady—isn't that wild?!" What it never actually ends up saying is whether or not Mr. Jimmy Springer sent this lady on her way, violently acted out his own neurosis on her, or happily engaged in sex with her. That must have been too much info for this tiny space. It seems that in terms of the human condition, nothing changes. Morbid fascinations have always begun with a lack of self-awareness.

PHIL

A morbid fascination. That's what Black publications like the *New York Age* in the 1920s and '30s and *Jet* magazine in the '40s–'60s had with people who were then deemed "female impersonators." Long known for its "Beauty of the Week," a centerfold acting as a public debut for burgeoning Black fem icons like Pam Grier and J'Net DuBois, *Jet* also regularly featured (very discreetly) between its pages a Black female impersonator by the name of Phil Black. Always placed with incredulity and in the context of mere innocuous entertainment, Phil Black was a regular feature in the magazine—but he was so much more than that.

Starting in the early twentieth century, Black was a pioneer of the drag and Ballroom communities—a hidden figure—standing there in plain sight during monumental moments, including that fateful day in 1967 at New York City's Town Hall, when modern house-Ballroom was born. Before that, his annual Funmakers Ball, started in 1947, became a blueprint for POC balls to come.[9] Creating balls from the ground up in his home state of Pennsylvania, performing in Atlantic City, and being the preeminent event planner of drag balls in Harlem, Brooklyn, and all of NYC, Black was the national face of drag and essentially the godmother of the people in attendance at Hughes's ball, queens whom he said came from "the eastern seaboard . . . from Boston and Philadelphia, Pittsburgh and Atlantic City to attend."

Later, in the '50s, Phil Black would allegedly work as an actress, first auditioning as a woman, securing major roles, and later revealing his male gender. He was paving the way. Always landing a gig. According to *Jet*, he even worked as a private detective, hunting down and reporting on married men out and about on extramarital dalliances.[10] Though the underpinnings of these facts being printed were meant to portray Phil Black as an underhanded or deceptive character, the larger implication was that he was a money-making machine at a time when female impersonators had little to no capital or hopes for steady employment. This was daring. This was radical. This was bold. Black was a boss.

You would never know any of this from solely reading *Jet*. In print and IRL, the sensationalism, patronizing curiosity, and verbal and physical aggression toward the LGBTQ community would last throughout the years of the Harlem renaissance and through the twentieth century to today. During that time, drag queens and transgender women persevered, continuing to stage balls, build whole communities from the ground up, attend functions, run thriving businesses, and exist in defiance of oppression. Now, imagine if they were the ones reporting on the culture.

Phil Black, we speak your name.

CRYSTAL

It was clear that Ms. Manhattan was too through before she even began. Her name was Crystal, and in fact, from all the way up in the nosebleed section of New York's Town Hall mezzanine, you could clock with crystal clarity the unabashed not-here-for-it expression draped across her face, that complex tough-as-nails daydreamer look that the winning drag queen of "Miss All-America Camp Beauty 1967" should perfectly embody. Defiant congeniality. Yep, she had that.

But honestly, they were lucky she even showed up. For weeks prior to the pageant, Monique, Crystal's friend/another Black queen regularly making the East Coast pageant rounds, had implored her, "Crystal, don't go, darling!" Monique had even said this taking into consideration Crystal's recent successes as one of the few Black ladies to break through into NYC's white drag contests earlier in the '60s. True, she was fair in complexion and beat to the high heavens with powder—but so what. Crystal was none other than the *reigning* Ms. Manhattan, and she was Black, for crying out loud! Still, for some reason, Monique had assured Crystal that none of that mattered. In fact, Monique had already made the decision herself to sit this one out. Her line of reasoning? The whole thing was rigged.

It happened almost every time. It got hard watching with hope the inevitable systemic and unconscious biases play out. The odds were already stacked against them—and for Monique, the case was closed. Plus, everyone knew that this year's Miss All-America Camp Beauty pageant was to be filmed as part of a documentary (what would eventually become *The Queen*). Putting on appearances would be the priority for the pageant makers, and already word on the street uptown was that the show's runner, Mother Flawless Sabrina, had had everything rigged in favor of Harlow, a waifish Sedgwickian blonde from Philadelphia who was essentially a poster child for the dominant white culture's definition of feminine beauty in the '60s.

Which was rich at best. No matter the time of day, it had always looked as if Harlow had unwittingly stumbled out of Warhol's Factory at 4 a.m. Yet, remarkably, she had somehow won her first pageant by just haphazardly showing up day-of, and in the larger drag world, the implication of such a standout first-time performance was that Harlow's youth, beauty, and superior fem realness were simply undeniable and effortless. Meanwhile, back on planet Earth, many of the Black and brown queens felt that *undeniable* and *effortless* merely described the racist structures that would allow someone so underwhelming and inexperienced to win any pageant, never mind her first! No, Monique would not be competing that day and had suggested Crystal do the same—but Crystal never backed down from a fight. She was going to go, and she was going to win.

Still, just below Crystal's hardened stage façade lay the vestiges of hope, a cool but soft faith commensurate with the miles of powder-blue chiffon, puffed-up bouffants, gingerly blotted beauty marks, and grace in the face of racism with which she'd adorned herself on so many pageant stages over the years.

So, when the day arrived, she carried herself like a lady throughout the competition, holding her head up high and trying (unsuccessfully at times) not to look forlorn, like during the swimsuit portion, when documentary cameras singled her out while some white queen did a languid and subpar rendition of the already depressing *Am I Blue?* by Billie Holiday, shit-grinning and bearing it through group song-and-dance numbers choreographed and enforced by Sabrina and her stagehand queens, trying with all her might not to roll her eyes and suck her teeth at the trite and uninspiring answers the other contestants gave throughout the "What would you do with the prize money?" section of the evening . . . clinging almost counterintuitively to her inner monologue—"I know I'm beautiful, I *know* I am beautiful, I know . . ."—in spite of society's deafening whispers suggesting otherwise. All this so that by the time they called her name as one of the top five queens primed to be Miss All-America Camp Beauty, Crystal had had enough, honey.

She was going to need them to hurry it the hell up and get on with it. At this point, they either saw her true beauty or they did not, and either way, she had already been catalyzed by a perfect storm of poor past pageant experiences, or to be specific, how Black and white the Black and whiteness of it all was: her complete and utter self-awareness; Monique's foreboding, and being told no One. Too. Many. Times. Like many a radical moment in history—Rosa Parks and the bus boycotts, Marsha P. Johnson and the Stonewall riots—circumstances can come together in an explosive chemical reaction that creates entire movements, and they're often sparked by Black women. Luckily for us, director Frank Simon caught it all on tape in his documentary *The Queen*.[11] Triggering an explosive climax to an almost stoic film, Mother Flawless Sabrina announces the third runner-up, Miss Chicago—then Miss Manhattan, Crystal LaBeija . . .

> **Sabrina:** Our third runner-up in the 1967 Nationals, from Manhattan, Miss Crystal, ladies and gentlemen—let's hear it for her!
>
> *Crystal is seething. Third runner-up?!*
>
> *She steps forward, mouthing, "Oh my god," to someone in the audience, but not as if she's shocked, instead in that throw-your-hands-up, "whatever" kind of way. As she walks over to the runner-up line, the crowd applauds even louder, to which she mouths, "Oh please . . . ," which is 1967 for "Girl, bye."*
>
> **Sabrina:** Okay, now we're down to the real nitty-gritty. And here are our three finalists. Come on kids, come on up here to the front of the stage, and let the audience have a good look at you.
>
> *Crystal does her best to stand by and wait for the niceties to end but has fully had it by the time Sabrina is ready to announce the second runner-up. She mouths something unintelligible to a girlfriend in the audience, before prematurely sauntering offstage and straight down the center row.*
>
> **Sabrina:** Crystal, where are you going? This is not the time to show temperament! Get back here and stay with the other finalists.
>
> *Crystal isn't having it. She's gone.*
>
> **Sabrina:** Oh well, you've got to expect losses . . . Okay we gotta continue with the business at hand. . . .

Sabrina goes on, announcing Miss Boston, then Miss New Jersey, as second and first runners-up respectively, before finally revealing the Queen of the 1968 Nationals: Harlow. Cameramen, drag queens, and judges storm the stage, jubilantly ambushing Harlow. She stands there in a weepy haze, mouth still agape, makeup all smudged. Two disembodied hands wonkily adhere the crown to her lopsided haystack of a wig. . . . Meanwhile . . . the cameraman exits, trailing behind Crystal and her friend Miss Fire Island, who have left City Hall and are now taking it to the NYC streets—their turf.

> **Miss Fire Island (to cameraman):** Do you think she [Harlow] deserved it?
> **Crystal:** She is *not* beautiful, has no qualifications, and is bo-dy-*less*.
> **Miss Fire Island:** Do you think she deserved it?
> **Crystal:** Darling, she didn't deserve nothing!
> **Miss Fire Island (to cameraman):** Answer me! You're not speaking from the damn camera; you have a mind. *DO YOU THINK SHE DESERVED IT?*
> **Cameraman:** (. . .)
> **Miss Fire Island:** I can tell by the smile on your face, you *know* she didn't deserve it.
> **Crystal:** You know she didn't deserve it! All of them and the judges knew it too. Cuz she was terrible. And her explanation for why she wanted the money—"to put it in the bank!" Ha, ha, ha! She's not getting any money, because Sabrina's not going to pay her. They're good friends. It's only publicity, and it's *bad* publicity, for Harlow and all the rest, cuz I'm declared as one of the uglier people of the world.
> **Miss Fire Island:** And next time, she should drop her outfit off at the cleaners, before she wears it onstage.
> **Crystal:** She better get the hell back to Philadelphia, because she's one of the worst—
> **Someone off camera:** They're in the dressing room!
> **Crystal (reentering Town Hall):** Where's Miss Sabrina at—

∞

I remember the first time I saw that last ten minutes of *The Queen*, sitting cross-legged on the floor of the dance space on West Fourteenth Street, where Michael Roberson and Robert Sember taught Vogue'ology. Time is of the essence in semester-long college courses, so I gather it was imperative they at least exposed us to the end sequence of the film that day. Thankfully. Watching Crystal lay into those white queens was exhilarating. I remember laughing out loud at how timeless a good read can be, reveling in how priceless good words sound in a New York accent. Her artful and ruthless delivery could make it easy to miss the sociopolitical implications of her tirade. The core principle: my Black beauty is clearly beyond your comprehension, so I suppose I'll just have to spell it out for you.

During the discussion of the film, most of my classmates agreed with Crystal—Harlow didn't deserve the title—but a few felt bad for Harlow, saying things like, "Aw, it's not her fault," and "But didn't she win fair and square?" Well, to a certain degree, the judges picking Harlow was not *her* mandate, but also, basking in your white privilege (whether activated by you or not) isn't exactly an act of innocence either. Plus, since such racial biases have been ingrained into each and every one of us since forever, watching only the final scene of *The Queen*, where Crystal flips out, could paint the skewed picture that she's just playing the raven-haired, bitter, older, evil queen to Harlow's thinner, paler, blonder, prettier Half-Asleeping Beauty. Luckily, we all know better than that.

Unfortunately, no one ever really watches *The Queen* all the way through. Instead they choose each time to revisit the last ten explosive (albeit important) minutes of a generally meditative 1-hour-and-6-min-long film. What with YouTube and other modes of modern information reducing pertinent cultural events like this down to thirty-second digestible bites specially made for our dwindling attention spans, there's honestly no way the girls could be expected to sit through a whole documentary from 1967—even if it is all about drag queens!

One example of such a salacious extraction is Aja, a contestant on *RuPaul's Drag Race*, who lifted this defining moment out of *The Queen* and folded it into twenty-first-century popularity by (uncannily) dressing up as Crystal for "The Snatch Game" segment of the show in 2018. Aja nails Crystal's scathing vocal affect and demeanor, slaying the judges and other queens with timeless and non-contextual one-liners, like "Where is Sabrina?! I will sue the bitch!" and "Fun facts about me: I will walk off if I lose—I don't give a damn what anybody thinks of me. And Harlow should never have won."

As fun, timeless, and savage as this disembodied read feels, what exactly is the value of this sensationalized primetime context of Crystal's plight? What does "I will walk off if I lose" convey to anyone without any further information? Did the D-list, part-time pop-singer advocates on RuPaul's judges' panel and the other queens come away with any greater meaning other than the fact that Crystal might be the world's most fabulous sore loser? It's hard to say.

Meanwhile, some of the most fascinating nuggets of twentieth-century queer anthropology are strewn throughout the rest of *The Queen*, including:

1. *Pre-Stonewall, pre-RuPaul footage of quasi-closeted drag queens of the 1960s tucking and suiting up for the show.*

2. *Various coming-out tales and anecdotal inklings of trans narratives:* A southern belle whose parents and entire town always accepted him as gay, meditations on what were back then cutting-edge sex-change operations, and the ins and outs of being drafted for war while queer in the '60s.

3. *Radio-era vocal affects that are somehow people's real accents:* Everyone in the film either talks like Bette Davis with a cigarette in hand, telling you a thing or two, or like an elvish-sounding announcer doing play-by-plays of the Kentucky Derby.

4. *An unconscious but blatant fascination with Black life and culture:* One stolen moment in the film shows a white queen mansplaining to three Black queens about their own skincare—"You know, they say that most Negro boys get bumps on their face from shaving, cuz when I was working, they had a magazine, *Ebony*, for Negro people. They have a special depilatory, especially for the Negro boys, that takes all the hair off and prevents [it]." Another moment in this same vein shows Sabrina excitedly explaining and pantomiming scenes from great Black performances that would later be folded into the pageant—"Now wait, there's Eartha, and then Josephine Baker comes on like this: 'Am I blue la la . . .'"

5. *Show creator/producer/host Flawless Sabrina's fervent and preternatural business acumen paired with her steely nurturing of the girls:* Early on in the film through a voiceover that could have been added any time throughout the filming process—say, after Crystal's tirade—Sabrina singles out Harlow as special, almost like her reluctant mentee . . .—*"I can't help but feel a certain responsibility for Richard [aka Harlow]. Although I certainly know I have no responsibility to him . . . I first met Richard at one of my promotional parties. . . . [He] started asking me questions, and he*

wanted advice on drag and everything. Well, first of all, I'm not interested in getting any new recruits to the drag bag. All I want to do is sell tickets."

6. *And finally, Harlow throwing a hissy fit over something of a wig fiasco, if such an oxymoron even holds up:* This pivotal moment is often overlooked. As a matter of fact, I had never seen or heard of it until I sat down to watch the entire film and, since doing so, realized how critical it is that these few minutes be submitted as "Exhibit A" in the case of *LaBeija v. Harlow* (1967). The section characterizes Harlow and fleshes out a little more holistically the dilemma at hand. It demonstrates that on many levels—outside the core principle that Black is beautiful and unsung, and that white mediocrity is woefully rewarded—Harlow *really* didn't deserve that crown.

Day of the pageant, in her hotel room, Harlow and her entourage raise hell over a wig that never even made it on stage. Harlow wasn't able to procure an appropriate wig, and so, all of her friends panic and fuss over her as if she were missing an appendage. One friend, also working as a stagehand later in the film, yells to another, "See if Cathy can get this full [wig]. Everyone can give you a full until it's time to give you one—[then] they give you *shhit!*" The mania in the scene is palpable. Harlow chimes in, "I want all those queens out of my room!" Her friend assures her, "They're all getting out right now, you just wait a minute."

Meanwhile, another girlfriend of Harlow—evidently, she requires a full-on entourage—works desperately over the phone to fix this wig emergency. "I'm in a spot and it's a matter of *life* and *death*, Carole, that I get a platinum blonde full [wig], and I mean life or death." Back in the other room, Harlow is in bed under the covers and looking super dramatic and ill. "I don't know what to do," she screams. "I'm interested in myself right at this point, and I don't give a fuck about anybody, to tell the truth. I'm very much interested in myself!" Gross.

Some other white gay then chimes into the camera, perhaps trying to put this mania into some kind of context. "An N–B–W," he says. "A natural beauty wonder. The first contest Richard ever entered, he won. A lot of these kids have worked their way up. . . . They worked for it. Richard never worked for it. Went into a contest, got on stage, was beautiful, the crowd cheered, the kid won. He never really experienced loss or anything happening to him." But this only proves to unendear us to Harlow and the erratic behavior of her entourage. I have to say, it's all a quintessentially white experience. By now, Harlow and friends seem to be near their breaking point.

"Richard, just relax!" his friend shouts.

"Do you know what I've been through today? My stomach is about to bust," Harlow shouts back.

"Just *relax*. You're acting like a little kid!"

"Well, that's exactly what I am!"

A Black queen assigned to the same hotel room looks on astounded as this privilege parade rolls out.

Harlow's friend gets the last word. "You're not that little, darling! You've been through worse than this!"

I'm not so sure she had.

You have the evening gown, swimsuit, Q&A, and talent segments— but creed is never a considered attribute of contestants in beauty pageants. I'm certain that if it were, the number of contestants would dwindle by at least two-thirds. No, fortunately, creed is not considered, perhaps because it's qualitative and immeasurable; yet, if we were to insert creed as a rubric for the winner of Miss Camp Beauty, Harlow's breakdown would prove that she's rich in entitlement, white privilege, pettiness, and people around her who will cosign all of the above. It would prove she didn't deserve the crown. This isn't to say that by this standard Crystal LaBeija necessarily deserved it—we have no evidence of her character outside of *The Queen*. But because we have seen Harlow in this unsavory moment, we can come that much closer to agreeing with Crystal—Harlow did not deserve it.

If you haven't already, I suggest you set aside an hour to check out the entirety of the film.

∞

Outside the dressing rooms.
Crystal: Where's Miss Sabrina at, cuz I'll sue the bitch. I will sue!
Stagehand: Did you sign the release?
Crystal: No, I didn't sign any release, and if she releases *any* bitch on me, I will sue the fool. She won't make money off of *my* name, darling. She can make it off

of Harlow and all the rest of the fools that flock to her, but not Crystal, darling. Anybody *but* her.

A Queen Off-Camera: LaBeija. *LaBeeeeeeeija.*

Crystal (answering): *Fantastique.* (Suddenly turning to camera) You can take all the pictures you want of me, but I better not see them on the street. Because it's over—get a picture with me and Harlow, and we'll see which is more beautiful, darling.

The crowd chatters disapprovingly. Harlow to the side, looking like a shaken puppy, surrounded by her entourage woo-wooing her. Sabrina walks across to the dressing room entrance.

Sabrina: The judges—

Crystal: The judges didn't have any taste, it was with you that the judges was with, darling. You were in it! Two weeks ago, Monique told me not to come. That's why Monique is not here in dress, because she is one of the—

Sabrina: Monique is a friend of ours!

Crystal: Monique was *not* here as a friend of yours. She's a friend of mine, darling! Monique, will you tell her why you didn't come?

Monique comes up to warmly console her.

Crystal: Because she knew it was fixed for Harlow! She said, "Crystal darling, don't gooo, because you're not going to get it." That's why *all* the true beauties didn't come!

Sabrina: It's in bad taste, and you're showing your colors, you should have—

Crystal: I am! I am doing it bad—but I have the *right* to show my colors! I am beautiful, and I know I'm beautiful!

Lots of commotion.

Another Queen Off-Camera: Don't talk about she's showin' no color! Don't you tell her that she's showin' no color!

The voice of this particular off-camera drag queen is a dead ringer for a young Dorian Corey, who is credited as having been in *The Queen* along with eventual mother of the House of LaBeija, Pepper LaBeija. Though credited, these Black beauties aren't easily found in the footage. We're sadly left to scour the film to guess as to their whereabouts. Also, "showing your color"? We'll return to that. . . .

Sabrina: No, you're taking it the wrong way—

Off-Camera White Woman: May I say this to you—

The woman sounds a lot like Cathy, Harlow's friend who earlier called the shop about the wig.

Crystal: Taking it the wrong way? Shit—she looks bad! And no way or what you say can do [anything] about it.
Pan to Harlow looking sad, cornered, weepy.
Crystal (Pointing down the hall to Harlow): Look at Harlow's outfit! That is quite— don't bother her, darling, don't bother her, It's not Harlow's fault. It's not her fault. She can't help it. (Addressing Harlow) Cuz you're beautiful and you're young. You deserve to have the best in life, but you didn't deserve [this]!

Harlow's wig patroller Cathy is squawking, whining, and pleading something unintelligible at Crystal.

Crystal: Miss Thing, I don't say she's not beautiful, but she wasn't looking beautiful tonight! She doesn't equal me—look at her makeup! It's terrible! And, and—
Sabrina: Crystal, wait a minute. Did you complain to the judges?
Crystal: No. I didn't, I wasn't thinking, really.
Sabrina: But why don't you show the judges and complain to them?
Crystal: But they told me, Sabrina, that you had it fixed for Harlow. Everyone knew about you having it fixed for Harlow for weeks and weeks ahead.
Sabrina: Now, we listened to you. I listened to every word you had to say. Now wait a second, hold it. There's a party after here. Every one of the judges is going to be there. You may feel perfectly free, I'll cart you over myself, and you can talk to each one of em. Most of those people I never saw before in my life! I don't know them. I went down to the Dom—now wait a second, dear. You listen to me. I went down to the Dom one night trying to influence Mr. Warhol to come up here as a judge. We sat down there for two hours and couldn't even get an audience with Andy Warhol. He was running around the Factory making a movie or something.
Town Hall Worker: Everybody go out!
Another Queen Off-Camera: What you say?
Town Hall Worker: Everybody go outside, that's what I say!
Phil Black (drag legend): Everybody out—let's go!
Fin.

Showin' your color. An illuminating turn of phrase if not a dated figure of speech meant to comment on some unsavory characteristic unwittingly revealed by its owner. They're acting out. Showing their ass. Revealing their true selves. The tone of it automatically sounds sage and insightful. Yet, the implication of such language coming down on a Black drag contestant like Crystal from the upper power dynamic of a white event coordinator like Sabrina has the feel of a schoolmarm correcting the socially disruptive actions of a child—because all children are practical sociopaths before socialization, and in a certain era of America, all Black people were spoken to like children.

But that word, "color," demarcates another aspect of this era gone by. Sabrina, whether wittingly or unwittingly, likely subconsciously, chose this phrasing, using the term "color" as in "colored folks," as in dark non-white people, as in how unappealing, dangerous, or even deadly showing your Blackness could be in the '60s; how assimilation was expected if you were fair enough or well-off enough to pass; how Crystal and countless others had to continually beat their faces with white powder in an attempt to downplay their color—just to even be contenders in a pageant; how Blackness is the culmination of all the colors, a safe haven for the universe's thriving spectrum, yet we should aspire to whiteness— it's complete and utter absence? I'm sorry, but no.

Sabrina's way of describing Crystal's outrage was poignant, but not in the way she'd intended. It revealed more about the times and, honestly, about Sabrina, than it had anything to do with Crystal and her core argument that the pageant was rigged. Frankly, Sabrina's pageant, like "justice," the economy, the prison-industrial complex, education, employment, or any system in this great nation, whether or not it was fixed, the whole fucking thing was fixed! And Crystal indeed deserved to actually show her color by saying so.

As lore has it, on this fateful day in Manhattan's Town Hall in 1967, Crystal LaBeija's vitriolic self-expulsion became the reason you and I are here today. It's said that at the behest of the Black and brown legends in attendance that day, early twentieth-century iconic drag foremothers like Phil Black and Dorian Corey, Crystal made a shrewd move—she withdrew from future white-run downtown pageants and, with her friend Lottie, returned uptown to organize pageants and balls in Harlem, an almost century-old safe haven where Blackness and Black fem-realness were not only understand but honored. There they held the genesis event titled "Crystal & Lottie LaBeija Present the First Annual House of LaBeija Ball at Up the Downstairs Case on 115th Street & 5th Avenue in Harlem."[12]

The profound effect of Crystal and Lottie's action cannot be understated. It caused a seismic shift, laying down a cultural foundation that was rooted in protest and thereby unshakeable.

A 2018 Billboard.com article perfectly paints the results of Crystal's courage:

> That overall feeling about drag pageants set the groundwork for what we now know as the ballroom scene. . . . Lottie convinced her to host a ball for Black queens. While it wasn't the first ball of this sort, it was the first to be hosted by a "House" [LaBeija]. And within the 10 years following that founding in 1972, the ballroom scene was flourishing.[13]

No, Crystal, Sabrina, and the world didn't know what they were in for that day in 1967, but like a sci-fi, time-heist film where the spark of a revolution can be pinpointed to a singular moment in time, I'm almost certain that if the Black-and-trans-hating-yet-appropriating white heteronormative gays had a time machine today, Miss All-American Camp 1967 would be the day they'd undo—or try to emulate.

SABRINA (OR JACK)

Flawless Sabrina's apartment was the kaleidoscopic innards of a queen's jewelry box. I'd kind of gone there expecting as much. That inkling was triggered by my decade-long love affair with Jennie Livingston's interviews in *Paris Is Burning.* I just knew Sabrina's Upper East Side apartment would match the camp of that cascading green feather boa propped up behind Dorian Corey as she meditated and monologued on shade from her vanity mirror, how it just *had* to smell like fresh baby powder mixed with the dust gathered between drag performances. Or perhaps it was comparable to the smoky lamplit fog swirling around Pepper LaBeija as she ruminated the rules of being a house mother, an ambience something like that jungle of scarves where harems tend to hang out. Accordingly, Flawless Sabrina's tchotchke-lined home didn't disappoint—it was basically the inside of a genie bottle.

The opportunity to meet with Sabrina had unfurled fatefully. It was 2014, a Biennial year for the Whitney Museum of American Art. In previous years, usually by some random acts of grace, like arriving on a pay-what-you-want day or a boyfriend's older sister covering my admission—I'd attended every single Whitney Biennial since 2004. Even when I'd lived in Boston. But this one was special. As part of the 2014 exhibition, the famous drag queen and legendary pageant coordinator Flawless Sabrina was offering tarot readings for twenty dollars, and there was something of a live exhibition put together by Zackary Drucker and Rhys Ernst, artists of trans experience and Sabrina's mentees. Even as a dirt-poor student in the city, I knew I had to be read, so to speak, by the legendary queen. I immediately bought a ticket and waited for the email confirmation. When it came, it looked like this:

Ricky C Tucker,

This message is confirmation that your booking was created.

Details of the new booking:

When: Sun 4/13/2014 7:30pm to 8:00pm
Title: Tarot Reading with Flawless Sabrina
Price: $ 20.00
Status: Payment received
ID: 13156811
Full name: Ricky C Tucker

Greetings!

Thank you so much for booking an appointment to have your tarot read by the legendary Flawless Sabrina!
His apartment is located at:

5 East 73rd Street New York, NY 10021
It is located between Madison Avenue and 5th Avenue
Apartment 4B - Jack Doroshow

Upon arrival, please ring the buzzer for 4B for entry.
Please arrive on time; Flawless only has ten-minute windows between appointments.
Enjoy the experience, it will be truly magical!

Best,
Zackary Drucker and Rhys Ernst

I was at a pivotal moment in my life and already knew a lot about Sabrina. The reading was, for me, that future thing we're always dying to fast-forward to.

It was on the verge of spring, and the sun was setting as I approached Sabrina's building, which was shorter than most of the ones flanking it but still maintained the austerity of its address, 5 East Seventy-Third Street. It had white marble columns, and Central Park began at her street's end. I rang the bell and was buzzed up.

When I arrived at door 4B it was slightly ajar, and before I could creak it open, one of those jazzy radio-era voices met me where I stood. "Come on in, hon! You can just leave your things right by the door!"

I did as I was told and made my way toward the voice, which seemed to be coming from the living room, just off the entrance.

"Hello, my darling," it said as I entered the room.

I turned to my left, and there sat Sabrina behind a dark wooden desk at least three times the size of her slight frame. Her head was shaved clean, and I just remember the colors she was wearing were loud, along with a gold chain and other paraphernalia that suggested she might be moonlighting as a cosmic raver and headed to a party right after my reading. The wall to her right was lined with progressive treasures of yesteryear, a promo image for *The Queen*, a portrait of a stoic-looking Obama on a postcard, an alien throwing up a peace sign, gold tinsel, a mannequin bust wearing space goggles, and on and on and on . . . It smelled of aged wood and cigarettes but like the lovely kind from your Mee-maw's house.

"Please join me," she said, pointing to the chair on the opposite side of the desk.

"Oh, thank you," I responded.

"You're very welcome. My name is Jack—and you're Ricky?"

"That I am. It's very nice to meet you."

"Lovely to meet you. We have very little time before my next reading starts, so let's get down to business. Sound like a plan?"

"Sounds good to me."

"Wonderful. Let's begin . . ."

I had twice been introduced to Mother Flawless Sabrina (aka, Sabrina, aka, Jack Doroshow) years before she read my cards that day. The first time was circa 2010 through Michelle Handelman, a queer-centric multimedia artist and my part-time roommate who back then was dividing her time teaching at the School of the Museum of Fine Arts Boston and creating films. Her meditative depictions of non-heteronormative people queering spaces were fantastical, cinematic, and set in New York City and never-binary universes. Both Michelle and her films were always a fresh-air supply in a world brimming with patriarchal bullshit. Being a cool teacher and all, she regularly encouraged my art-criticism endeavors, my love of *Paris Is Burning*, and my eventual move to New York. Flawless Sabrina was a heavy feature in Michelle's films at the time. It seems that, over the years, Sabrina started to evolve along with the greater aesthetic of the drag art form, veering away from well-kempt bouffants, glittery gowns, satin satire, and pleasant if not campy pageantry, and leaning heavily into drag as an act of aesthetic nihilism.

In Michelle's video installation, *Dorian, A Cinematic Perfume*, an instrumental mind-bender based on Wilde's *The Picture of Dorian Gray* and its themes of decadence, narcissism, and the meaning of art, Sabrina is the melted, unhinged version of everything she once was. She is defiantly presented as aged, sometimes wigless and with a shaved head, sometimes donning a blonde wig so voluminous it would make Cindy from the B-52's shudder. Bold colors, black pleather, and studs galore; rouge lipstick running down her face like the Joker gone S&M. Her look is clownish but in an active, joyfully upsetting, Pennywise sense. She writhes around speaking gibberish, spattering like a golem without all the angst.[14]

I mean it's cool. It kind of warms your heart to know that there is a space for drag and queer artists to grow old, not just gracefully but *artistically*, anarchically. Yet, it also casts shade over the same heart to know that while those spaces are created broadly for white queens like Sabrina and Leigh Bowery, the same cannot be said for Black and brown Ballroom icons like Lee Soulja who have been infusing a shaved head, leather, lace, spikes, and the insides of a child's coloring box—basically the avant-garde—into their artwork and attire for decades. The disparity in visibility and reverence is profound.

But I found Sabrina's maniacal writhing and angular poses delightful. It was clear that she had found a new lane late in life. White LGBTQ artists like my friend Michelle Handelman, Zackary Drucker, and Rhys Ernst publicly heralded Sabrina before her passing in 2017, making way for her to appear on platforms broader than that of indie films, platforms like the Whitney Biennial. Meanwhile, the Ballroom community tends to be back-doored into these spaces in voyeuristic, non-legendary, brand-dampening capacities—if they're even let in. This was honestly the crux of the matter in 1967, and it still is today.

My second encounter with Sabrina was watching her in *The Queen*. In it, she felt like someone I might have wanted to know—she was to-gether, industrious, and art-loving, and she maintained a socially adjust-able level of biting camp. When you first watch the film in its entirety, liking Sabrina only complicates the matter of making credible Crystal's accusations about her rigging the competition in the name of whiteness. Like some of my white classmates in Vogue'ology, you may think or even say Crystal's just a spoilsport, in the name of objectivity or whatever. But when does this inquisitive, "balanced," or devil's advocate line of ques-tioning become gaslighting? Does it empathize with the white queen be-cause accusations of racism feel too mean? Is it because Crystal's so full of rage? Well, she oughta be.

At a certain point, we have to stop asking the questions, "But do you *really think* Sabrina meant to discriminate against Crystal and the other Black contestants? Then why would she even invite them there?!" We know that racism is an institution that is the bedrock of the United States of America. The worth of white Americans is dependent on the oppres-sion of others. As little sense as it makes, I will not debate this fact. It simply stands to reason that if America's inherent racism goes without saying, which we know it does, then it can absolutely, almost certainly, operate unconsciously. All in all, no, I don't think Sabrina rigged the pageant in Harlow's favor, but I also don't think that Harlow was a supe-rior beauty. Her winning that award was definitely a nod to white, thin waifishness—the poster child at the time for fabricated white superior-ity—the rock upon which the entire Western world stands. What makes *you* think Sabrina—though kind, industrious, maybe even wise—would be exempt from operating within this system? *That* seems naïve to me.

I wish I could have been there on Crystal's behalf that day in Town Hall's dressing room, there amongst all that gaslighting, the "come now's," the "you can see for yourself's," and the basic claim that she was "showing her color." I would tell them that no one, especially in 1967, is beyond systemic racism and wouldn't be for the foreseeable future. Then again, had I done that, Crystal's eruption might have been quelled, and we wouldn't be here right now considering anything.

Jack was deliberate and calm as he laid the tarot cards on the dark table one by one and upside-down from his POV, so I could meet my fate face-to-face. That's generally how I like it. We both studied what to me, in my novice understanding, was a Canterbury Village of cup makers, monarchs, and mystics arranged in three groups and framed by a fresh pack of fluorescent pink Peeps (the bunny kind), half a cup of coffee, a small glass of Cherie, a stem of water for me, and a pack of More brand cigarettes.

"Do you mind if I smoke," Jack asked, looking up from his trance and reaching for the pack.

"Oh, of course not. Actually, can I steal one from you?" I grew up in a town called Winston-Salem (two brands of cigs) and went to a high school named R. J. Reynolds (the company behind those two brands), and I'd never heard of "Mores." I needed to know. Plus, the stakes were so high!

"But of course."

We sparked up and went right back to looking down in silence. This is what we saw:

Middle set of cards, lined up vertically:

King of Wands, Nine of Wands, Eight of Wands, Six of Wands, Five of Wands, Five of Swords, Ace of Wands

Upper-left corner, lined up horizontally:

The Fool, Justice, the Lovers, Four of Pentacles, the Chariot, Judgment

Upper-right corner, vertical:

King of Cups, Eight of Cups, Ten of Cups

If you're a tarot head and reading this, have a field day with interpreting my cards; however, six years ex post facto, I'm only able to retain a few key takeaways Jack laid out for me that evening. At some point in the future I'll have my dear friend and Vogue'ology classmate (the one our teacher Robert Sember lovingly refers to as my wife) Colin Bedell (aka Queer Cosmos) reverse engineer the reading for me, but in the meantime, this is what I remember about Jack's breakdown.

He went straight to the Fool, to which I replied, "How dare you." He laughed and assured me that the Fool, despite his name, is quite the fortuitous card.

"Are you going on any last-minute trips or jumping into any new endeavors?" he asked.

"Well . . . I'm trying to decide which grad school to go to. Got into a handful. Waitlisted for Cornell. But I'm leaning more toward one of two writing programs in England."

"Well, the Fool is always ready for an adventure . . ."

We both smiled.

Somewhere in the cards the South African I'd met in New York and whom I'd fallen madly in love with showed up, but he always does. Even from across the globe. I remember a lot of reference to magic. Jack had done a lot of these readings for the Biennial, and it stood out to me that mine stood out to him. The general feel of the entirety was that I was powerful at manifesting my desires *when focused*. That I should realize it now and harness it asap. The reading flew by.

"So, you know exactly what to do. The world is yours. You just have to grab it."

"I think I'm going to England."

"You're the boss, Applesauce."

THE INTERVIEW

w/Lee Soulja, Part 1

Lee Soulja wears so many hats: Performance artist. Event organizer. Archivist. Activist. Father and founder of the House of Soulja. For those in the culture, he is a Ballroom Legend, and for those in the broader NYC nightlife scene, he is a legend and a mentor. To others, he's kind of a hidden figure behind many great Ballroom events, but I've come to find that he was also there when hip-hop was born, disco died, and performance art was resurrected as pop. I'm honored to be a holder of his story—but I'm getting ahead of myself.

In this first conversation, on October 17, 2018, I'd been helping Lee write a proposal for funding for one of his many but most important projects: NYC Center for Black Pride, an archive, outreach, and events organization for which he serves as executive director. We talked about

Black Pride's history and how Lee was readying for World Pride 2019, which also marked the fiftieth anniversary of the Stonewall riots. We quickly got into the importance of preserving Ballroom history. There's honestly so much more to say, but I'll leave it there for now.

RICKY: So, you've been running NYC Black Pride for about ten
    years now?

LEE: More than ten years, actually. I was a part of the planning com-
    mittee when POCC (People of Color in Crisis) was doing it. They
    [Black Pride] used to bring community leaders in to be a part of the
    planning committee, and Michael Roberson, who's like my brother,
    actually initiated doing Black Pride programs with the Ballroom
    community, Black publications, and outside promoters. I'd already
    been helping the founders of Black Pride for a while, and after that
    original Black Pride ended and POCC closed. I took the two found-
    ers out for lunch and asked them about letting me run Black Pride.
    The two of them looked at me and said, "Knock yourself out." So, I
    renamed it NYC Black Pride, incorporated it, and then I just kind of
    moved forward.

RICKY: What was the process of evolving Black Pride into *NYC* Black
    Pride like?

LEE: Obviously, my first journey was how do I get people back to work-
    ing with Black Pride here in New York after everybody lost money
    in the 2008 recession? Right? I spent a lot of those first years trying
    to work with the community, get sponsors, and make money back.
    When Michael and POCC ran "Pride in the City," aka Black Pride,
    they not only brought the community together, but they were also
    able to amass substantial funding for the events. When I inherited
    Black Pride, that then became my task.

RICKY: That sounds like Michael. So, he and POCC brought in mean-
    ingful conversations about LGBT and Ballroom issues?

LEE: Yes, they brought the whole community outreach part into it.
    When I took Black Pride over, I thought about how everybody
    already knew me as a club promoter and a performer. I can throw a
    club party with my eyes closed. Actually, at that time, I was part of
    a promotion team that threw a big party here in New York at Mars
    2112, a space-travel-themed space. That party was bringing in 1,500
    people a week. Like I said, I could throw a party. But watching all

of these Prides that were popping up all over the country, it really just occurred to me to ask, what are we *really* proud of—that we could throw a party? That's not what Black Pride meant to me, and I wanted to figure out a way to expand on what Michael had started at POCC and make it more about a cultural celebration. So that first year, I started pulling people together that were in the community and telling them that I wanted to make the NYC Black Pride committee more diverse than it had been and more representational of the many pieces of our community.

RICKY: Tell me what you mean by more diverse.

LEE: Well, I decided I didn't want to be a Black gay man trying to dictate what a lesbian event should look like. I didn't want to decide what a trans event should look like and so on. So, I figured I needed to engage the community to be a part of NYC Black Pride. I decided to invite all of these people that were promoters or doing special events that were catering to different segments of our community to say that Black Pride is for all of us—so what would you like to see? Then there were other conversations around POCC's award ceremony and its role in Black Pride. It made me stop and think, *What do these awards really mean for our community, who are we awarding, and why are we awarding them?* Then the bigger picture of it was thinking about the young people in Ballroom and the LGBT community who feel this lack of a sense of value for themselves, which to me is a big part of why I think the epidemic of HIV is where it is with our community. Of course, if you don't see any value in yourself, or you don't see anyone valuing your life, then why would you protect something that has no value, right?

RICKY: Absolutely. Great questions. I've heard Michael say something similar in his theological work about what happens when you're taught by society that your life as an LGBTQ person of color is an abomination. How would you think you're anything other than that? Why wouldn't you act accordingly?

LEE: Exactly. So, I also do community work around young LGBT people. I mentor people, have conversations with youth graduating out of foster homes. I talk to them about life as the LGBT grown-ups they're about to be. I say, "*Now* you're going to deal with it on a bigger scale, because the world at large is not happy about who you are." So just grounding them, you know? I also help them plan events and showcase their art, performances, and stuff. I mean, I'm a visual artist myself. I'm known for my bizarre costumes.

RICKY: I've seen them! They're amazing . . .

LEE: Thank you! I had to figure out at one point how to change that from the façade of what I was doing in nightclubs as a club kid in the day, to people wanting me to open fashion shows or use my pictures at different events and stuff. And I began to realize this is a product and I'm marketing myself now as a visual artist, not a club kid. I try to help young people do the same.

RICKY: It sounds like when you took over Black Pride you transformed it into a program that provides a lot of community services.

LEE: Yeah.

RICKY: So, you do events and outreach. What do you envision the future of NYC Black Pride to be? Obviously, these events have to keep being a main attraction. . . .

LEE: Right. Those services have not gone away. Under the process of running NYC Black Pride over the last ten years, and giving out Heritage Awards, I learned so much, working with the Schomburg Center for Research in Black Culture and the LGBT archives that are there, I realized that a big piece that's missing is documentation, talking about, presenting, and *saving* LGBT history—which includes ball culture. The Schomburg has the archives, but it's a depository. It's just a space for safekeeping of records, papers, and artifacts. But you really don't have access to it unless you are going there for something specific, and how would you know specifically what to go there and ask for if you don't know it exists? So, the first thing is that we've got to start documenting our history and our people and who they are. We need to be able to then digitize all media, like Polaroids, flyers, etc., and connect them to the Schomburg and the New York Historical Society, the Smithsonian, and other institutions. This takes funding and a lot of work.

RICKY: That's huge.

LEE: Exactly. When I went to those entities and asked if they'd be interested in partnering to make an archive, they wanted to know if I'd be able to create something that would connect people and drive them there. I thought, *Well that's just what I'm going to do.*

RICKY: You told the Smithsonian you'd get back to them?

LEE: Yes. So, I'm working to create the archive now, and I know there's a huge need for it. When they opened the African American History Museum in DC for the Smithsonian, they actually threw a ball, and everyone there was telling the Smithsonian to contact me, because they knew I was creating this whole archive. They have history and documentation there, and it's so sad that Ballroom, something that's so historically important, is not equally represented. We now know that Ballroom, the first drag balls, started in 1869 in Harlem—2019 will be Ballroom's 150th anniversary. That's hugely significant to Black history, never mind LGBT history. That's exactly 100 years before Stonewall. There's so much to that, and nobody is telling that story. So, NYC Black Pride, to me, began with the idea that our story is not being told. Our story is not being documented. So, how do I do that? How do I create that space and also inspire other Black Prides across America to realize that this is what Black Pride *really* is about? It's about us celebrating who we are, our culture. Not a bunch of circuit parties.

    So, when I go to DC, I should be able to learn the history of what Black gay life was like in those early clubs and how they organized and started. Then we can do the same thing for DC, Detroit, and Philly. Every single Black city that has a Black Pride has a Black LGBT history. And there are Black people that are doing amazing community work and public things that we should be celebrating. We should be able to know who those people are in order for the newer generation to feel like these are the people they come from, that they can aspire to. We have to learn who these people are.

RICKY: How did you start doing that work?

LEE: I decided to create this thing called the NYC Center for Black Pride, a place that kind of puts into context Black LGBT history. It's basically an educational center, and within that will be this Ballroom archive, because it's important and under the umbrella of Black LGBT history. It's a space for history and people to come together.

    It's important to reach out to our community, so I try do that in different ways. I'm preparing right now for Thanksgiving dinner, which will be my fifth year giving a dinner for people in the Ballroom and LGBT community. So many people here in New York don't have family to celebrate with or don't have money to go to a Thanksgiving dinner. There are people with HIV that don't want—because of stigma and stuff—to utilize Meals on Wheels and all of those programs. So, I do this community dinner every year the day before Thanksgiving. Then I do an event to support the NYC Health Department with the Red Ball, which is an annual ball on World AIDS Day. I usually do something around New Year's too. I've basically expanded Black Pride over the last ten years to be beyond just the once-a-year festival in August.

RICKY: Are awards still in there somewhere?

LEE: Absolutely. I do the Awards Ball at the Schomburg. Then there's the huge beach party that I throw. I also do this off-Broadway show called *Songs for Marsha* [P. Johnson].

RICKY: Awesome.

LEE: Yeah, it's great. I'm so grateful for that one because it brings us back to that notion of why Black Pride even started. It's because of people like Marsha P. Johnson and Sylvia [Rivera] and Stormé [DeLarverie]. Next year's going to be World Pride, and it's the fiftieth anniversary of Stonewall.

RICKY: Is the Schomburg still creating a Black LGBTQ archive?

LEE: Well, the Schomburg actually has two tasks now. They've got these LGBT archives—what are they going to do with them now that they don't have a person like my friend Stephen there anymore, someone who spearheaded it and was logged into the community? He was the real reason why I started to do the awards at the Schomburg, because he was like, "You have your finger on the pulse of who's doing what and what's happening in the community. We could use you as a feed for the archives for new events that we should be made aware of." Now he's not there anymore, which makes what I'm doing even more important. I am necessarily moving forward with the center, but now I've got to reestablish a new connection to the Schomburg. Stephen said, "When you're ready to do that, hit me up, and let me know. I'll help you to navigate that."

RICKY: Oh, good. That seems promising.

LEE: And I have some friends, like I said, at the Smithsonian who said the same thing: "When you reach the point when you want to sit down and have a conversation about how there could be linkage between our organization and the Center for Black Pride . . ." Everyone is itching for the real history of Ballroom to be written down.

RICKY: Most definitely. Documented—seen.

LEE: Exactly. Especially because Ballroom is so global now, and the information is just not there. So, I go back and forth between the New York Historical Society and the Schomburg. There's so much information there. I've taken a couple of interns out of Columbia University, and we just started digging. We were all over the place, and I realized how this historical stuff is so scattered that it's going to take a long time to archive it. It's a project in and of itself, just taking information and centralizing it in one place to tell the story. Hopefully, one day we can be that place for people to learn more.

RICKY: Yeah, even if it were just a digital platform, that's a huge undertaking.

LEE: Right. There's so much, like the Black newspapers that talk about where the very first balls were held. We found out that those Black newspapers—although the New York Historical Society has some— *all* of them are at the Schomburg. But again, Schomburg ain't gonna pull those out for you. You really got to be specific in what you're looking for.

RICKY: This archival aspiration seems to be the differentiator between the past Black Prides and this current NYC Black Pride iteration that you're talking about.

LEE: Oh, big time, big time.

RICKY: And I think that's a huge point of leverage when looking for funding. Also, what about memories and oral histories? VHS tapes of balls, people voguing, etc.? Getting those digitized. That's another layer of archival matter, and another big lift.

LEE: Right. I mean, I have lots of those tapes too. So, yeah. But here's a big part of the problem: I had a large conversation with Jennie Livingston. I've known her since she did *Paris Is Burning*. She filmed it over four years, and when Miramax bought the rights to all stuff, I said to her, "Where is the rest of that footage?" She said, "Lee, that stuff needs to be digitized. We're going to lose it." Then she said, "It's going to be expensive, but history-wise, somebody needs to do it." I thought, *Yeah, they do. That has to be on the list of things to do—get that stuff and digitize it!*

RICKY: My God, it's so important.

LEE: But that's money. So, what she was kind of saying to me was that this is such a great project but wanted me to realize how quickly it's going to grow into a beast. We're collecting LGBT history and trying to link different parts; imagine the kind of computer database we'd need to build to house this stuff. But I know there's a lot of money out there for it. I've done my research and found out that there's money available for the creation of learning spaces, especially if it's something that is made accessible to youth and community and builds awareness. There are so many angles to it, but it's necessary for us to know who we are in order to know where we're going.

JOSÉ XTRAVAGANZA

AKA: José Gutierez Xtravaganza
HOUSE: Xtravaganza
CATEGORY: Old Way, New Way
SUPERPOWER: Flexibility
FAMOUS BATTLE: José Xtravaganza vs. Willi Ninja
NOTABLE QUOTABLE: "Street voguing is something that you feel. . . . It's like acting out your dreams."

W hen you think about the temperament of a typical voguer, that scene in *Indiana Jones and the Temple of Doom* comes to mind, you know, the one where the Thuggee cult leader tears out a man's heart before dunking him in lava as human sacrifice—but Father José Gutierez Xtravaganza is no typical voguer. With composure and grace, your end by his hand is an agile demise. Through lush freeze frames, lines that blossom and bloom in sequence, exotic contortions, and a beguiling smirk that creates a kind of spellbinding sleight of hand (performance), José is the Poison Ivy of voguing, wholly intoxicating—yet fully lethal.

It's the sweetness he emits while at werk that is most compelling about José, a complex fragrance that's equal notes lily of the valley and Dominican on the Lower East Side. Cutting his teeth on Vogue during the time when disco was evolving into house, hip-hop into various dance forms, and Ballroom into the competitive mainstream, this ballet-trained New Yorker sits at the intersection of opposing centrifugal forces, making him destined to be an ambassador for his community and the reigning prince of vogue. Madonna marveled at the seemingly infinite number of rapid-fire elegant poses that José, a diminutive force of nature, was able to conjure up at the age of fifteen. Since then, he has toured the world as a dancer/choreographer, been in numerous films and music videos, and already a reigning legend, become a crown jewel in ball culture's tiara, letting everyone across the globe know that a ruby rose does indeed grow on the LES.

CHAPTER 3

VOGUE

w/Arturo Mugler

Learning to vogue, the five elements, and getting your life

There's a sink or swim element to traveling to a new foreign city alone that gets me jazzed. But being more of the "I want to pretend I live here" type of tourist as opposed to the "When's the next double-decker to the Louvre" American cliché, I find the only thing more fun than being in that new city alone is traveling there for work. It means you automatically arrive with a network, even if that is just your event contact. Plus, I like a stretch of vacation days to be anchored—in the middle if possible—by a professional activity, something to look forward to, a chance to shine in a new context, be it a public reading, a university lecture, or, in the case of Toronto, "on the beat."

In January of 2019, knowing that I was working on this book, Michael Roberson forwarded me an invite to the Journey to Black Liberation Symposium and the Black Liberation Ball 2019, hosted by the Harbourfront Centre, an arts and culture organization in the heart of Toronto. I perked up immediately as I pored over the contents of the email—the description read as promising:

Date: Thu, Jan 17, 2019, 3:44 PM
Subject: Journey to Black Liberation Symposium and The Black Liberation Ball 2019

Greetings and salutations,

I hope this new year has been a prosperous one so far.

I am excited to announce that we are just over two weeks away from the Journey to Black Liberation Symposium and The Black Liberation Ball at Harbourfront Centre, in Toronto. The symposium will take place on February 1st and 2nd, 2019, a part of the Kuumba Black History Month festival.

The Journey to Black Liberation Symposium and The Black Liberation Ball is co-curated by The Black Daddies Club (BDC) founder Brandon Hay (Toronto), Michael Roberson Maasai Mason-Margiella (Ultra-red/C-RRED/Adjunct Professor Union Theology Seminary New York City) and Twysted Miyake-Mugler, founder of the Toronto Kiki Ballroom Alliance (Toronto).

The focus of the Journey to Black Liberation symposium is to have a series of cross border conversations between various Black communities around the world engaging in discussions that are affecting us on a micro as well as macro level. Our goal is not to just bear witness to the oppression and injustice, but it is to create a series of conversations across networks of Black activists, academics and other stakeholders looking at sharing ideas, strategizing, educating each other and community building in efforts to achieve Black liberation globally. The goal is to touch lives, enrich lives and also change lives in the process.

The theme for this year's Journey to Black Liberation is *Black Love, Honesty and Healing in the 21st Century.*

The Black Liberation Symposium is free with recommended pre-registration, there is an admission fee for The Black Liberation Ball. Below is the line-up for the 2019 plenaries.[1]

I'd never been to Toronto (or anywhere in Canada for that matter), but I had been wanting to attend a few balls to freshen up on what the girls were up to these days. It would be work, research to be specific, but that kind of work was sure to be a blast. Also, based on the flyers that were attached to the email, one of which featured a freeze-framed Pony Zion dancing in mid-air, I got the impression that all of New York's Ball-room scene was going to be there. Plus, the timing was just right. Those few weeks between New Year's and my birthday, in late February, are always the epitome of the doldrums—insert adventure here.

I immediately bought a ticket to the Black Liberation Ball and then signed up for a few of the workshops that focused on a range of discussions centered around community self-reflection and leading-edge Black/queer theory, like "Ballroom Has Something to Say," "For the Love of Money: A Conversation Around Sex Work and Black Bodies," "What Are Black Fathers Teaching Their Sons About Love?," a runway workshop with Twiggy Pucci Garçon, and what I would consider the centerpiece of my program schedule, the voguing workshop with icon Arturo Mugler, a room where I was almost certain to feel at home; I just needed to get there.

Another reason I like working on vacation is because something always seems to go awry during the strictly vacay portions of my solo trips to new places. While mountain climbing in Wales, I experienced a height-related, anxiety-fueled vertigo the locals called "crag fast," a condition that renders you suddenly immobile and irrationally afraid you're going to just tip over and fall off the face of a mountain. It was so bad toward the end that I had to crawl on my hands and knees to the summit. My friend Andy called me Spider-Man the rest of the way up to relieve the tension. That top-notch British humor.

Traveling to Toronto ended up being no exception. I should have suspected this would be the case by the very fact that I had to take one of those almost always broke-down double-decker buses, a company that I won't mention but will say that every time I take one of their buses, I instantly vow to never set foot onto one again. That is, at least until the next time. I mean, they're struggle buses; if they don't break down first, they end up dripping onto you mystery water from the ceiling while the loud and wrong person sitting next to you uses speakerphone throughout the duration of the trip. But a flight would have been exorbitant at such short notice, and I'd already dished out a good dime to stay in a fancier than normal condominium for the first half of my trip. I'd be in an apartment on the hip-but-not-fancy as usual side of Toronto for the second half.

I regularly make fun of Canadians, like my good friend Ted Kerr from Edmonton, Alberta, for using made-up elvish-sounding words like "toque" and "dink" instead of "toboggans" and "dicks." It's nonsense. It basically all stems from how jealous I am of their free healthcare, unlocked front doors, and generally even-keeled dispositions. So, when my double-decker bus pulled into customs roughly *four hours late*, the last thing I expected was to be discriminated against by a Canadian border patrolman.

I walked in half awake, having only slept a couple of hours, which was more than expected on that bus, so it never occurred to me that I'd need to quickly get it together for some Mountie-looking discount customs Kevin, but turns out I did.

"Passport?" he demanded.

I groggily checked all my pockets from the bottom to the top, finally pulling it out of my inside jacket pocket and handing it to him. He looked inside.

"Why were you born in England," he inquired sternly.

"Because I was born there."

"But why do you hold an American passport?"

"Because I'm an American." I wasn't relenting, mainly because I didn't know what about any of this was coming across as so curious to him. Both of us becoming increasingly frustrated, he moved on.

"Occupation?"

"Writer."

"No, your real job."

Now I was fully awakened, save for a flash daydream of pulling out one of my New School business cards that read "Senior Writer–Marketing & Communication," charging it up with kinetic energy like Gambit from *X-Men*, and throwing the projectile explosive right into his face.

"Writer." I said, with the blunt emphasis of a word made redundant. But that didn't faze him.

"Why are you here?"

"Research for a book."

He narrowed his eyes at me a beat. I raised an eyebrow at him that I intended to read as a defiant armfold. He begrudgingly stamped my passport. I took it and walked off.

The sun was rising when we reached the city around 7 a.m., revealing the streets of Toronto's waterfront to be blanketed by knee-high stacks of snow. I called for a car and waited, trying to shake my rude awakening at customs before it arrived. It helped that when he got there, my driver ended up being a personable and refreshing counter to my "I *knew* Canadians were secretly horrible!" theory. He chatted with me a perfect amount for that early hour, sporadic, unoppressive, non-spinoff patter connoting a genuine curiosity about my life as a writer rather than maintaining a pregnant racist suspicion about it. His SUV was broad with seat warmers, and he was engaging; unfortunately, all of this conspired to be just distracting enough for me to leave my phone in the back seat of his car. I only realized it as he pulled off, chasing after him for a good three blocks to no avail. Crap. The security code to get into the condo was in my phone, and on the way back to the high-rise, I stepped in a freezing pile of street slush. Luckily, the attendants in the lobby helped me get in without the security code, even though my Airbnb had specifically asked me not to bother them. I think they weren't supposed to be renting their property out or something, but by that point I was exhausted and like whatever dude. I lugged my things up to my room, drew the blinds, and collapsed fully dressed onto fresh sheets.

In my mind, I needed to at least attend the voguing workshop at noon and the Black Liberation Ball later that night, otherwise my work trip would have been a bust. Cell phone be damned. So, I spent the next three hours asleep instead of attending the first two Ballroom workshops and panels of the day, and then roughly half an hour pretending that that spotless condo overlooking Toronto from on high was indeed mine, staring out the window and burning my tongue on complimentary coffee because time was ticking. Then, in order to begin the process of getting my phone back, I jumped willingly into a gig-economy customer service K-hole and, with no customer service line to call or a phone with which to call it, flailed about in the ethers of an automaton hell, yelling transcripts of frantic laptop emails into the canals of deaf digital ears, not a single human in earshot. I hit send, crossed my fingers, and then had to get ready to go.

Toronto's Harbourfront Centre on Queens Quay West was basically down the street from my Airbnb, and when I walked in, the tall-ceilinged halls were quiet, oddly mimicking the sound insulation of all the snow on the ground just outside its many windows. Off in the distance, coming from what I imagined was a multipurpose room somewhere, I heard music that might have been featured on any playlist by preeminent Ballroom DJ MikeQ, that repetitive 180 bpm's of "boots and pants" kick drums and hi-hats perfect for supporting a bewitching hand performance, a spin, and a dip. I felt a sudden sense of ease. Less alien. I followed the signs down the hall to Arturo's vogue workshop.

Harbourfront's dance space was gigantic, expansive white floors against massively windowed walls. The crowd there was mixed across age, gender, and race, but the dancers in the room could be easily spotted. They stretched and prematurely gave hand and duckwalk performances to set themselves apart. It was interesting to me that none of them were Black or Latinx, but then again, this *was* mostly a class for beginners—in Canada—so that may have explained it. I continued skimming the room from the doorway. Bureaucratic ladies standing against the wall, staunchly assessing the class size . . . a range of middle-aged to older women, smiling excitedly, some wringing their hands . . . three young Black ladies in their twenties having a discussion about what voguing even is (interesting, is that because they're African Canadian?!) . . . and at the front of the room, perched on the stage's edge, smiling and brimming with the excitement of an upcoming performance, were two young Black men who I gathered were the workshop's facilitators. As a friend to the community, and a voyeur for the afternoon, it was important for me to introduce myself, so I made a beeline over there to do so. While I was in transit, one of them, a full-bodied man with knowing eyes and a wise beard started voguing, and from the registration PDF, I knew that this must have been Arturo, our instructor for the day.

"Hi, Arturo?"

"Hello," he replied.

"Nice to meet you," I said, shaking his hand. "I'm Ricky Tucker, a student, colleague, and friend of Michael Roberson's."

"Oh, okay. Nice to meet you too, Ricky," he said, brightening.

"I don't wanna bother you too much, before your class and all, but I'm visiting from New York because I'm writing a book about Ballroom."

"Very cool."

"Thanks, I like to think so. I'm doing research while I'm here at the conference, and planned on sitting in the back over there and taking some notes for the book, if that's okay with you? I didn't want to be back there like a creep all class and not introduce myself."

"Ha! That's no problem at all."

"Great, thanks. And I may hit you up for some questions afterward, if you'll be around."

"Sounds good."

I introduced myself to the other man standing with him who turned out to be Twysted Miyake-Mugler, an incredible voguer who was one of the Torontonian organizers of the weekend and an up-and-coming bridge between the New York and Canadian scenes. His eyes were kind, framed by what many of my girlfriends have deemed ironically and unnaturally unfair long lashes on a man. His smile was fleeting and fun, kinda like he always had a shady secret. I made his acquaintance and went about my work, walking over to the furthest wall from the door and slumping down onto the floor. I nestled into the rote writer-DNA-igniting acts of making myself small, turning on my laptop, and then its voice recorder.

There on that studio floor in inhospitable Toronto, having just activated my New York Ballroom familial connection and observing seasoned dancers warming up along with soon-to-be first-time voguers breaking a sweat, a sense of relief washed over me. I was home in that foreign place. Finally.

VOGUING WORKSHOP W/ARTURO MUGLER, TORONTO
February 2, 2019, 12:21 pm EST

Arturo decides to get things started by throwing 'em in cold—without warning, he puts a house track on over the loudspeakers. This indeed sparks a vibe, and people start moving. He says to them, "To start, I just want to see what you can do, and I'll critique you and fix you as we go along. Don't be afraid. . . ." From the back of the room, just finishing up their obligatory stretches, a handful of professional dancers move forward and start showing off their advanced vogue skill sets. A young Black man wearing a red top busts out some austere old-way angles that get us going. As Arturo nears, a circle naturally begins to form, the class creating a human spotlight made for whoever dares step into it. A young Asian woman in an electric-yellow dress does so, fem rolling her hands up to the sky, her long hair waterfalling as she watches them ascend. She spins out of the circle. A small group of middle-aged women marvel at the performance and start clapping to the beat. I join in. Arturo is now walking the perimeter of the circle, tapping folks into it. A young white woman in a leopard-print dress launches in but slows the vibe down several beats, throwing hands from side-to-side in a deceptively casual but deliberate way, then playfully using her dress as a prop for seduction. She is taking her time, and it is werk-ing. Arturo taps in an older Black woman in a stunning yellow, black, and blue kente print, and though she's clearly new to this Ballroom brand of strutting, she's no stranger to gettin' it. She body rolls and shakes her dress from side to side. After a few more pro and not-so-pro exhibitions, the music stops, and Arturo comes in like a cool Cheshire Cat. "So . . . I see that everyone's at different levels," he says. "Yasss!" shout the dancers. "And that is all good," he says. "Now, I want everyone to space out." He waits as the class moves into a typical set of dance instruction rows. A woman from Harbourfront takes this quieter moment to run over to me from across the room. "Don't you want to join in?" she asks. "Oh, no thank you," I say. "I'm working on a book about Ballroom, so I'm just here to observe and take notes. Thanks, though!" Crestfallen, she smiles and runs back to the opposite wall to continue observing. Arturo is ready to teach. "Let's do some catwalks!"

Vogue Element 1/5: Catwalk

Catwalking is a driving engine of vogue fem, a rhythmic hybrid of dance and runway. With a clear trajectory in front of you and a lowered center of gravity, you step one foot over the other like you're traversing a straight line, your hips swaying femininely with every step forward. As you get the rhythm—tah, tah, ta ta ta—your forearms and hands move forward and back or up and down in opposing directions, which without practice can feel like walking and chewing gum concurrently. Because of its defiant feel, you'll often see folks enter into the frame of a vogue fem category using this element. Done well and at a fast enough clip, it means walking into the room followed by a trail of flames.

After explaining to his students the logistics of catwalking—how you want to lower yourself to five feet or your lowest level—Arturo walks around the room gently lowering folks by their shoulders, displaying the severity of the gravity drop needed to properly catwalk. Even folks who are only five feet tall are expected to reduce their height. "If you feel the strain in your knees," he says, "you're doing it right." #Hardfacts.

As I watch him float around the room, I'm reminded of what it takes to pull the fierceness out of your students, or to even just get them to come out of their shells and participate. Being an instructor of vogue means being a dancer, a motivational speaker, a stand-up comedian, a personal trainer, and the shadiest bitch in the room. You have to inspire like twenty to thirty new voguers, often through humor, to work past their comfort levels (to embrace pain) lest they be shaded into dust—the less bloody, newbie version of a chop. Spinning all of these compartmental plates can come off as wholly compelling if not fully manic. Frankly, both are a kiki to observe, and watching him, I'd say Arturo is more of the compelling variety. At one point, he runs over and stops a woman who is taking too full a stride while catwalking one foot across the other. "Wait, wait, wait," he says, stopping her. "It's not a lunge, girl! Watch me." He catwalks about fifteen feet in front of her, effortlessly sashaying there and back again. Great technique. I practically heard timpani playing along as his hips swayed. "Now, you got great skinny calves, but Ima need you to push that hip *out*," he says. Positive reinforcement followed by a critique. Super effective. On the way over to his next case, I hear him scream-whisper, "Chile, I need to stretch!"

He wanders over to a tall, older woman wearing an outstanding amount of gold crinoline. "Uh, honey," Arturo says to her. "What's up underneath this frock you got on?!" She's not sure how to answer that, so she just starts giggling. "I need to see what's going on under there. That's too much fabric!" Not grading on a curve, it seems that Professor Mugler's pedagogical practice is twofold: (1) no pain, no gain, and (2) work with what you got! While talking to a tall white male student, he's a tad less flirtatious. "You're not low enough." He lowers him by the shoulder. "Stay down—don't come up." Arturo steps back to observe the man who's clearly a dancer but has fallen into the technical trappings of impersonating instead of embodying. Arturo rests a kind hand on his shoulder for a beat. "Stop forcing your arms . . . relax . . ." He takes this as an opportunity to emphasize the importance of being loose and "cunt" (those are two separate ideas) when performing the hands portion of cat-walking during vogue fem. Arturo shows the man what he's doing wrong with his hands, robotically serving left and right, and then demonstrates the correct feminine flow. "Don't overthink it. It's not about how hard you're doing it. It should be graceful. . . ."

Vogue Element 2/5: Hands

Hands are interesting because they can be their own separate performance and often are. In terms of vogue, with femininity as the baseline, hands can go fast or slow but should always tell a story: of how ugly your opponent is, how pretty you are (in the case of Willi Ninja), boredom through yawning, dainty nose-tapping refinement, and on and on. Personally, I lament the current trend of throwaway hand performances, i.e., hands that are literally thrown hap-hazardly from one side to the other, yes fem, but without a lick of narrative to tell. Why even bother? No. In the name of Ninja, I want Mummenschanz crisp hands that cuntily mime out every major and minor plot point of the goddamn *Odyssey*. Thanks.

Back in Vogue'ology, on our very first day of theory-free dance practice, the feeling in the studio was comparable, frenetic with anticipation and self-consciousness. No one, men or women, was venturing as courageously far into the fem end of the spectrum as Professor Pony Zion would have liked. We were far from his first vogue class, and I remember him notably softening his tone and switching up his approach.

"So, listen. Y'all are going to have to get more cunt wit it. And yes, we use the word 'cunt' here; it's not a bad word. See these," he says, holding a letter C with each of his hands and slowly and sensually twisting them around his nipple area, his dancer pecs as diesel as gladiator plates under his tank. "These are your breasts. Do this." Everyone follows his lead. "And see this," he starts seductively running his hands, one after the other, up the length of his inner thighs, like a hot waterfall running upstream. "And that is your cunt. You have to imagine that you are fem and be that." In that moment, every gender and age in the room learned the transformative power of pulling desire from our imaginations and turning it into hard facts. Professor Zion helped us find our inner women, and our collective imaginary cunts were wet.

Arturo then has the girls (everyone) break into rows of roughly five or six, each of them meant to catwalk to the front of the room with cold unadulterated conviction. As they do this, I notice that (as in any class-room) each row of people is marked by their comparable levels of experience, and then, in descending order, the most daring and experienced dancers are ready to roll in row one, the least red-2-go in like row five. No matter the cohort, everyone has a peer set and a direction in which to grow. A lot of the time, your level of confidence has a lot to do with your row. I myself have been in both rows one and five in my life.

Dance is a real source of joy and sanity for me. I didn't always honor or even admit that.

One time during karaoke, a friend started giggling at how badly I was singing a song, which kind of irked me because he's a trained musical theater nerd and clearly was jumping at the opportunity to be cooler than somebody, but ya know, a broken clock gets it right twice a day. Anyway, once I was done botching the track, I looked over at him and said, "You know, I'm a writer, teacher, and dancer, in that order—I never claimed to be a singer." That confirmed list of what I indeed was and never claimed to be was enough for him to fuck off, but after having articulated it like that for the first time, I suddenly realized it was true. Gasp—I *am* a dancer.

So, in Boston in 2010, right before my move to NYC and right around my Saturn return—my astrological return to self—I started renting out the dance studios at my job at Northeastern University on Fridays at 7 a.m. Getting there at that time meant I would rarely have to compete with students or anyone else signing up for a studio (or worry about anyone walking in on me), and it was just enough time to dance for like an hour and a half, run over to the gym for a shower, and be at the admissions office by 9 to be on time for work. After being depressed for so long in my early twenties, I was excited to explore the few ways that I knew for a fact were my sources of joy—and then exploit them to no end.

NU's dance studios were wrapped in ballet bars and wall-length mirrors, equipped with major sound systems, and built with ample enough insulation so that even in that far-flung corner of the Curry Student Center, you were sure not to bother anyone, or be bothered yourself. I was concerned about that at first, maybe because the dance that I was drawn to was like a butch queen, hip-hop, modern dance combo, and I wanted to explore that unhampered, or I guess unashamed. Plus, dance was personal to me, and even tucked away in an off-to-the-side studio that almost no one was using, this was still my workplace. Even in Boston, queerness had a stigma.

It took me a few months of Fridays to find the courage to really dance the way I'd wanted to. Things started off slow. I tried falling back into old choreography, mostly dredging up stuff from Janet Jackson videos like "If" and "Rhythm Nation." The choreography to Aaliyah's "Are You That Somebody" was a particularly dazzling jewel in my crown, and once I had a sturdy repertoire of music videos under my belt, I leveled up a bit.

About a year into this habit, I ordered a unitard. Don't ask me why; it just seemed to bolster my increasingly accurate use of the studio's ballet bars. Every Friday turned into Tuesdays and Fridays, and the only reason it wasn't every day was because I'd convinced myself I needed to diversify my workouts by running the rest of the week. And I was afraid of overexposing myself to and therefore ruining the act of dancing, one of the things I love most. Now I know how impossible that is. I started choreographing original dances to songs like Robyn's "Fem Bot" and learning the dance to "End of Time" through meticulously rewinding and starting spliced together bits of Beyoncé's concert footage with her performance at the Roseland Ballroom. Still, even while channeling the ubiquitous Sasha Fierce, I would never go too deep into anything too ladylike, never vogued without looking over my shoulder or out the studio door window to be sure I was actually alone. I didn't want to be caught letting go. I didn't want to be clocked femming.

Then one Friday morning, in preparation for a dance party I was going to later that night, as a warmup, I decided to freestyle to a song that is definitively fem: "Throb" by Janet Jackson, a rare house track produced by Janet's mainstay collaborators, Jimmy Jam and Terry Lewis, that gets you off your seat and causes you to blush, the song's climax being the sound of Janet climaxing, her moaning, swearing, and riding empty air until the beat redrops like a culminating thrust. It's easily the cuntiest song on the *Janet* album and surely her most voguable track to date.

But that day in the studio, I just let go. Pre my Vogue'ology training, I intuitively put together a hand performance in front of the mirror, spinning, splitting, serving up my hand-framed face to the gods, body rolling, and nay-naying with delight to Janet's pulsating track. When I was done, I grabbed my towel draped over the ballet bar on the far end of the room and then did my obligatory walk over to the port window to make sure no one had been watching, except this time there had been. A young guy, maybe fourteen years old, Black and ostensibly queer (whatever that means, but whatever, I *know* he was), had been watching me the whole time, his eyes so glued to the window that he didn't move until I actually opened the door—then he leapt out of his trance and out of the way. He was wearing a unitard with black gym shorts over it.

"Hi," I said.

"Hi, um, I'm sorry, is this dance studio B?"

"Nope, that's the one next door."

"Oh, I reserved it, but the door is locked."

"Facilities has the key," I said. "Their office is that door just across the courtyard, but if they're not there, I should be done in here in about forty-five minutes."

"Oh, okay, thank you."

"No sweat."

I closed the door and instantly flushed with the hot embarrassment of being caught in the act. I hid my face in my towel for a good fifteen seconds, reliving and regretting the stunned look on that kid's face, how his face was positively on the verge of being pressed up against the studio window, his mouth agape, his wide-eyed astonishment . . . the sense of wonder bubbling up inside of him . . . ? It occurred to me that I'd seen that look before in classrooms when, out of nowhere, an illuminating turn of phrase connects two seemingly disparate thoughts, igniting something new in a student. It's the switch that connects the current that finally lights the bulb. It wasn't an embarrassment. It had been an "aha" moment I'd witnessed.

It may sound weird, but I suddenly felt a sense of responsibility to be fem, and from that point forward I decided to at least work toward being free of homophobic restraints by my own hand, especially in the hallowed space of dance, one meant for me but also rich with the power to affect others. Through watching me vogue and twirl and such that day, that kid, I hoped, learned that by the very virtue of it being a deep personal desire, embracing a true side of himself can affirm him, is generally innocuous to others, and in its greatest capacity even feeds the culture. That's what I learned that day. In short, it is our fucking birthright to fem.

That sentiment, the idea that bodily freedom can be a path to personal and social freedom, that it can teach others, and be a direct route to thriving—even shining—is one of few things in this world that I know to be true. A heady concept but one my friend Jonovia Chase is able to articulate more concisely:

> To me everyone should have a little something special in them. I used to do this thing—I think a lot of people do it actually—when I needed a moment at work, so you know, I'd go to the bathroom and vogue a little, give a little something in the mirror. Whether you use it on the Ballroom floor or not, voguing is for everyone within the culture. You should feel you can use it to express yourself whenever you feel you want to do so. It should be in your back pocket—you never know what's going to happen! You never know when a battle might pop up, or when you just need to relieve some energy, to feel like you're that girl.

"Five, six, seven, eight, and switch . . . and pop . . . Yeah, I know it hurts!" It's round two of the catwalking rows, "The Bomb!" by the Bucketheads is playing ("These sounds fall into my mi-yee-i-yee-ind"), and Arturo is no longer playing around. In the interim between rounds, he's added choreography to the mix, a complex routine culminating with duckwalks, a move that, like the rain, makes my knees hurt just knowing it's coming.

Vogue Element 3/5: Duckwalk

Thankfully executed in small bursts, duckwalks are exactly what they sound like, squatting down on your haunches and kicking your feet out like a duck as you walk forward. It is an impressive display performed by the steel-willed and young-kneed.

"I know you're older, girl," Arturo yells to a woman in the last row who's given up on the duckwalk bit and life, "but that don't mean shit!" To a man catwalking, he shouts, "More hips, you got a lot of em—push it!" I giggle along with a few other bystanders, including the Harbour-front folks, who intermittently juggle that with being spellbound.

Row two, that earlier group of three gorgeous Black women in their early twenties along with two others, comes catwalking to the front of the room, knocking the strut, hands, hips, and spins in the routine out of the ballpark and turning the duckwalk at the end into a self-congratulatory celebration, kind of like a touchdown dance. "Yasss," Arturo screams.

It's so thrilling to watch; I start seat-dancing the choreography from my place against the wall. A less confident row comes through. "Even if you mess up, don't stop the catwalk," says Arturo. "Just keep moving. Keep on moving . . ." he sings. "Don't stop like the hands of time." Soul II Soul songs are great motivators.

After a few more stellar performances, you can see that people are really starting to get the hang of it, but you can also tell that they are getting pretty zapped. Arturo intuits this. "Everyone tired? Yeah? Good," he teases. "If you need water, get it now." The rows evaporate.

Now a small circle, the more experienced young dancers from row one keep it going. They compare how they each approach the harder bits of the routine. The girl in yellow shows off her duckwalk, spinning while low on the ground but then bringing it back up and falling back into a dip and split, her long hair tossed back in victory. Her friends golf clap, while one of the older women screams "Ooh!" in encouragement.

Vogue Element 4/5: Spins and Dips

The pièce de résistance of modern vogue. You spin or twirl, whether fast or slow, into a dip down onto the ground, typically in a stage split in which one knee is tucked behind you, the other leg straight in front of you. When asked in Vogue'ology by a tentative student how one might go about performing the dip portion of the spin and dip without hurting one's self, vogue icon and superhero Pony Zion, known for leaping off stages and into impossible dips, simply said, "You try to be careful, but honestly, girl, sometimes you just gonna eat it!" In other words, no pain, no gain. And finally, post-dip, while you're already on the ground, you may as well do some . . .

Vogue Element 5/5: Floorwork

An element that, at its full height, is a heated, unrelenting, gracefully composed knock-down, drag-out competition on the floor. Often in front of the judges in a bid to win them over, two voguers slide and maneuver sensually on the floor, sometimes contorting and shaping themselves around one another as a means of conquering the other and displaying superior flexibility. It's truly a sight to behold, and it's one of the shadier and more expressive elements of this already engaging category.

Back from the break, Arturo adds increasingly difficult bits and pieces to the choreography. Arm circles, body rolls, and intricate hand configurations are thrown in to solidify the routineness of the routine. Again, he keeps challenging his students but is also open to their needs. "Let's pick it up—ta-ta-ta—boom-boom-boom!" is met equally with, "Slower? Okay, let's try it slower—five . . . six . . . seven . . . eight!" For every, "If it's easy, it's not gonna be good enough" there's a drill sergeant-esque, "You wanna learn—don't do easy shit." It sounds harsh, but it's thrilling to watch and be a part of.

He adds a shimmy to the dance and yells, "All that rack you got— let them girls work on they own." At one point, a scruffy young white dude who looks like he's a dancer but like only studied in modern dance studios where the "freedom" of choosing to wear deodorant or not is way too entertained, slows down and stares blankly ahead. Arturo calls to him, "I need to know what's going on in that head." The scruffy dude replies, "Nothing's going on." "Then that's why I need to know," says Arturo. "You're doing the moves—but I need you to make it a *feeling!*"

Finally, in the last fifteen minutes, Arturo organizes the rows back into a dance circle, a space for this new family brought together by art, physical hardship, and the love of learning, to show out. Everyone gets their moment in the spotlight. During this time of fem affirmation, here are some of my favorite Arturo exclamations:

"Do it like you're feeling sexy . . . Yes! See how you let go?!"
"Touch yourself, yes, get real cunty with it—this is the time to use
    all that good shit."
"You're selling your face, your gorgeous face on a platter."
"Yes! You got a boyfriend?! Mmhmm. That's why."

Once everyone in the circle had done their thing, we all applauded
our instructor. Arturo then thanked the group and offered his services in
the future by way of his social handles. It was done, and like that we were
returned to earth from some foreign fantasy realm, albeit for some of us
a more familiar one. The class began chatting each other up, folks of all
experiences and demographics electrified and united over vogue. I stayed
seated and small, trying to remain an impartial wallflower while I checked
the notes I took for integrity, to use them in the future as I am now. My
next workshop was supposed to be a talk featuring the Ballroom legend
and actress who scathingly plays Elektra Abundance on *Pose*, Dominique
"Tyra" Jackson . . . What was the time? And did I have time for lunch?! I
patted my pants pocket to check, quickly remembering after a few hours
of pure joy that I'd left my phone in that car the night before! And it was
still missing. . . . Maybe the car service emailed me back? Nope. I checked
my other emails . . . one from my friend Cristina, reading:

Cristina Cacioppo
Sat, Feb 2, 2019, 11:45 AM

Hey -

I just texted you and got a text back from someone who says they found your phone.
Did you lose it?[2]

I replied that I had! I hit send, thanked god, and then thanked her for
Canada. I sat and waited for Cristina to email me the contact info of the
beyond amazing Torontonian who the night before had found my phone
abandoned in the back seat of that car and who would later that afternoon drop it off to my second Airbnb location clear across town—free
of charge.

At that moment, the lovely lady in the kente dress was walking over.
I'd noticed her tentatively eyeing me all class long and had recognized her
self-consciousness about dancing so flamboyantly. I subsequently tried

to be as encouraging as possible through clapping, etc., to relieve her of some of that. Smiling, she grabbed her purse and water bottle from the wall next to me. Her brow was still a little sweaty from putting in the werk. "Ya know," she said laughing, "it's much harder than it looks!"

Touched by the proximity of old and new and how clearly time was a circle or a series of concentric ones getting us back to where we already are, I laughed too. "Oh, trust me, I know. And well done."

CHAPTER 4

THE CHILDREN

w/Jonovia Chase, Twiggy Pucci Garçon, Gia Love, Luna Luis Ortiz, Michael Roberson, Robert Sember, and LaLa Zannell

Mothers, fathers, LGBTQ youth, and lost and found families

A FLAMBOYANCE OF FAMILY

Whether it be family, a free lunch, or inspiration, it's funny how we find what we most need when we need it most.

I'd heard of Marlon Riggs, or, rather, sang of him, since the year 2000, mainly because his name is planted in "Hot Topic," the broke-down Sesame Street–style Le Tigre song I probably listened to a million times over the course of twenty years. Incidentally, what's great about this song is that it's pretty much just a list of seminal artists that the band members who made up Le Tigre, Kathleen Hanna, Johanna Fateman, and Sadie Benning, loved throughout their riot grrrl days. Since I discovered the song at nineteen, I promised myself that at some point before I died, I'd look up every single artist whose name they dropped. But what has ended up happening more often is that before I can even remember to engine search them, these artists happenstantially reverse engineer themselves into my life. Names like Eileen Myles, Justin Vivian Bond, Angela Davis, and David Wojnarowicz were lyrics that became flesh through interviews I've conducted with them, literary stages I've shared with them, chance visits they made to my grad school, and books (*Waterfront Journals*) gift-wrapped and Valentined to me by ex-boyfriends, respectively. Actually, I was stunned to find out that my friend and Vogue'ology teacher, Robert Sember, was integral in managing and preserving David Wojnarowicz's personal belongings after his death. I feel like we're all one random question in an elevator away from finding out we're surrounded by titans. Just one of the perks of remaining curious, I guess.

Also, the irony that through "Hot Topic," Kathleen Hanna, a white woman in pop culture (yes, like Madonna and "Vogue"), revealed to me art made by Black queer people like me is both annoying and encouraging. I wish I'd found Marlon Riggs beforehand, but we should all know about one another no matter the source of our information.

Anyway, like those impressive, hundred-dollar words that have somehow evaded your cognition your entire life until they suddenly don't, out of nowhere the name Marlon Riggs popped up three times in one day. I was like, "Wait a damn minute—I know that name from somewhere . . ." Le Tigre was where, but I'd never really let his name sink in before. The first of the three times I actually paid attention to his name was when my friend Todd said it to me directly. "You know, if you're looking for content for the book," he said, "you should check out *Tongues Untied* by Marlon Riggs. Might be useful." He was a little too eager in his recommendation, which can be a turn-off, so I noted it, said thank you, and went about my business. Then, later that same day, I was skimming the merch on the Very Black Project's website. My dear friend and dancer André Singleton is a cofounder, so I like to patronize the cool and unapologetically Black brand as much as possible, but outside of any friendly obligation, their apparel is awesome and coveted by many people, including celebrities like Spike Lee, and therefore runs out pretty quickly. I'd had my eye on a Very Black tank top (which I ended up buying) when I noticed there was a special-edition shirt with the name Marlon Riggs and *Tongues Untied*, his seminal film, printed onto it. Curious. Finally, that night, I asked my friend and film programmer Cristina Cacioppo if she'd heard of the guy, and she said, "Of course! I screened one of his films a few years back. Why, haven't you heard of him?" "Suddenly, I can't stop hearing of him," I replied. So, I relented, found the right streaming platform, and set aside a couple hours to finally watch *Tongues Untied*.

I loved it. I am not a poet or a poetry head—as a prose writer, the forced rhythms of spoken word regularly set my nerves on edge, and I've only ever snapped my fingers at a poem ironically—but the subject matter of this film and its mostly lyrical content, it's frankness, shot through me like an ice-cold bolt of lightning. Because the rhythm of Riggs's words is nothing compared to their truth, because the revelation that Black gay men go through a like set of traumas doled out by, yes, white folks, but, first and foremost, by their Black brothers and sisters. Their families.

Africanah.org, a diasporic art archive, bills Riggs's masterpiece as "an elegiac, erotic, and challenging portrait of 'black men loving black men' in the face of racism, homophobia, and the attendant alienation experienced in being African-American, gay, and a gay African-American"—all entirely apt.[1] But what any curatorial description of *Tongues Untied* is likely to omit is the stark feeling of relief that comes over you as a Black gay man, hearing Riggs, Essex Hemphill, and other members of the Black, gay intelligentsia in the film speak what you've felt your whole life: That the irony of straight Black folks marginalizing their gay brothers for being themselves is crushingly hypocritical. That homophobia is often a precondition of or a preempt to unwanted, unrequited, and unmitigated desire. That nasty words like "faggot" are unnatural yet frequently come from the mouths of children—the ones tainted too early. That being Black and in love with a white man can truly be the loneliest place on earth.

But for me, the most intriguing snippet of *Tongues Untied* is around the middle, where Riggs inserts an ode to motherhood—or rather, the families we find in lieu of it—by way of the iconic voguers of Greenwich Village circa '89, which, by the way, is roughly a year before both Madonna's "Vogue" and Livingston's *Paris Is Burning* were released.

Set to the glistening streaks of city streetlight, a bright-eyed version of my very first vogue teacher, Derrick Xtravaganza, vogues while wearing a red tank top, using his hands to exactingly slice the air in front of him before daintily using them to wave off any worldly concerns. He's near the ground and in front of a green-sweatered cutie who knows he is, using his hands in myriad ways to frame his sweet face. After some more of the girls, Vogue queen supreme and innovator of the category Willi Ninja comes in, pantomiming in mesmerizing slow motion, lightly tapping the corners of his shoulders to accentuate with dexterity the prim and properness of his gray pinstriped suit. She means business. Ninja's arms form a horizontal S and flow like the queen of carnivale's plumage. You can't take your eyes away. Marlon Riggs's voice comes in:

> Mother, do you know I roam alone at night? Wearing Colognes, tight pants, chains of gold? Searching for men willing to come back to candlelight. I'm not scared of these men. Though some are killers of

sons like me. I learned there is no tender mercy for men of color. For sons who love men like me. Do not feel shame for how I live. I chose this tribe of warriors and outlaws. Do not feel you failed some test of motherhood. My life is borne fruit. No woman could have given me away anyway. If one of these thick lived wet black nights, while I'm out walking, I find freedom in this village, if I can take it with my tribe, I'll bring you here, and you will never know the absence of rice and bridesmaids.[2]

Caught in relative time, slow-motion Willi Ninja finishes out the scene with his signature beauty-compact move, "holding" it in one hand while primping, preening, and posing like he's applying powder to his refined face with the other. A trail effect sets in, practically immortalizing him like Durga, the many-armed Hindu goddess. He closes the compact, stands up, and then pantomimes using a curling iron to pull a flowing pretend truss slowly away from his head; it illusion-falls like a mortal Shirley Temple coil.

The scene made me cry. Why? Well, there's its ballet-like aesthetic. The slowed-down presentation of Ballroom folks voguing in their original context, the Village in the late 1980s, all lines and graceful angles, the world's greatest city their backdrop, is like watching scores of flamingos descending on a legendary lagoon. Far be it from me to run a metaphor into the ground (who am I kidding—I *live* for an overextended metaphor), but the collective noun for flamingos is a "flamboyance." A flamboyance of flamingos. A flamboyance of voguers. A flamboyance of family.

Plus, you know when someone keeps bothering you to watch something, like, say, *Breaking Bad* or some shit because they think it supposedly applies to you and how you are, and then you watch it and it doesn't apply to you at all? Or like, when they say you look just like someone and then you get a glimpse at the person, and they look like who done it and ran? Or better yet, when a friend says you should check out this gay shit because you're gay, and then you check it out and it doesn't have a goddamn thing to do with you? Well, watching *Tongues Untied* was none of that. In fact, it was the opposite. Todd was right; it did apply to me, and the sheer friend-awareness of it all brought me to tears. It was what I had needed exactly when I'd needed it most.

Also, like I said, I don't often love poetry, but when I do, it hits me pretty hard, and Riggs's poem hit me pretty hard. It underscored for me the outrageousness of someone who'd rather their child be homeless, walking the streets, a reluctant sex worker, or even dead than be gay. We all know how insane and archaic this type of exile can be, yet it persists past 1989, when the film was made, and up until this very moment. Even more tear inducing is the idea that finding a family like the folks in Ballroom, hand-picked and talented, a flamboyance of family, can be the precious gift that fills seemingly unfillable voids like homelessness, alienation, sorrow, the hunger to be seen—a sense of purpose. The supplemental nature of house-Ballroom parents adopting LGBTQ homeless youth could be and often is discounted in terms of its legitimacy, perhaps because it points out through its deep intimacy, fierce support, and unconditional love for tossed-aside children, the rich cruelty, ineptitudes, and toxicity of heteronormative biological families. In fact, complete and utter non-Ballroom strangers, career foster parents who could care less about the well-being of these young folk, take in LGBTQ youth as a means of collecting a government check and are better supported culturally and financially than the house mothers and fathers who every day lay their lives on the line for their children.

I cried because I wanted to go there—there being in that crowd, watching Ninja and the others vogue for their lives. My geographical proximity would have been perfect. I worked and went to school in the Village. But alas, I was twenty-some-odd years too late. I've certainly been in the presence of vogue icons, including Derrick, who was in the movie in 1989, and later in 2011, a fantastic teacher and voguer who made those sharp, punishing arm angles seem carefree and effortless.

But Willi Ninja? Willi was a virtuoso, serving vogue lines that were equal parts ancient hieroglyphics and bold innovation. He seemed to perfectly occupy the great Ballroom dichotomy: he had the soft lyricism of a mother when he spoke and the exacting delivery of a sensei, the founding father of a martial art form, when he vogued. He'd prettily dab his face with powder while wearing the smirk of a cat who just ate the canary. Being around him would have been something else, and while watching *Tongues Untied*, not being around him stung even more because I realized that through his dedication to mentoring and mothering young folks before his passing, there was only actually a degree of separation in several directions between me and Willi Ninja. And just earlier that day I'd interviewed icon Lee Soulja. When I asked him my obligatory, "How'd you find Ballroom?" question, he told me that Willi

Ninja was his inspiration. From what I can tell, he seemed mad cool to be around.

Lee Soulja confirmed that suspicion. Willi Ninja was, indeed, cool as fuck, if for no other reason than the fact that he nurtured Lee back when he was a twenty-year-old up-and-coming dancer in the 1980s. More advanced in his age, technique, and career, Willi gave Lee a unique blueprint for being a gay global talent, while also nurturing him socially by being his gateway into the Ballroom community. Soulja remembers most things, including their first meeting.

> I got booked to do some [dance] shows in Asia . . . and I was going to work for a Terry Mugler fashion show over in Tokyo. I met Willi Ninja backstage. I'm a young kid, I'm a little cocky, and he was like, "Oh, you bout to dance?" and I was like, "Yeah, I'm 'bout to turn this out!'" I was doing good, and the crowd was like, yeaaaah. When I came back-stage afterward, Willi was like, "Good job, kid." So, then I wanted to see what he could do—Willi went out there and *ate it up*. He was doing 360s with his legs and double-jointed contortions, and dropping to the ground. . . . Let me tell you, the crowd stood up! He was voguing and they *loved* it over there. I was like, okay! He showed me. . . . So, after that we started talking and realized we were both from New York City and the whole thing.

Their love of dance fatefully brought the two New Yorkers, Lee (twenty-one) and Willi (twenty-six), together all the way across the world in Japan. The encounter was a crazy act of providence sparked by Lee following his personal joy (dance), which is often how young folks in ball culture find the person who integrates them into the community. Shortly after that first meeting, Willi started that integration process with Lee.

> When we came back [from Tokyo], Willi hit me up and said, "I want you to meet me here at this club. I wanna show you the dance I was doing, voguing, and where it comes from—c'mon, let's go out and have a good time!" And so, Willi took me to my first ball. When we got to the ball, he didn't introduce me as, Oh, this is my friend Lee; he was like, "This is my little brother, Lee." So, automatically, this was the

thing that attracted me to Ballroom, because the next person was like, "Oh, you Willi's brother? Then that makes you my brother, cuz he's my brother." Or another one was like, "Oh, Willi? That's my uncle!" I walked into the club not knowing anybody; the next thing you know, I got an instant family. I'd never experienced that, not in nightlife or hip-hop—the way the whole family thing kinda came together. Everybody was like, "Okay, sit here." The tables would have food sometimes. They were like, "Here, take this, you need anything, you want anything, you comfortable?" Everybody was so attentive! It was that warmth that you felt when you went home. That's what it was like at this ball. I will eternally be grateful for my friendship with Willi.

There may be a couple of reasons Lee had never experienced from the jump such a familial dynamic while dancing in hip-hop and club-kid circles. Though these subcultures are formed around common activities and artistry, they aren't always built out of the direst necessity. Sure, breakdance, for instance, was a performance genre that was in many ways created as an answer to a socioeconomic deficit, mainly the institutionalized poverty of Black and Latinx kids in the South Bronx. It was dance, and that is a safe haven for straight and queer children alike. And it was indeed an artistic buck against a system that was holding an entire generation down, and along with graffiti and hip-hop, they were a powder keg of creativity, one resulting in a cultural fallout the reaches of which none of us can truly assess in our lifetimes.

But Ballroom's house system exists on a more personal and visceral level. Yes, Ballroom is a response to classism, racism, transphobia, and a list of other chronic cultural constructs, but at its core Ballroom is an answer to an act against nature: parents disowning their children. Even in more modern non-nuclear families or adoptive situations, your parent or legal guardian exiling you from the family hits you dead in your DNA. These are the people meant to protect you from cruelty and to love you unconditionally, not to be the source of your greatest trauma. This kind of excommunication plays out on a cellular level, your nervous system triggered any time someone henceforth tries to get close to you. Your self-worth is often mixed up in it and constantly in question, a feeling understandably commensurate with how sexually desirable you feel, because desire is what got you here in the first place. Your light is dimmed, your body branded. No. It's not societal; it's biological. And when Mother Nature sees a vacuum, she fills it.

This, I think, is what Marlon Riggs, Lee Soulja, and nearly every person I talked to from every branch of New York's Ballroom family tree (which hasn't been drawn yet, but I'm working on it . . .) is saying. Built out of the human need for lineage and legacy, the house system is a clan barreling toward posterity with a common cause: freedom. And on an individual level, just like with biological families, these houses, Lanvin, Ebony, LaBeija, Pendavis, Mugler, et al., provide LGBTQ BIPOC youth an opportunity to metabolize centuries of generational trauma. Every gay parent, every gay child, is a chance to start anew. Though these relationships are fraught with some of the same codependencies and dysfunctions other families face—drug addiction, poverty, sexual and physical abuse—the very fact that they exist, that they fill a void, is one of the more providential wonders of the world. And through this preciousness, their potential to change lives is limitless.

Everyone in Ballroom has an origin story of how someone in the community took them in and/or under their wing, became their gay mother, father, sister, brother, aunt, or uncle. And nine times out of ten, once they were properly acclimated and had standing in the community, those children then made a habit of extending that same familial kindness to other newbies.

Twiggy Pucci Garçon, Ballroom legend, runway choreographer for FX's *Pose*, cowriter of the Ballroom documentary *Kiki*, and chief program officer for True Colors United (the LGBTQ youth homelessness org founded by Cyndi Lauper), put it to me perfectly, saying:

> At the onset of house balls, house mothers became literal parents. We've been that support system in some capacity or another, particularly when biological families reject or kick young people out. We're chosen parents, maybe—that's the word that people always use—but parents, nonetheless. . . . You know, in the homelessness movement, there's this thing called Host Homes, which is basically when a person or family becomes a host for younger people. They get a sort of stipend, if you will, to basically host this young person in their home. It sounds like foster care, but it's not. Some of them are really almost like roommate agreements, and then some of them are totally different, where

they're almost like families. Now, every house in Ballroom is structured differently, but house parents have shown up in the same way for decades—but without the financial support.

So, what makes a "good" or at least an effective house mother? I'd say that's as subjective as judging any mother, her background and parental desires paired with that of her children—and the consequent dynamic. I asked some legendary Ballroom family members what mothering means to them, either in terms of their own approach to mothering and mentoring young folks, or how they've been mothered/mentored themselves. Unsurprisingly, the answers were as varied as the individual yet as familiar as motherhood itself. There are single house mothers, working minimum wage to feed and house their children. Civically engaged mothers who understand that community is everything and that it truly takes a village. Mothers who are less hands-on but will hold your hand while they help you paint the town fluorescent pink. However unperfect, but always on time, these modes of mothering stem from the desire of these Ballroom legends to pass on the valuable lessons they've learned over the years, and they're an effort to end the cycles of trauma inherited from children's biological mothers. It's important to carve out the space for—to speak the names of—what Riggs so aptly named "This tribe of warriors and outlaws," who, every day, ensure that future generations of queer Black and brown children "find freedom in this village."

We speak your names.

GAY AND TRANS MOTHERS

There are certain parental figures in Ballroom who come up in almost every conversation with folks, mothers and fathers with vast levels of influence who, in their personal attentiveness to their many children, almost seem as if they had a master plan to critically and infinitely change the culture for the better. And often, as with their biological counterparts, that parental goal is born out of a sense of their own mortality. Arbert Santana is one of those people. As unfortunate as it is to hear that before his death he did in fact have a plan to use motherly love as a means of creating a living Ballroom archive in the hearts of each of his children, it's even more inspiring to know that it definitely worked.

LEGENDARY MOTHER ARBERT SANTANA (HOUSES OF LATEX AND EVISU)

As told by friend Robert Sember:

It was the desire to nurture that made me a mother. But being a mother wasn't easy. Being a single mother was even harder. One of the hardest things to deal with is being a mother and watching your children die. We accept our own death, but it is very difficult to see our children die.

—ARBERT SANTANA LATEX EVISU (January 22, 1965–March 3, 2011)

In the year and a half prior to his death, Arbert and I collaborated on the development of the Ballroom Archive and Oral History Project. We spoke of it as a project for the rest of our lives and as an investment in the survival of the scene, which we measured, implicitly, in the notion that it would outlive us. This hope was not based on an abstract notion of the end of a community, for the Ballroom community has lost and continues to lose many of its members at very young ages. It is at the intersection of populations that have the highest HIV-infection rates in the United States, are the target of brutal and frequently murderous homophobia and transphobia, and are the target of the social violence that is the condition of the poor. Only in his early forties, Arbert was another of these deaths before his time.

When Arbert and I embarked on this project, Edgar, a mutual friend, shared with me his sense that Arbert was aware of his failing health and that his investment in the project represented a desire to leave something important for the community. He wanted to make something that would continue to "mother" even after his death. The logic would be, I suppose, that if he took care of the community's collective memories, memory itself would become a form of care.

He spoke often to me of how the death of his mother made him more aware than ever before of the painful consequences of loss. He grieved his mother passionately. He could be comforted but was ultimately inconsolable in the sense that grief is lonely work. This loss threw into relief his mourning for the Ballroom "children" he had lost over the years. In one of the public presentations of the archive and oral history project—a discussion between members of the Ballroom scene and feminist and queer studies scholars—he referred to the "unnaturalness" of a parent losing a child. The performance of this observation captured much of what is at stake in the house-Ballroom community. He intended no irony in his description of himself as an effeminate gay man and a mother who has lost her children, a number of whom were actually older than him. This is not a drag performance. Like so much else in the Ballroom scene, what is at stake in this mothering is the power defined by the relationship between what "is" and what is "as if."[3]

Although she is no longer a mother of the House of LaBeija, LaLa Zannell is the embodiment of familial love, as evidenced by the fact that in her empty-nest days (at only forty-two), she still continues to do the work of personally, professionally, and legally helping LGBTQ folks of color in her role of trans justice campaign manager for the ACLU. But her story speaks to *all* mothers in that it underscores the importance of avoiding the motherly burn-out and how nurturing others starts with self-care. It's a hard lesson that moms have to learn—be they Ballroom or otherwise.

LALA ZANNELL (FORMER MOTHER, HOUSE OF LABEIJA):

When I was growing up a young little fifteen-year-old trans girl in Detroit, I was trying to find myself, and there were so many people in Ballroom who were already affirming what I was before I even knew what I was. I knew I wasn't a boy, and I knew there was something going on within my mind and spirit which was having me not comfortable in my own body, but I didn't have the words to explain it, until I saw fem queens from Ballroom hanging out in Palmer Park, one of the few places we had to go and be with community. I remember walking in the park dressed as fem as I could. I had to sneak out of my mother's house at the time to dress back then. A voice told a group of what I had thought was cisgender women, "She is going to be cunt when she grows up." They called me over to them, snatched me up, and said, "This is what it is. This is what is possible," after having a long conversation explaining who they really were. I was a Prestige and Mid-West mother of LaBeija back in Detroit; then I became mother of LaBeija in Atlanta.

Houses in Detroit were very family-oriented—we were a family. Houses in Atlanta, on the other hand, were very territorial depending upon what house you were in. But also because I was new in town, everyone was trying to test me or figure me out. It was just a different kind of atmosphere, so competitive, but there were still small pockets of people who still needed this sense of family. It was a culture where everyone was amazing and talented and wanting to be seen and fighting for validation. I didn't need that. It was not in line with my values.

As a mother, I just wanted to love on people and get love in return. But at that time, I was working a full-time job as a shift manager at Starbucks, getting up every day at four in the morning to catch the bus. I had my chosen kids to take care of, and my house was the place everyone came to stay ball weekends, and I was also in a relationship. And I was still trying to find myself, battling extreme dysphoria and the balance of my womanhood—all while being a house mother. All those things were becoming too much. I began to put my needs secondary to the chosen kids, and culture. Some shifts in the house leadership came, and I was removed from the house. I felt so relieved but also hurt at the same time. I said I would never be a member of a house again.

Time may have healed some old wounds, and one of my Ballroom husbands, Luna [Luis Ortiz], was in town for a conference, and he came up to my job and we chatted. Luna was like, "Nah, Girl, you need to become a Legacy." He had just opened up his own house and wanted me to be the mother. "Come up to New York!" I told him I didn't really do Ballroom like that anymore, but he dragged me back into it. [Laughs] I ended up moving to New York in 2014 after becoming homeless in Atlanta after losing my job at Starbucks due to discrimination.

Because [New York] was the center of Ballroom, one of the first things I had to do was go to the piers. I was craving seeing all these people being their authentic selves, whether that was in the voguing corner, the kiki reading corner, the shy corner—even the folks that were LGBTQ and homeless knew that they could sleep on that bench and no one was going to touch them. They were going to be safe. One of the favorite parts of my trips to New York back in my old Prestige and LaBeija days was going to the piers, and I could not have moved to New York at a better time because it was starting to be the end of the pier era I loved and [that] was home to so many. . . . Gentrification was starting to take away our history in the West Village.

I can remember my first time seeing Sania [Ebony], who just had this confidence where you couldn't tell her *nothing*. In the wintertime, she was wearing a fur coat, stilettos, and lingerie underneath! I was like, girl. That energy, that fashion, that spunk. She was just this confident Black woman. A lot of the fem queens in New York gave that flare.

And I met so many people like Michael Roberson, who is my chosen brother now, who had the same ideologies as me, and [I] wished I would have crossed paths with someone like him in my earlier days, because he has the same vision I have for Ballroom, how he's grounded in history, spirituality—I'm a preacher's child. And me being trans has never affected my relationships; my mother's a pastor, and my family affirms me. So a lot of my experiences are different from other people's in Ballroom. I understand that other people have been thrown out and have been broken. So, because the culture freed me and helped me find myself, I felt I had a duty to do the same for others. I was so trapped in it that I forgot about my family many times, which years down the line caused disconnect and repairing. They would joke, saying, "You are going to be with your other family this weekend."

I know my family loved me, but it was something about my Ballroom love because they fully understood me and what I meant to be in this body in this world. So I was able to offer love back to those who were not as blessed as myself. I always used that to create a space of love, like there is a place that affirms you. And whoever I love, my mother loves. All of my kids become my mother's grandkids. I came from that, and Michael was just so grounded in that. This is what Ballroom is about, but this is also what being Black and queer is about. I believe that you're not going to succeed or be successful without some type of spiritual belief system. Whatever you believe, you need that. Those moments have helped me through life. So I appreciate Michael for creating spaces for those difficult conversations.

So I will always support Ballroom by trying to keep its family roots and trying to really merge advocacy with organizing and healing in the community. I think I'm able to do that better now because I'm not a member of any kind of entity. I can work across houses to create better opportunity for my Ballroom family. I get to do what I want. I like that."

Just as with any other mother-child relationship, you can see familial traits passed down from one to the other, and if her son Luna is any indication of who the founder of the House of Pendavis, Avis Pendavis, was, then she was a present and devoted, politically engaged, firecracker, and a hoot and a half to be around. Her fierce commitment to her children who survive her is evident in their firm sense of self and in the heart-warming way in which they evoke her. When we spoke, it seemed as if Luna could have gone on about Avis for hours, a method of oral resurrection signature both to Avis's doting son and to ball culture at large.

FOUNDING MOTHER AVIS PENDAVIS

As told by her son, Luna Luis Ortiz:

I was an uptown gay—I didn't know life existed downtown! I was mostly up on like 149th Street, 141st, and I thought that's what it was. One day, November 16, 1988, I met my friend Wade at New York Public Library over on 145th Street. We were hanging out there all the time. He told me they were having a Thanksgiving dinner at HMI, the Hetrick-Martin Institute for the Protection of Gay and Lesbian Youth, and so we went.

When we got there, all I saw was a whole bunch of beautiful Black and brown folks at the center. They were voguing, and I was in awe. I was very shy, so I asked my friend, "What are they doing over there, what is that?" and he said, "Oh, those are our sisters! They're voguing—you don't know voguing?" I was like, no, but I was in such a trance.

Then, being the new girl on the block, everybody was asking Wade, "Who's your girlfriend?" I had my cute lil flattop and all back then. [Laughs] Everybody was in their own groups, even though we were all in the same space. The LaBeijas were together, the Pendavises were together, the Xtravas were over here, the Ebonys over there. . . . I was introduced to the Pendavises and eventually ended up hanging with them, probably because they were like, "Hey, what's going on?" They were more approachable. They spoke to me. At the time, it was Karen Covergirl and people like that. So, I ended up hanging with the Pendavises, and then they all kept being like, 'Oh, you need to meet Avis, you need to meet Avis,' and finally I was like, "Who is this Avis y'all keep talking about?" They told me she was the house mother, and then I said, "What's a house mother?!" So, I was getting schooled directly. Then, on December 5, 1988, I went to Avis's house, and that day I became a Pendavis. She saw me smile and she was like, "Oh my god, that smile! He's going to break a lot of hearts," but I didn't. [Laughs]

I know people always say this about their house mother, but Avis was *the* best mother. Any time I talk about Avis, and if there are people in the room that knew her, they kind of nod their heads because they understand what I'm talking about. If Blanca [Evangelista, from FX's *Pose*] looked different and was maybe a little older, a little thicker, then Blanca would be Avis. She was so involved in your life that it was just incredible, and for me, that's the truest mother. She didn't do drugs or anything, you know? She just educated us. She didn't care if you walked a ball, okay? She wanted you to finish school or have a job—to her that was the most important thing in the world. She even came to my graduation at Harvey Milk [High School] because she was so proud that I finished school. And I remember when she came in, everybody was so excited that I got Avis out of the house, because she was more of the 'Come over to my house to see me,' kind of house mom. She really only came out for her appointments and probably to go shopping. She was always at her house, up on 157th and Broadway, right near my neighborhood, and what's funny—you see, it's all connected—what's funny is that just a few blocks away I used to see this *really* tall woman coming in and out of cars. She had furs, and she was really glamorous, and I didn't know who she was. I thought, *Wow, she's so glamorous*. It wasn't until I joined House of Pendavis and Ballroom that I discovered that she was Dorian Corey. I'd actually seen her around first, but just didn't know. Later, I'd meet her and some of the other mothers through Avis, and that's how it all came together. All of this happened within two years. I ended up taking a "Ballroom course" taught by the pioneering mothers.

GIA LOVE (FORMER MOTHER, HOUSE OF JUICY)

A hug. A meal. A word of encouragement. If nothing else, we remember our mother's affection for us and the ways in which she expressed it. Though she is a mother who got her groove back, modeling, and becoming an avid social activist since stepping down as mother of the House of Juicy, Gia loves on her kids as if she never stepped down, and this is the case every single time I've seen her out in public, her arm around a kid, posing with them for a picture, her undivided attention beaming down onto them like a sunset glow. It's also evident in the way she recounts her time as mother. Her method? Work smarter.

I'm not currently mother, but I am the Queen Mother. Essentially what that means is that I was the mother of the house once before—and I was a really good mother—but I still have a lot of influence. Because

I'm old. I'm twenty-nine years old, and I have a lot of stuff to do. I can't go to Juicy practice every week like I used to or go to every ball. And honestly, I'm not even interested in that like I used to be. So that's why I'm the Queen Mother—the older girl who's not out there [walking balls] but still deserves the mother position. I'm both at the same time. It is simply acknowledging what I have done as mother.

But when I was active as mother, I was working more on the community-based level, not only contributing to the kids' side of things but also with how the kiki [non-mainstream] balls look, and working with partners like CBOs (community-based organizations), you know, being that middleperson. With the kids, specifically, I was really building their craft, self-esteem, letting them know that they're enough and that they're talented and that we'll find some way for them to be seen, even if the community doesn't see them in that light. We would manage them and make sure that they got their time to shine and really be at the forefront of whatever they're doing. We were creating opportunities for kids who probably never had a Thanksgiving dinner with family, stuff like that. Having cookouts and really loving on people, showing them the love that they didn't get from the people they thought they were supposed to get it from—because we accept them for who they are. We accept them for the reasons their families or friends who they grew up with may not accept them. We allow them to be their authentic selves. Every mother doesn't mother like this.

FATHERS

Famous quotes by my father, Ricky Tucker Sr.:

1. "There are no fat Tuckers!" (But what about Grandpa? I ask.)
2. "He doesn't count—he's old!"
3. "Men don't hug; they shake hands." (I was five years old.)
4. "You want something to drink from the machine, boy?" (Sure, anything fruity, I respond.)
5. "ANYTHING FRUITY?!"
6. "Hahahaaaa" (in his incongruously high-pitched laughter in response to that baked-beans commercial where the dog says, "Roll that beautiful bean footage!")
7. "Hold this gun, I'm going right there to the ATM. Watch my back." (In broad daylight.)

8. "Here's some money for the movies. I'm gonna drop you off for a few hours while I go to Freaknik with this girl. Page me when you're done. Don't tell your stepmama."
9. "Taste this sandwich and guess the secret ingredient." ("Kraft Italian dressing," I say.)
10. "Well, I guess you just know every damn thing, don't you?"
11. "You're very nonverbal, you know that?" (Me: . . .)
12. "You know I used to beat your mama, right?" (No. I did not know that.)

A famous quote from my mother:

13. "I'm sorry your father is such an asshole." (We both laugh.)

The Savannah sun was particularly oppressive that day, and at the time, I remember thinking to myself, "Why'd they have to move *here* of all places?" My dad had retired from the US Air Force in my preteens after being stationed in more exotic, curious places like England (where I was born), Japan (where my little brother Jordan was born), Saudi Arabia, and Germany. Yet, for whatever reason, even though he and my stepmother were both from *Miami*, they'd picked up and moved themselves and Jordan to Savannah, Georgia—in my mind, the swampiest place on earth. It was a city where the smell of roadside boiled peanuts paired with a constant undercurrent of swamp sulfurs lingered in the air. The mere memory alone threatened to jumpstart a dry heave.

I was thirteen and had been there on my biennial summer visit. Divorced parents. The fact that they were ever married is beyond me. Practically hearsay. One July morning, without any subtlety, my dad woke Jordan and me, got us dressed, and drove us out to the running track to explicitly address the issue of my fatness before sending me back to my mom in North Carolina. I guess over the past few weeks he'd seen enough of my expanding angsty self. The time I spent sitting around his house eating grilled ham and swiss sandwiches and Doritos and drinking Ecto Cooler. Or tearfully watching the video for Seal's "Kiss from a Rose" on VH1. Or lying on the floor on my stomach in front of the CD player in the spare room, crying to the *My So-Called Life* soundtrack I'd scored from the Peaches record store in the strip mall with the movie theater where I'd seen *Clueless* three times just to get the hell up out of that uptight child-unfriendly house. Also, *Clueless* is an amazing film.

Jordan, on the other hand, was five years old, little, spry, and slim like I used to be before all the trauma had settled and gelled around my teenaged heart and torso. At that point, unlike me, Jordan was presumed straight and not a reminder of a failed marriage. My dad carried him on his shoulders as we ran, barking at me his best impression of whatever drill sergeant it was who used to torture him.

"Let's go," he huffed. "Yep, we're gonna start coming out here every day—come on, keep up!"

I was trailing behind. "Can . . . we . . . take a break?"

"A break?! Boy you kill me. I'm over here older than you and carrying Jordan, and I'm still running faster than you!"

I stopped to catch my breath. "How about . . . we run to each of these poles and then . . . take a break in between?"

"We haven't even run two miles yet."

"We haven't?!" Jordan yelled from above.

"Was anybody talkin' to you?" Jordan zipped it quick.

"Alright, Ricky Tucker. We sprint and then walk for ten seconds after each of them lampposts. *Now, let's go!*"

We ended up running through the soupy Savannah air for what felt like forever, but maybe it was five miles? It's hard to say. Everything was whirring by. Other humans. A slew of static hemp lampposts. Endless weeping willows nodding nonchalantly, as if it were only a cool 75 degrees out—meanwhile it was more like 100. The heat, on top of all the starting, stopping, huffing, and puffing, began to melt together and pour like hot liquid over my scalp and behind my face, radiating outward and making me want to hop out of my own skin just to get away from myself. Finally, he was like, "Alright, that's enough for today."

The scorched stretch of pavement between the parking lot and my dad's Ford pickup set off brain-frazzling flashes that made it hard for me to see. And gravity seemed to be pulling me down toward it. My father opened the car door, and the last thing I remember is sinking, nearly but not quite reaching the back seat, and saying, "Daddy, I don't feel so good . . ."

"Ricky? Ricky?!"

"..."

"Ricky, can you hear me?!" An unfamiliar voice says. You're being poked and prodded and jostled.

"Ricky, if you can hear me, say something."

"Ricky, if you can hear me, say something," you manage to say.

"Ha-ha. Very good."

"Thank God," a familiar voice finally says.

It suddenly occurs to you to try to pry your eyes open, and when you do, you open them to a blinding lamp over your face and a crude introduction to your splitting headache, already in progress.

"Great. You're with us. Wonderful. Can you tell me your name?"

"Ricky Courtney Tucker II."

"Do you know who the president is?"

"Bill Clinton?"

"Bill Clinton. That's right. Very good."

Only now realizing that you've been through something, you panic and quickly try to sit up, but before you're fully erect, a firm hand grabs your shoulder and pushes you back down onto the table.

"Lay down, boy," your father says. "Just wait a minute." You're both relieved and scared.

"Mr. Tucker, he's going to be okay. Can you come with me, please?"

It's just you and a nurse now.

She strokes your forehead and asks, "How you feelin', hon?"

"I want apple juice," you say.

She laughs.

So, you've had a heatstroke and need to be monitored for the next couple of days. Your father called your mom, and she is furious. Told him she's gonna fuck him up. You smell kinda horrible, like gathered BO enzymes, because you passed out after running miles in the hot Savannah sun, but there's an IV in you and all kinds of vitals wires glued to you and going every which-a-way, and you can't figure out how to shower properly without disrupting them. No one's explained it to you. You finally get your apple juice but only after hours and hours because you were severely dehydrated and all you would do is just throw it right back up anyway. Only vital fluids and ice chips for now, the doctor says. He asks if you have sickle cell anemia, and you say no, but your little sister with a different dad back in NC does, which is probably why you're so calm and at home right now in this hospital, well that and because earlier this year your favorite aunt and two family friends died of AIDS-related illnesses, the last of which you found out about a couple of weeks ago. When informed about it, your father had said, "Your mama told me about your lil friend. I'm sorry to hear about that," on his way out of the room.

"Why," you ask the doctor.

He says it's because you have very high liver enzymes, which is a typical indicator of sickle cell, or at least the recessive trait, two of which (one from each parent) it takes to make the disease. You must have the trait. He urges you to drink eight glasses of water a day and stay vigilant about your exposure to heat for the rest of your life. You promise to do so.

You watch TV to fill up those couple days that turn into four. It kind of feels like a vacation compared to the vibe at your dad and stepmom's place. Then your dad pops in. He closes the door behind him, pulls up a chair, and comes oddly close. "Alright now, it's time to come home. This place is costing me a fortune," he says, as if you'd asked to be hospitalized there because you'd heard word of their unrivaled amenities and renowned, nonexistent bedside manner.

"Okay," you say.

Good, you can tell he's thinking. Now that he's at ease, he takes his close proximity as a chance to lapse into an anecdote about some friend of his, which is weird because your father is not the storytelling type unless the plot involves the trials and tribulations he went through to find the right sparkplug or that time four summers ago when you stupidly did that task he asked you to do but you did it the hard way instead of the right way—'member that?! You're hilariously hopeless. Well, this time, the yarn he spins is about a military "friend" of his whose son just came out to him and how his "friend" is embarrassed, furious, and distraught. He lets you let that sink in for a beat before bringing it all home, saying, "You know, if I ever found out my son was a homosexual, I'd kill him."

No. You did not know that.

THE LOST & FOUND

Moving to New York is a wild but harrowing experience, like being shot out of a cannon and into a bouncy house, where you're expected to jump up and down nonstop and until further notice. . . . When I first moved to the city, in 2011, I only had fifty dollars, an acceptance letter into the New School, some boxes, a U-Haul, and an apartment off Wilson Avenue in Bushwick that my friend and screenwriting partner Andrew and I had scraped the money together for several months prior. All my savings had gone into that, and we almost hadn't gotten the place, because I couldn't find a cosigner on my end. Still, I was so ready to start jumping up and down.

Back in Boston, just before my move and last day of work for admissions at Northeastern University, I'd gotten a random phone call from a number in Georgia. "Ricky Tucker," it said when I picked up the call. "This is your daddy."

I froze. My heart rate skyrocketed, making it nearly impossible for me to hear and properly process whatever it was he was saying on the other end. The gist of it, I think, was that he'd divorced my stepmother, married again for the third time, become pseudo-Christian, and had talked to my mom on the phone. He'd asked, and she told him I was indeed gay. And he was okay with that.

"Okay," I responded, nonplussed. He supposedly wanted to make things right. After my heatstroke, I'd basically continued seeing him every other year or so, right up until I ran away from home at nineteen. Since then, I hadn't spoken to him for ten years. So the idea that he'd changed since then wasn't a stretch in terms of time, but it was a little farfetched in terms of who he actually was. Anyway, I heard him out, found compassion for him and the messed-up childhood that he'd also had—but proceeded with caution . . .

We started emailing back and forth. He'd always fancied himself an amateur DJ, so he sent my mom and me stacks of these mix CDs he made and sold to barbershops in Savannah, hours of not-too-shabby Top 40 R&B and dance playlists with his voice occasionally interrupting songs like "Getting Jiggy with It," saying things like "Deon's Barbershop! The one and only place for cuts. Yeah . . ." My mom and I laughed about it on subsequent phone calls. "What in the world . . ." she'd say.

Despite that cringe-worthiness, with my impending move to NYC, and not a cosigner in sight, I thought, maybe he's really looking for redemption. Maybe he *had* changed, the man who for sixteen of my first eighteen years of life only paid $150 a month in child support, immediately calling me on my eighteenth birthday to let me know he was having it stopped posthaste, even though I was going to college later that year (which made stopping it against the law). Maybe his new church-y wife helped exorcise his worst demons. Maybe he'd curbed some of the excessive drinking and was no longer what my mother referred to as "the Budweiser King." Maybe he could help me secure the apartment and, by proxy, a new life, and for him and me, perhaps a new start. I anxiously put together an email to send him, asking for the help. This is what I sent:

Subject: Your Son Needs a HUGE FAVOR
Ricky Tucker tucker.ricky@gmail.com
July 28, 2011
9:55 AM
To: Ricky Senior

Good morning,

So, I got into the NEW SCHOOL in Manhattan, and I'm moving there in September after going back to England for a little bit for a trip.

My roommate and I found an apartment and filled out the housing application. I used my mom as a guarantor (cosigner), but they said she doesn't make enough. I need your help, I think. They want us to wrap everything up this morning. I tried to give you a call last night, but your number has changed.

I really hope you can help me with this and be a cosigner. I wouldn't ask unless it was super important. Either way about it, let me know you got this. I attached the guarantor form.

Love, Ricky T II[4]

My nerves were shot that entire day, waiting for him to respond. When he did, it was about eight hours later, and this is what it said:

Ricky rickyt@onlymyemail.com
July 28, 2011
6:38 PM

Hello Ricky Tucker,

I just got this around 4:30pm this afternoon. . . . didn't check my email earlier. . . . too busy. . . . anyway, let's get right down to business.

At the 2019 "Escape from Arkham" Kiki ball in the Bronx, NY, Two-Face vogues and slays the competition.

The Joker, master of ceremonies. "Escape from Arkham" Kiki ball in the Bronx, NY, 2019.

Starfire, spin . . . and dip. "Escape from Arkham" Kiki ball, Bronx, NY, 2019.

The Flash, mid-dip. "Escape from Arkham" Kiki ball, Bronx, NY, 2019.

Batgirl, working the crowd. "Escape from Arkham" Kiki ball, Bronx, NY, 2019.

Unadulterated Starfire. "Escape from Arkham" Kiki ball, Bronx, NY, 2019.

The category is: Fashion. Latex Ball, NYC, 2015.

The category is: "If I only had a heart...." Kiki Legends Ball, 2015.

Kia LaBeija and a friend. Latex Ball, NYC, 2015.

The category is: Sex Siren. Latex Ball, NYC, 2009.

Left to right: Kevin Aviance, the late icon Hector Xtravaganza, and Jeremy Xtravaganza. Latex Ball, NYC, 2015.

Mike Mizrahi serving up face at the House of
Khan Ball, Washington DC, 2006.

Ballroom legend, and NYC nightlife royalty Lee
Soulja. Latex Ball, NYC, 2009.

The category is: Face. Latex Ball, NYC, 2009.

The category is: Team Body Battle. Latex Ball, NYC, 2009.

The children at the Red Ball. Brooklyn Expo Center, 2019.

A young woman basking in the spotlight. Red Ball, Brooklyn Expo Center, 2019.

A stolen moment with the girls. Red Ball, Brooklyn Expo Center, 2019.

Having a ball. Red Ball, Brooklyn Expo Center, 2019.

Michael Roberson (back wall, center) and young LGBTQ/Ballroom folks gather at the H.E.A.T. Retreat in Catskills, NY, February 2020.

I cannot co-sign for your apartment at this time. My mother once asked me the same thing and I turned her down as well. In these crucial times in America, and the way the economy has been, we can just barely manage with what we have. I cannot extend myself to do this because if for some reason you miss a payment, I would be responsible, and I will not put myself in this position. There are allot of questions I would normally ask but it doesn't matter because I will not be doing this.

You are 30 something years old maybe 31. I would have thought with all the running around that you do you would have your credit good enough to get an apartment . . . Your mother cant co-sign, okay no problem . . . how about your roommate's mother and father?

I don't really know your character because we have been out of touch for allot of years now. Really, I don't know what you have been up too. But all of this does not matter because I cannot do what you are asking. . . . so no point in going on.

Take Care and hope you have luck with this venture.

P.S. I won't even begin to ask why you left Boston. . . . and decided New York City which is a very expensive place to live. . . . Fast pace and dangerous as well. . . . That would be another day of talks . . . Later. . . . [5]

Finally, this is how I responded:

Ricky Tucker tucker.ricky@gmail.com
July 29, 2011
8:36 PM

Hello Ricky Tucker,

I ended up getting the apartment, on my own merit. They initially said my mother wouldn't do as a cosigner because of her salary (I currently make more than her) and because both my roommate and I are students (he's in grad school). Our credit is fine.

While we're discussing worth, please don't tell me again how you turned down your own mother and my siblings when they were in need. It just illustrates how you're consistently ineffective. I'd rather not know. Just say you can't do it. The other people I asked to cosign (whom I know a lot better than you at this point) simply said, "Sorry, I can't at this time." NOT, "No, I can't, but ya know, I won't even give my wife a ride to the bus stop, so . . ."

I'm leaving Boston because I'm almost done with my degree at Northeastern University and I want to complete it at a better school. I applied to and got into the New School for creative writing. I also got a competitive scholarship because of my published writings. I'll have my degree in a little over a year. I'll then be 12 credits into my master's. I'll eventually get my PhD, and then I'll write a book that you'll be not so thrilled about because you'll either be frightened by your own reflection, or worse, like all the light snatched from a room—you'll be remarkably absent.

You may not have been in contact with me for a while, but there's nothing ambiguous about my character. You see it and everyday it leaves you awestruck and confounded. By the way, I'm 29 and I will be until Feb 28th of next year. Forget the Co-Sign, scratch anything to do with finance from this point until forever. Call me on my Birthday. Show me something different. You're not off the hook.

PS, I'm gonna need a new phone number for you, the one I called last week belongs to some redneck now.

Your Son, Ricky T.[6]

He never replied. That was almost ten years ago now. I have not spoken to him since.

So I moved to the city, leaving any hope of a real relationship with my father behind and jumping headfirst into my career as a full-time academic. I used that fifty dollars I had to buy as many groceries as possible and an unlimited train pass. That would get me to school until I met with my aunt Jackie, who worked for the MTA at Jamaica Center and came across many a MetroCard abandoned by businessmen on their way out of town. Side note: My mom is originally from Brooklyn, so I have an aunt in every borough—literally—and even though none of them are rich, I wouldn't have survived undergrad in NYC without them. Thank you, Aunt Sandie, Aunt Jackie, Tati Elsie, Aunt Sylvia, and Aunt Gizette.

I was so excited to start at the New School. I went to every orientation event I was invited to and even went to the ones I wasn't. It didn't hurt that they tended to have boxed lunches and snacks there. I filled up my complimentary New School bachelor's program tote with whatever lunches weren't taken. Got my tuition's worth early.

One evening in that first week, I went to an orientation event called something like "What Classes Should I Take?" which was a valid question, because I was having real trouble narrowing it down. The New

School courses were all so cool sounding! "Old Weird America," "Trans Genre," and "Writing for NYC Magazine and Newspapers" were some of the courses that I would eventually take, but at that orientation event, I discovered "Vogue'ology." It was the first time it was being offered, and the event leader made it a point to highlight it as such. I enrolled in it immediately—it was the first class I signed up for—and it forever changed my life.

I believe we're divinely rewarded for taking risks and making space for new experiences to move in. For new people to move in. Taking the risk to move to New York and dropping everything for the education I felt I deserved yielded my own personal intellectual renaissance. And letting go of a father who would never be who I needed him to be freed up the much-needed space for two profound father figures, Michael Roberson and Robert Sember, the co-instructors of Vogue'ology who were not only gay and therefore gay-friendly but also intelligent, hilarious (on purpose), kind, thoughtful, generous, and on and on and on. As they say in Ballroom, they and the first Vogue'ology cohort became my "gay family" when I needed them most.

And like truly hands-on parents, Michael and Robert often intuited what I might need and sprang into action to help, and without me even asking. Even though I was twenty-nine years old, like the thousands of LGBTQ kids disenfranchised from their families, I needed a foundation of understanding and consistency, and that foundation became Ballroom.

During the time he was teaching me in Vogue'ology, Michael Roberson was also attending school at Union Theological Seminary and working for GMAD (Gay Men of African Descent), an org in Burrough Hall that was founded in 1986 by the Reverend Charles Angel to provide a space for Black gay men in New York City to support each other in fighting the AIDS epidemic, homophobia, and racism. There, on Thursday nights, Michael hosted groups of gay Black men or Black folks who at one point identified as gay men, to have conversations about sex, relationships—life. We were an intersection of New School undergrads, Union grads, and Ballroom folks who were usually from the House of Garçon as Michael was its father at the time.

He'd promised us a two-way MetroCard and dinner if we showed up, and all we had to do was hang out, talk, and listen. I'm sure the ball kids were used to such a setup, seeing as how at that point in the city (circa 2011), the life of a young LGBTQ Black person meant the potential of finding large swaths of folks like themselves through various channels of public health and nonprofit organizations. Through HIV/ AIDS testing efforts with GMHC (Gay Men's Health Crisis) and New York Public Health—continued partners with ball culture from the '80s and on—community enrichment initiatives, after-school programs like the ones at Harvey Milk High School in Astor Place, and so on. To me, however, being surrounded by people like me was what I had imagined taking your bra off after a long day felt like. A relief. Plus, like I said, I was hungry for food and ideas, and we usually ended up getting Domino's Pizza between intense conversations about self-worth, desire, sex, and God. We covered a lot of ground. Shared our personal experiences. I was finally able to hear in depth, outside the confines of Vogue'ology, Michael's musings on how as a Black gay man, you're taught by the greater Christian-hetero-patriarchal culture that your life is an abomination, that you're deserving of the poverty, persecution, HIV/AIDS, and struggles you face day to day. So when the time comes to protect yourself, of course you'd cave in to the type of pressure that leads to life-risking behavior. You've been told from day one that this is your destiny. His articulation of that stays with me to this day. I've seen it in my own behavior and used it as a field guide, a north star to self-care, faking it till I made it. Even if we think they aren't, such biases against ourselves work unconsciously like a pirate train conductor hijacking the wheel and throwing our futures off course while we placidly sip tea and stare out the food-car window at the passing desert expanses. Next thing we know, our life is derailed.

But it wasn't all grave cautionary tales on wellness and self-care at GMAD. We kiki'd often. I always crack up laughing when I think about how this one time, during a conversation about the effectiveness of preventing STI infections by using condoms during oral sex, Michael walked us through its importance and the many hazards one might face—reckless lovers, intoxication, apathy, nihilism—when putting that desire into action. Where in the past, say in sex ed courses some of us may have taken as tweens, ones where fear and judgment were the primary pedagogical practices (I'm looking at you, North Carolina), it may have been suggested that using a condom during oral sex was a mandated action to take in spite of our desires, but at the Gay Men of African Descent meeting in New York City, Michael Roberson, father of the House of Garçon, public health advocate, theologian, and maternal heart, let us know that desire isn't wrong, nor does it fade because you take the appropriate action, saying, "Of course you don't wanna use a condom for oral sex—dick tastes good!"

Throughout those couple of months of sparkling conversation over pizza and train rides home that made this often-alienated gay writer feel a part of something, I marveled at the wholesome, heavy, and hilarious energy of our cohort. How my decades of embarrassment about my proximity to femininity and subsequent protective layering fell away, being all loud, queer, and wrong on the A Line home, calling each other girl and people not with us wanting to be a part of our cohort. How, under the right conditions, despite the bullying from my father and because of kindness from *real* men who happened to be Black and gay, I could smoothly transition out of being "nonverbal" and into a state of candid vocal reflection. How so many of us gay Black folks have been traumatized not only by the greater culture but by those we love most. How I constantly manage the fact that Black women have been some of my greatest abusers; yet, as a Black man and their son, brother, and nephew, it is my job and privilege to uplift them, as they are our most marginalized group yet deserve to be most cherished. How admiringly Ballroom folks, and seminary and liberal arts students all looked up to Michael, for many as the father they never had, others the one they never knew they so desperately needed. He was resourceful, critically engaged, full of loving-kindness—yet not afraid to push us. Of course, flawed, but at last, a functional parent.

Recently, in preparation for this book, I got "my two gay dads," Michael Roberson and Robert Sember, together to answer the million and one questions I had about Ballroom. Whenever I lose footing, find myself ambling about, lost in the many cultural paradoxes that make up this community, talking to the two of them always knocks my thinking back into alignment. We spoke for two hours, which didn't even begin to scratch the surface of it all, but part of that conversation was me asking Michael about his approach to fathering. In fact, since the advent of this book, I've asked every single house mother and father about their credo when it comes to parenting, because this found familial structure that works as an answer to LGBTQ youth being renunciated by everything and everyone they love is the very foundation of the house system in Ballroom.

So, I asked Michael, gay father to countless children in several Ballroom houses over the years, what he modeled his approach to fathering on. Here is his response:

MICHAEL ROBERSON (FATHER OF THE HOUSE OF GARÇON, MUGLER, ETC.)

Black women. It really is absolutely that. The older I've become, the more like my mother I've become, and it's so interesting to me. The relationship between my exterior, being nurturing in so many ways, but also patriarchal in other ways. It's okay to not always try to reconcile that fact, to not have to reconcile what seems like a dialectical tension. But yes, my approach absolutely comes first and foremost from my mother. Robert [Sember] knows this probably more than anybody else, because he's heard over the years the way I speak about my mother. She was absolutely fucking everything to me. My mother was God; she was goddess. My construction of cosmology when I was young was my mother, then God and Jesus. Therefore, for me, the trinity goes: Black women, God, and Jesus.

From Michael's perspective, it seems that here on earth, we're surrounded by holy trinities: Jesus, Mary, and Joseph; the Father, Son, and Holy Ghost; man, woman, and nonbinary; and the archetypal nuclear family that has been reconfigured in Ballroom as house mother, house father, and the children. And, to Michael's point, if we're tuned in enough with the world around us and are radically self-aware in Ballroom, we are lucky enough to get to embody all three.

In terms of the greater culture, Michael might seem to stand out in his willingness to integrate the spirit of his mother into his fathering; but, if you shadowed other gay Black fathers, or anyone in Ballroom for that matter, you'll find that everyone's *theoretical* approach to parenting is also primarily an iteration of that of their first and most formative role model—their mother. But the very fact that Michael offered "Black women" in response to the question "What is your approach to fathering?" is what makes Ballroom unique. Within this culture, a quintessential act of masculinity (fathering) can be driven by classic femininity (mothering), and *Black* femininity in particular—the most marginalized group who again and again care for the greater good, the type of tender, put-upon yet persistent nurturers consistently known for and expected to save the world from itself. The unrelenting manifestation of Gaia.

Michael's honest, self-reflective answer about his mother brings nuance and warmth to fathering, an act that could easily be defined as cold, blunt, and absentee based on our cumulative past experiences. And in his thoughtful, deliberate parenting of young people, Michael also dismantled centuries of binaries, not just in some theoretical vacuum but in the sort of direct action that transforms generations. Through this type of fathering, he is reconstructing old narratives about parenting BIPOC and LGBTQ youth and instilling in his kids across houses, across decades, the potential for emotional and spiritual generational wealth. The chance for collective recovery.

However, the framework for Michael's parenting includes not only who he wants to emulate, his mother, but also who he does not want to emulate:

> My parenting also has everything to do with what I always wanted my father to be. To some degree, that desire has probably allowed me to stay in these relationships with my kids for so long.
>
> My best friend, Michael Lee, oftentimes says, "You act like you birthed these kids, like you can't walk away from some of these relationships. . . ." And I always say to him, "Parents don't walk away from their kids." Because, in my mind, being abandoned is a whole thing for me, and so, I'm always wanting to not be that. I want to be the very thing that I wanted my father to be. But, you know, I'm a Pisces/Aquarius, so my Aquarius is theoretical and conceptual.
>
> So, for me, that translates into seeing who my mother was and wanting to be who my father was not, which then translates over into my style of leadership, because parenting is leadership. And that leadership translated into my work. I found my very first mentor in a Black woman named Sharon Shields, who was my boss when I worked for the Kansas City Board of Education. She really extended my notions around leadership and public health.

And this is the way. After a decade of learning alongside and critically engaging with the Ballroom community and dozens of hours of interviews with them, I can say that there is somewhat of a "typical" trajectory for young folks to enter into the culture. This path tends to contain at least one if not all of the following points of entry:

1. **Point 1: Gay Adoption (Classic)**—You're a young LGBTQ BIPOC, and your parent or guardian hates that unchangeable fact. You are expelled from your home. *Or* you never had a home or a family and—because you are the way you are—it feels nearly impossible that you'll find one. Someone out there, an adult from the house-ball community, has been in your shoes, and they see you. They take you under their wing. Suddenly, you're a part of something bigger. Suddenly, you have a gay father or trans mother or queer siblings. Suddenly, you have a home.

2. **Point 2: The Arts**—Young LGBTQ BIPOCs are historically drawn to dance, singing, lip-synching, costumes, and the whole shebang, and you're no exception. Your escapism spins off into an interest in after-school programs and extracurricular activities that enhance your craft as an artist and connect you to other folks who are also marginalized and talented and need somewhere to put it. It's the twenty-first century, so stumbling upon and longingly watching voguers slay on YouTube or clips from *Paris Is Burning* become the conduit for an affinity for fiercely fem formations, and this fated artistic alignment of the stars converges into an aptitude for voguing.

3. **Point 3: Your Peers and/or the Piers**—Birds of a feather. The kid on your block, in your family, or from the aforementioned after-school program is the one who tells you about balls and the one who subsequently brings you to your first one. And if you're from the NYC area, all it takes to have a run-in with this enticing middle(wo)man is a stroll past the Chelsea Piers at just the right time. Again, the girls are the pushers, voguing the gateway drug.

4. **Point 4: The Not-for-Profit Sector**—Public health. LGBTQ centers. Black empowerment organizations. Urban welfare. Since the HIV/AIDS crisis in the 1980s, Ballroom has been dovetailed with these organizations, working together to gather research data and get resources to the folks who need it most. In many instances,

that resource was and is Ballroom. Plus, you're from New York, one of the best publicly funded cities in America, and because of this, from a very early age, though part of a marginalized group, you're the beneficiary of the city's many free channels for personal and professional enrichment. These orgs aren't a panacea by any stretch, but such regular brushes with the nonprofit world provide you with a sense of civic duty, self-worth, and, perhaps most importantly, through people like yourself, a glimpse into your future.

Now, these are strictly my observations made from through-line narratives gathered from friends over the years, so I wouldn't say that a young person would *have* to arrive at being a part of ball culture through one of the above channels, but I would say the chances are great that they would. Although, if ever there were a savvy sixteen-year-old who, through pure cultural osmosis, arrived at their first ball and miraculously walked vogue fem without escort, introduction, or induction, it would be one of these children who are consistently wise beyond their years because they are native to New York City.

Case in point: one time I met a professor friend and his two small children (roughly four and seven years old) at a midtown patisserie to hand off some files I put together as his research assistant. He offered to buy me a pastry as a thank-you for coming all the way out from Bushwick. I allowed it. I perused the glass case, landing on a glossy slice of tarte Tatin, and asked myself aloud, "Hmm, I wonder if that's apple . . ." The four-year-old came over to me and said coolly, "It's pear." He was four, and it was only two words, but "you poor dummy" was implied in there somewhere. Of course, he was right—it *was* pear, and I don't know how he knew that. There was no sign saying it. Well, actually I do know how he knew. He was a four-year-old from NYC. But I digress.

More often than not, LGBTQ youth excommunicated from their biological families find the path to Ballroom via points 1–4: peers, gay parents, the arts, and city organizations—but typically it's some combination thereof. And though I ingratiated myself into the community in several different key ways—though I am not a member of a house, don't walk balls, and was initially brought in through Vogue'ology, a university course (and at the ripe, over-the-hill age of twenty-nine)—my induction into Ballroom still follows this traditional schism and is therefore a good example of it.

1. My ex and I rented and watched *Paris Is Burning*. The arts/peers.
2. What inspired me to enroll in Vogue'ology in the first place was my love of dance and *Paris Is Burning*. Many folks in the ball community say something similar. Dance is by no means my profession but something I need to do to stay sane, like meditating or taking deep breaths. When I was five, I learned most of the choreography to Janet Jackson's "Pleasure Principle" music video and many of the ones after, like "Alright," "If," "You Want This," and so on. I finally got real with myself during my Saturn return (roughly, age twenty-seven/twenty-eight), and decided that I would always need access to a dance studio, or at least a makeshift one, to run through choreography, to feel like myself. Vogue'ology allowed for that and so much more. The arts.
3. In Vogue'ology, we participated in events connected to ball culture and had regular guest instructors, like Derrick Xtravaganza and Pony Zion. Shortly after enrolling in the course, my cohort and I dared to venture out into the world to attend kiki balls and talks wherever Michael and Robert were in the city, thereby exposing us to the community. Peers.
4. Michael, one of my two gay dads, invited me to GMAD, where I was personally introduced to the Ballroom community. Gay adoption/organization.
5. Robert, my other gay dad, invited me to the Hetrick-Martin Institute for LGBTQ youth, a program hosted at Harvey Milk High School, in Astor Place, that through mentoring, provides many Ballroom kids the theory and lexical tools to be leaders of their community. Gay parents/organization.

The Hetrick-Martin Institute in particular was thrilling and a lot like GMAD, but for me, as a twenty-nine-year-old college student engaging these young people, HMI took me out of the position of peer and into that of a learner if not a voyeur with the potential to become a teacher. We met every Friday afternoon and it was a blast. I love kids and, again, free pizza, culture, activism, and conversation, and as much as those weekly meetings in the East Village served as a grooming space for young up-and-coming community leaders in Ballroom, they were also equally a crash course for me in how to organize around an idea: freedom. I learned how to air grievances in an open forum and build community in the constant fallout of inequality.

We covered so many bases in those halls and meeting rooms of Harvey Milk High. Because of the age of the HMI cohort, roughly sixteen to twenty-five, I was, for the first time, introduced to folks from the kiki scene, essentially the little league of Ballroom, for lack of a better term. In a structure that perfectly mimics that of biological families—in an almost Oedipal framework—those young people from the kiki scene who came to Hetrick-Martin expressed a fiery passion to be acknowledged by their elders, the legendary icons that make up the main/major Ballroom set. Though under their tutelage it seemed many of the kids felt left behind by, antagonistic toward, or in dire need of a level of acceptance from their predecessors. Back in class at the New School, it was compelling to hear from Michael the logistics of this hierarchy, how the kiki scene works as a sort of nascent staging ground for aspiring legends, and then later in the week, hearing from their end the visceral anticipation and sometimes resentment the young folks of kiki held for this process. Like all families, it seemed that, in the case of Ballroom, the growth of children into adulthood signified, on a metaphorical level, the death of their legendary parents. And like all families, the severity of this process was in direct correlation with, say, a house mother's desire to step down from a category like vogue fem and train their daughters to successfully walk it with a nod to the past and an eye on the future. Eventually, however, the young folks that I met in those rooms a decade ago were groomed to be the very agents who would today close the gap between the two factions of kiki and mainstream, perhaps through their hard work from ball to ball, legitimizing their talents across categories as superior voguers, runway darlings, immaculate faces, and avant-garde bizarro innovators; or maybe through their achievements as community builders and icons in their own right. Or, as the scene began to gel as a sub-sub-culture, maybe the girls just stopped caring about acceptance. It's likely a combination thereof that moved the needle, as Twiggy put it in our interview:

> That need for validation has changed. The kiki scene has evolved in such a way that you'll find people in it who give zero fucks about what mainstream Ballroom is doing or not doing. The kiki scene is their own

scene, and that's good for them. It has its own legends, its own icons, its own hall of famers, its own structure, all of that stuff. But then there are people who come into the kiki scene that want to use it as a training ground to eventually join a mainstream house, to use those connections and what they learned about people or the category they walked or whatever to enter into the mainstream.

Sometimes, because of where I was in my own journey to find a confident voice as a leader, I was overwhelmed by the boisterousness of the HMI cohort, stunned by how in control and sure they were as teenage and twenty-something leaders, where I always seemed to just be gaining my footing. So, I chimed in with an insight or pertinent question here and there but mostly committed myself to being a present listener.

I also learned more about the chasmic disparities between the experiences of women in Ballroom (both trans and cis) and gay men within the community. They reasserted that yes, ball culture was started by defiant trans ladies like Crystal LaBeija and then jettisoned through the twentieth century and into the future by trans mothers like Pepper LaBeija, Dorian Corey, Avis Pendavis, Angie Xtravaganza, and countless others who instilled in their houses and children unique traits and values that are the very life essence and lineage of the culture. Yet, as time went on, the misogynistic trappings of the heteronormative world infiltrated the community, gay men aggressively claiming the spoils of being the founders of ball culture, while the trans women who actually laid everything on the line to spark such a genesis were pushed to the wayside, dismissed as feminine and weak. "Man. Kind." is such a funny word for what we are.

And similar to the inevitable misogyny that seeps into families, and into subcultures that are meant to be their antidote, the subject of race in ball culture came up from time to time at Hetrick-Martin. It seemed the privilege and favoritism that results from colorism, the harsh reality that even in Ballroom, amongst a POC majority, Black bodies continued to experience marginalization from their Latinx, Asian American, and white brothers and sisters, including when it came to walking and winning particular categories like fem realness, were also in proximity to whiteness and historically an unfortunate advantage. Crystal and Harlow, and the case of the 1967 Miss All-America Camp Beauty, along with the overwhelmingly Latinx and fair-complected voguers Madonna chose for her tour come immediately to mind, but these disparities in color and fortune happen every day. But that's no surprise. This shit plagues every corner of the earth.

But the presence in those rooms of preeminent and future leaders of the community is what impressed me most. I was standing next to greatness. I watched as vibrant young people like Jonovia Chase and Gia Love found their thirst for leadership at HMI, becoming civically minded, breakout students of Ballroom in their own right. They were both bright, funny, and bold but sometimes shy, always gorgeous. Being a humble witness to their journeys these last ten years or so has been an honor, like watching a time lapse of orchids defying gravity and ascending from the forest floor and up to the heavens. Gia and Jonovia are now both public speakers, and Gia is a model and an activist for Black trans lives; Jonovia, a Ballroom coordinator for FX's *Pose* and lead organizer for House Lives Matter. They are women who in many ways have become the living embodiment of the dreams of their gay parents and mentors at HMI. To leaders like Robert and Michael, Ballroom friend and medical anthropologist Edgar Rivera Colón, and community mobilizer, educator, and HIV/AIDS preventionist Aisha Diori (a legendary cis woman advocating for all women in the Ballroom community), Gia and Jonovia are caretakers of the future. I spoke to them individually about their origin stories, the gay and trans mothers and fathers who reared them into their current evolutions, and how their sisterhood stands as another familial saving grace.

W/JONOVIA CHASE (HOUSE OF LANVIN)

JONOVIA CHASE: Now, when I moved to New York City, I really discovered dancing—I'm a dancer—and being part of a dance troupe in the city allowed me to once again be in very close proximity to Ballroom in a new way. I started to get into YouTube to watch people vogue, and I was like, "Oh, these are all people that I am completely in awe of." Voguing was a phenomenon to me. Who doesn't want to be able to move and express themselves as such, you know? It became a really big part of our extracurriculars, social gatherings—it was a thing that we just did.

Then I was in a dance company over the summer of my sophomore year of high school called Young Dance Makers, and of course the Latex Ball is every summer. That's when this boy named

Raymond took me to my very first Latex ball. Outside of him, I would completely accredit Kevin Omni from House of Ninja—he walks old way [vogue]—for helping me find Ballroom. When I was taking dance classes at Broadway Dance Center, I stumbled across him doing Old Way in the hallway, and I approached him. My friends knew that I had aspirations to vogue and wanted me to join a house. They were like, "You should ask him what house he is in." I did, and he said House of Ninja, and of course because of *Paris Is Burning*, I was like, Oh my god. I was so in awe of Willi Ninja's history and his moment in the movie. It's what really struck me most. And so, [Kevin] invited me, and I wound up joining my first mainstream house. I found the kiki scene shortly after that.

But other folks like Twiggy and my father, Michael Rober-son, were around and influential in my early stages in Ballroom. Through them, I was a Garçon and more deeply rooted in Ballroom than when I was a Ninja. And definitely my sister, Gia. She's been an anchor to me. So many people are behind you in this community.

RICKY TUCKER: You know, I watched the kiki documentary about two weeks ago, before I talked to Gia, and that part where they filmed the two of you just standing in the snowy street and facing the camera is breathtaking. I kept rewinding back to it. It's mesmerizing. It brought to mind those pictures in Harry Potter, how the people in them are kind of still but they smile and move, and then it loops like a GIF? Well, I told Gia that one of these days, as a thank-you, I'm going to figure out how to make an enchanted portrait of you all's scene and frame it for both to hang on your walls.

JONOVIA: My god, that would be so beautiful. The irony of this is that I was just looking at a picture of us from kiki earlier, and I was going to post it.

GIA LOVE (HOUSE OF JUICY)

GIA LOVE: I talk a little bit about this in the *Kiki* film, but I grew up on the debate team. My friend was on the team. I knew that in order for me to not be bullied, I needed to be really tough because my gender expression was always feminine. It was like I needed to do that to protect myself. So, growing up I didn't have behavioral issues, it was just a performance so I could be seen as tough, so people wouldn't bother me, because when I behaved in a soft and submissive way, which was natural to me, I was bullied.

My friend Lamar, who was in debate, was much older than me by like a few years. Basically, I feel like we were—and I'm going to say this because this is a Ballroom book—like the Banjee cunt. So, even though I was a very good debater, the best debater in my league, I was Banjee. I was from the hood, and still, even with my intellect, that was my existence, that was my story, a hood story. A Banjee queen doing policy debate and just navigating white spaces. So, Lamar was that as well.

Lamar used to vogue, and I related to it. It was a performance; it was an expression of femininity in a very attractive way. So, I was fourteen years old, and he took me to the Pier, and he started to introduce me to some of the girls in Ballroom. That was my introduction. And then he took me to HMI for the first time, and I went to vogue on Friday, and I was just in awe. The community, the [crying] . . . sorry, I got emotional with this just now. Just seeing . . . I had never seen so many people like myself in one space. I was so used to being the only one. And there we were being celebrated, like people clapping for you, and it wasn't a joke.

I was just talking to a friend about this. I said, "A lot of people that I know have abandonment issues because we come from these communities yet we cannot exist in these communities, so we're literally fighting for our lives and to find a space to thrive, and Ballroom is probably our first time having that. Even in debate, as a queer Black person, I was praised for my intellect but not my personhood. That wasn't elevated until the last tournament that I debated.

RICKY TUCKER: What happened at the last debate?

GIA: My best friend and I debated together for the last time, and we wanted to make it dramatic, so we did like a performance debate and vogued our talking points. We were seventeen years old, and we won the tournament. So, that was like the first time I really mixed both things, and that was my transition into Ballroom. At the same time, I met Jonovia in the tenth grade. Jonovia's a dancer and a performer, but I'm not a performer. . . . Sorry [weeping], all of this is triggering, in a good way.

RICKY: I'm sorry, honey. It's okay. Oh, my goodness . . . Can I just tell you something, as an aside really quick?

GIA: Yeah.

RICKY: I was talking to Robert [Sember] and Michael [Roberson] the other day, and it took me back to when the three of us were on stage at the Schomburg [Center for Research in Black Culture] for the House Lives Matter symposium. After our presentation, you got up to speak. I was sitting next to Robert at the time, and I remember looking over at him and saying, "Gia is magnificent!" And he goes, "I know." And then that just took me back to when I used to tag along with him to HMI years ago and seeing you and Jonovia and a bunch of different people, and just the arc of your growth and self-actualization—it's awe-inspiring. I just wanted you to know, that's what I see. Every time I see you on a screen, I'm just like, this girl is phenomenal.

GIA: Thank you. Sorry [takes a beat] . . . So, I met Jonovia in tenth grade. I went to an all-boys school for ninth grade, so it was just a lot going on at that period. I met Jonovia when I transferred to Washington River High School, because they had a debate team; that's why I went there. She was really quiet; we were cool, but we were not really friends like that, and actually, she wasn't really giving Jonovia steeze yet. Then, in eleventh grade, the bitch came back to school with a Playboy-bunny bag, tight-ass jeans, and she was gay boots, okay? That's when we became close.

When she joined the House of Ninja, Lamar was taking me to these kiki balls at the same time. It seemed like she was in Ballroom learning, and I needed someone to come into that space with me because, as I was seeing, Ballroom was a place where people who have been abandoned and seeking refuge could go to be celebrated. But before you break into Ballroom, from the outside looking in, it can be a very intimidating space to enter. They say we're some of the most judgmental and welcoming bitches, and ain't it true.

So, one day I heard about this ball at the Bronx Community Pride Center, and I hit up Jonovia and I was like, "You want to go?" I didn't walk balls before that, but the reason I started to walk balls is because of Jonovia. I didn't want to walk, because I just wasn't a dancer or whatever. And then she was like, "Oh, you're tall, you would be good walking runway. I'm going to teach you how to walk runway." So, she started teaching me to walk runway, but the thing is, when we got to the ball, she was nervous. Finally, I was like, "Well, then I'll walk, and if I walk, you have to walk." And she did. So, that's how I got started walking balls. I walked so she could walk, and because she was good, then I became good.

Even through separate interviews, the love between Jonovia and her sister Gia is palpable. When one walks, the other walks. When one is good, so is the other. It's inevitable when talking about gay and trans parents in Ballroom that the idea of siblings comes up. Past the obligatory brother- and sisterhood of being a part of the same culture—a comradery that to LaLa's earlier point can *quickly* be undercut by competitiveness between houses, and *shadily* undercut, I might add—siblings can be formed in different ways, like in the instance of having the same gay/trans parent, being in the same house, or simply by having a bond so close it's almost prenatal; the air-sealed tightness of Jonovia Chase and Gia Love's sisterhood is just that.

From those Fridays haunting the halls of HMI at Harvey Milk High and watching the two of them in their youthful effervescence, to sitting next to Jonovia a couple of years ago at the Schomburg in Harlem and watching as Gia commanded the stage during the House Lives Matter: Journey to Black Liberation Symposium—I marvel at the women these two sisters have become. Their groundedness. Their ability to laugh about grave issues. Their integrated activism. Their lexical prowess. Their self-actualization and its subsequent glow. As I mentioned while talking to Jonovia, nothing is more demonstrative of their inner light and the importance of family and how it feeds that inner light to me more than a stolen moment in the documentary film *KiKi*, starring J + G and produced and co-directed by the iconic Twiggy Pucci Garçon.

Like many a profound cinematic shot, the kiki moment in question is quite simple, painfully fleeting even, which is central to its brilliance. It's a tight frame. In it, Gia stands to the left, warmly but defiantly staring at the camera dead-on. She's wearing a winter beanie, her dark hair flowing down around her fur hood; Harlem, a brick-lined snow globe all around her. In front of and just to the right of Gia, her little big sister Jonovia wears a simple part in her hair that flows down past the frame. A playful

Dorothy Dandridge smile threatening to rise from her face like the warm dawn rendering the city frost innocuous. The camera holds there for roughly ten seconds. They're gorgeous. It's stunning. It is oxygen.

Just seconds prior to this bracketed moment of Zen, Gia is randomly verbally attacked by a kid (maybe like thirteen years old?) while walking down the street in Harlem. He shouts out "faggot" at her. The moment is pregnant with heartache. Gia admits to the director, "Honestly, I'm triggered." The moment could be seen as a breakneck metaphor for the lives of queer brown kids, that pathway from having a home to being lost to found again, going from safe to unsafe to safe again—being found.

They are courageous spaces, most often literal shelters from the storm. They're a kiki in the face of tragedy. The truest reflection of our own beauty to date. An amen to our potential. The resetting of our course. The acknowledgement of our worth. That's why our gay families are so critical.

Gay families are everything.

LEIOMY MALDONADO

AKA: The "Wonder Woman of Ballroom"
HOUSE: Amazon, Prodigy, Mizrahi
CATEGORY: Vogue Fem
SUPERPOWER: The infamous hair flip known as the "Leiomy Lolly"
FAMOUS BATTLE: Leiomy Maldonado vs. Keith Evisu
NOTABLE QUOTABLE: "What did you do to make your mark on the world?"

Leiomy's grace and agility are a raging fire. Not the mere flicker of a single flame, prancing tippy-toed atop a candle wick like a prim and proper ballerina that dare not spread out, take up too much space, some tragic fire afraid to catch. No. Maldonado is that sprawling, awe-inspiring fire tornado you see on the news, born of destruction, crackling embers thrown to the forest floor—relentless—kicked back up and reignited by the wind and spun into an all-consuming fire whirl, an explosive and elegant display—a phenomenon you never even knew existed.

Or is she the legendary fiery phoenix? Every stage-jumping, hair-flipping, tornado-inducing performance a new life giving you lyfe, infinitely rising and falling, spinning and dipping into the ground and back up again, leaving the stage momentarily only to return, sparking as many encores as she and her subjects see fit. Because it's fucking deserved. She is the core paradox of Ballroom: a fierce beauty with soft, Olympic-level athleticism.

This trail-blazing dynamo also reincarnates through her professional lives, from being the heroic vixen (though vilified) on *America's Best Dance Crew*, to sitting on her royal throne as a judge on *Legendary*, to her own vogue evolution into Florida Ferocity on *Pose*, to lyrically shattering multiple ceilings as an ambassador for Nike, to rightfully sitting upon her throne as the heir apparent authority of all things vogue fem.

CHAPTER 5

CHURCH

w/MikeQ and Lee Soulja

*Clubs and balls as hallowed ground, house music
as gospel, and the Theology of Vogue'ology*

THE FALL FROM MT. OLYMPUS

Studio 54: Night Magic, the fall 2020 exhibition at Brooklyn Museum is a disco-ball glitter bomb detonating the worst case of F.O.M.O. your deprived twenty-first-century heart has ever felt. It's a sparkling if withholding act of providence.

Filled with black-and-white and color photographs of an unbelievable mix of eye-catching strangers and high-watt celebrities alive between 1977, when the New York City discotheque was founded, and 1984, when its doors finally closed, the exhibition is practically an orgy of gold-lamé showers, cocaine flurries, mirror-ball sunbeams, and disco lightning raining down from Mt. Olympus, a rare, ephemeral convergence of the best parts of heaven and hell here on earth.

Save for a few rooms replicating 54's then cutting-edge, largely neon stage design, along with a poly-blend forest of DVF wrap dresses draped across '70s-thin mannequins, the exhibit is predominately 2-D: photographs, opening night's star-studded guest list (Liz Taylor, MJ, Liza, Bill Cunningham), programs from special events like Bianca Jagger's thirty-second birthday. Though unfortunately static, the exhibition does still provide a vivid vantage point into this golden age of photography, even if it at times feels like it's robbing you of a dimension, rubbing in the *almost* kinetic ecstasy you see running the show's length, only underscoring the pangs of having not been there (and never being able to go). But there is pain everywhere, as you're almost sure to see an upper-middle-aged person or two walking around the exhibit, joyfully reliving the ragers they used to attend there, and lamenting how even they must have had to come to an end.

Still, no matter the mediums utilized across the exhibition, the translation of what went down at that club travels effectively across multiple dimensions of space and time, making it very clear that this Studio 54 movement—the folks who made it a weekly if not nightly party, and the ones who waited in line for hours only to be turned away—was a frenetic meditation on the divine power of the dance floor, the DJ, and any group of people with a collective desire to be delivered.

When you walk into Brooklyn Museum, the first transcendent element to hit your senses is the music, hustle-inducing sonics that truly lift you out of the doldrums of what some people would consider a routine visit to a sanitized space, a museum, albeit one filled with art and its infinite potential to inspire. I, on the other hand, treasure a day at the museum as "going to church." Similarly, you arrive feeling the bluesy piano chords and the call-and-response of popular disco tracks finally given their breathing room—full extended mixes echoing off high ceilings—pop hymns heard appropriately in their cathedral.

They say that smell is the sense most associated with memory, but at the *Night Magic* show, hearing familiar songs like Thelma Houston's "Don't Leave Me This Way," Cheryl Lynn's "To Be Real," and Alicia Bridges's "I Love the Night Life," is most evocative, triggering in you a déjà vu rooted not in personal experience but in the collective unconscious, the feeling that you've either actually been there before, writhing around on-stage next to Angelica Huston and a harem of scantily clad go-go dancers, or that these era-specific melodies have turned on a sixth sense, in this case, your imagination, weaving a believable almost corporeal scenario where you're not at Brooklyn Museum but in 54's roped-off VIP section, whispering small talk through Diana Ross's waterfall tresses and into her ear, begging her to divulge what conditioner she's been using. An intimate moment amongst the gods.

Another club-characterizing moment in the exhibition happens in a video installation of a barely disco-aged Michael Jackson being interviewed by Jane Pauley. There's an air of fantasy to it because it's Michael, because the interview is in Studio 54, evoking the spirit of the subject at hand, and because another young man with a chronic case of the Peter Pans, the club's charismatic runner, Steve Rubell, is just outside the frame, smiling and bubbling with the prospects of what this interview and its free advertising could generate.

Jane Pauley asks Michael why people like he and Liza Minnelli would ever come to a place to dance for fun after dancing all day for work. With a sweet candor, Michael says:

> Because you're just being free then. Most of the time it's set choreography when we're on-stage, and it's stuff you have to do every night. When you dance here, you're just free. You dance with whoever you want to—you just go wild. Not only is it fun to dance, but it's fun to look at other people. You walk around and you see all kinds of things, like Darth Vader was here the other night. [Laughing] It was incredible![1]

There are several points in his answer where you might place curious emphasis, like on the part about dancing with whomever he likes, wondering with whom he'd like to dance yet usually cannot, and whether or not that criteria is gender and/or age based. Or if he has much input when it comes to this choreography he's forced to perform every night. Or if he thinks Darth Vader was a formidable dance partner, but I digress. The point is that to Michael, a god-like star at the time and a kid who at that point had it all and then some, the club was a rare opportunity to relinquish all of that. It was a chance to jump down from Mt. Olympus and party in the town square with humans, Darth Vader, and the other weirdos among them, kinda like when a CEO goes to Burning Man or Becky joins the Peace Corps.

In the full cut of this same video, Rubell corroborates this idea, telling Jane how he intentionally tries to provide such escapism as a credo, then goes on about the lack of paparazzi allowed inside, and how folks like Michael, Liza, Cher, Gloria Vanderbilt, and a litany of Olympians could just be themselves because of it. It is a noble sentiment perhaps and maybe *narrowly* altruistic if it weren't for it only serving the 1 percent, a group who, through monetary accumulation, was already experiencing a significant level of freedom, the likes of which some of us will never experience even a modicum of in our lifetimes. So, good for them—but what about everyone else?

Apart from the few regular humans deemed rich, cool, connected, beautiful, or vapid enough for entry into Studio 54, where did the marginalized poor, brown, and professionally queer partiers go "to be free"? Sure, a huge through line of both Studio 54 and the *Studio 54: Night Magic* show are the Black and unconventional (sexually and otherwise) it-folks like Michael, André Leon Talley, Pat Cleveland, and Grace Jones, who were regular attendees and performers at 54 and other clubs around New York City. Jones in particular is still one of the most awe-strikingly gorgeous, talented, and odd Jamaican female artists anyone ever laid eyes on. But like performers in clubs across America experienced during Jim Crow, being appreciated as an entertainer or socialite doesn't necessarily grant you a seat at the table or even a room in the hotel in which you're performing for that matter. Perhaps Jones got into 54 based on and later independent of her performances, and maybe she was treated by the establishment there like the queen that she is, but that does not mean that every minority was or that discrimination based on being the wrong race or having an inadequate relationship to fame or capitalism didn't take place. And in the wake of being marginalized from the Olympic arena, after they were drained of their F.O.M.O. and filled with rage, what did those "other" folks do? Where did we go?

CHURCH

A single song can be a portal into otherly realms, often ones you didn't even know existed.

Because my grandmother was a singer in New York City in the 1970s and '80s, my mother and her sisters grew up privileged in a couple directions, one of which was hobnobbing with famous Black musicians of the time, another was getting into exclusive clubs while underage. My mom had her fourteenth birthday party at the Copacabana. Seventies powder-blue seemed the color scheme; the pictures from the evening featured Harold Melvin & the Blue Notes, an added feature that was totally lost on me as a kid. Maybe I was practicing an adult New Yorker level of aloofness when it came to people namedropping—sometimes my Grandma and them laid it on a lil thick. But it was clear that all the ladies in my family lived a charmed life before I was born, roughly around the time crack began to decimate Black families like mine. When I posted pictures of my trip to the Studio 54 exhibition on Instagram, my mom left a comment that she and my aunt Veronica used to go there as kids, to which I replied, "I'd figured," genuinely not shocked, but definitely 10 percent mad I didn't get to go.

Anyway, after I was born and we'd moved to other places both near and far and landed in North Carolina, a lot of the music from those higher-profile times stayed with my mom and them and, by proxy, us kids. And even later, as a young adult, I went chasing some of those sounds, wanting to know more about the people who made them, more about my family in context to them, why I was drawn to them, and if the people who made them were like me. Turns out they were.

One track that I rediscovered in my early twenties was "Heartbeat" by Taana Gardner. If you know the song, you can peg it as soon as the nearly elastic bass line starts up and Gardner's angelic but substantial vocals glide in, like a melodic EKG warning of potential heart failure. The song maintains that groovy bass line and soaring vocals until it explodes during the bridge, when a backup masc choir rains down, while Gardner weaves in between those skyscrapers, telling us just how weak this all makes her feel—and how much of a freak it's making her become. The overall effect is that of everyone at whatever club it's playing in singing the song in unison. Like you're living a disco musical. Like a congregation in praise.

When buying CDs was still a thing, and the Internet still an innovation, I went looking for that song, which, once found, led me down a rabbit hole of new artists and cultural realms that would speak to me. "Heartbeat" was on a compilation by the DJ and production duo Masters at Work, two formidable disco creatives—Luis "Little Louie" Vega and Kenny "Dope" Gonzalez—eventually known for being central progenitors of the house sound of the 1990s, laying down tracks for dance-floor mainstays like Madonna (as mentioned before) and, Gonzalez in particular, working under the moniker Bucketheads to create one of the most enthrallingly voguable songs to date, "The Bomb! (These Sounds Fall into My Mind)." I've witnessed several vogue instructors use "The Bomb" as a perfect house-pop crossover track for training beginners. It just sounds like someone's fem queen debut.

Vega and Gonzalez came of age in New York City in the era of disco and were critically influenced by downtown clubs and uptown urban music innovators of the time like Afrika Bambaataa and DJ Red Alert. They were there when disco transitioned into house—and what a rejoiceful time and space to occupy. You can hear this in their mixing and curation of *Masters At Work Present West End Records: The 25th Anniversary Edition Mastermix*, the compilation where I finally found my

"Heartbeat" and many other tracks, like Loose Joints' "Is It All Over My Face," written by musical virtuoso Arthur Russell, and a slew of hits either mixed or produced by the great Larry Levan, a production genius and the decade-long DJ in residence at the legendary underground discothèque haven, the Paradise Garage.

If Studio 54 was the mainstream's Hellenic polytheistic home to tourist Olympians, their earthly timeshare dedicated to mind-altering ambrosia, exclusivity, and cash-cold capitalism, then the Paradise Garage took a page from Dionysus, the god of religious ecstasy, and ran with it, creating a rapturous, artistically elevated, egalitarian, panacean nirvana that wasn't a tour of earth but instead a hallowed space where "the meek" not only inherited the earth but transcended that realm—an answer to humanity's most-prevalent woes, a groundbreaking monotheism worshipping the one thing that matters: love.

And if 54 was a lengthy Homeric or even a Greek Orthodox hymnal, hearsay once removed from the source and once again by the bard, then the Paradise Garage was the advent of gospel, a joyful and faithful jubilance, a genesis sparked by very visceral oppression—and how it was overcome. This epic metaphor was made more literally evident by the music that was played there at "the Garage" by DJs like Larry Levan. Songs like Machine's "There but for the Grace of God Go I," utilizing scriptural lyrics, were played at the Garage at the time and addressed head-on the issue at hand, the fact that higher-profile downtown clubs, though virtual dance free-for-all's operating under Sodom-and-Gomorrah-loose mandates, didn't by definition cater to LGBTQ BIPOCs of the time. In many instances, they were hindrances for these folks to feel free. And while Machine's essentially dance-gospel hit, and other tracks like Larry Levan's mix of "Stand on the Word," a Southern Baptist feeling song with hand claps and a children's choir singing the praises of how great the good Lord's work is, may have been played at Studio 54 as well, these things take on a completely different context when lifted out of the devil's den and returned to the house of the Lord.

So, after the Masters' West End compilation, I continued my education by seeking out more on this time period, landing on books like Tim Lawrence's *Life and Death on the New York Dance Floor, 1980-1983*, which plays theoretical connect the dots between the various clubs at the time, like the Paradise Garage, CBGB's, 54, and the Loft, but also with music genres of the era, including disco, noise, hip-hop, and post-punk.

I also watched films like *Maestro*, a documentary that follows the transition of sounds like Levan's particular brand of underground disco into the house sound mixed by people like Frankie Knuckles, and then on to EDM across time, geography, and demographics. Through many of these disparate elements during the late 1970s, it seemed the Paradise Garage ended up becoming more of a sanctuary of sound for the city's most subjugated demographics, a hallowed dance space with a thoughtful, incredible sound system, a place where people weren't "Blacks, Jews, or gays" but just *were*, because being all of those things was the common denominator, an impossibility once one left the mixed congregation during those wild nights in that building at 84 King Street in SoHo. Not at 54, and not even at the predominantly Black clubs uptown that catered to a burgeoning hip-hop and, therefore, machismo-hetero set. Yes, Grace Jones did indeed perform at the Garage, but more notably, Black and brown men danced with each other in droves and with abandon. Freely. And while I haven't heard mention of him being there, if he were, I'm sure Darth Vader would have been more than welcome at the Garage, finally able to spread out and be himself, helmet off—Dathomirian burn scars and all.

This open ambiance is what made it so that ball culture became a cornerstone of the space at the Garage. Folks that I've spoken to from the community who were around during this late '70s, early '80s period in downtown New York talk about having either vogued there firsthand, or seen people vogue there, some perhaps for the first time in their lives, wondering with a dire curiosity what it even was those queens over there were doing, where it came from, and where they might find more of it. Like the impossibly tight constraints that created the big bang, progressive movements like Ballroom and house music are born from finding crawl spaces of freedom in seemingly inescapable dire socioeconomic conditions. The two art forms share a genesis, and according to many folks in the community, the Paradise Garage was in fact a paradise where they were found. It was their Garden of Eden.

When I got to New York, in 2011, and took Vogue'ology, Michael Roberson, who was attending Union Theological Seminary at the time, broadened for our class this dance-floor-as-religious-experience concept by bringing in Ballroom's prominent archetypes as key figures in the metaphor. He explained how the MCs and DJs can be both pastors and choir directors with their bombastic narrations of walked categories, fire-and-brimstone levels of shade throwing, and melodic use of scripture and gospel—often the only reason folks even show up to "church" early on a Sunday morning (or at a ball, 4 a.m.). Then he explained to us how, in this scenario, the audience at a ball is the congregation, dancing, shouting, catching the Holy Ghost, and carrying on. All dressed in their Sunday best, everyone in this holy trinity comes into the space ready to give praise to (or read) one another, and each time, coming that much closer to salvation.

Carving these sacred spaces out on the ball floor isn't just an innate instinct; it's also an answer to a great loss, as many of our Black and brown folks, having been raised in Baptist and Catholic churches, were made unwelcome once ostracized by their families. It should go without saying that not all Ballroom community members were raised in supportive religious homes like ACLU trans justice campaign manager LaLa Zannell, whose father was a pastor and whose mother and other family members embrace both her and her LGBTQ family. Because LaLa is able to retain complex multitudes within herself, never having to choose between her biological and chosen families, never feeling they're even at odds with one another, but instead, lovingly fusing the two communities together, Lala was never forced to divorce herself *from* herself. But hers is an exceptional case.

Since many of the folks "in the life" are brought up in Black churches, this connection between dance spaces/balls and religious experiences fills a loss stemming from missing their spiritual roots, communal spaces where likeness is found and thanks are given. What could seem like a default aesthetic choice about a gospel-inspired song played at a ball, a church-ish hat worn to accentuate realness, or the hot plates of free food that often line the back walls and feed the congregation at many a ball are actually ways of rejoining those spiritual institutions that taught them to love, sing, and praise all their lives. Maybe folks in Ballroom miss that house they used to go to every week to tap into that soul-enriching element. It's unfortunate that many of them are no longer welcome, or if welcome, simply don't feel safe. Luckily, the Lord is omnipresent. And her sense of irony is on point.

The Ballroom as church metaphor may not have necessarily originated with Michael, but he is a far-reaching community leader, father, mentor, and theologian, and so his take on the comparison is ubiquitous as well. Recently, I asked Michael's daughter Twiggy about the divinely spiritual feeling people get at balls. This is what she said about the experience:

> I was born and raised in the South in a Baptist Christian church. I've always been sort of rooted in religion and spirituality. Coming into Ballroom, I've discovered how colonizing the religions that I grew up with have been to my mental and spiritual thought process, and since then I have decolonized quite a bit. To be completely honest, a lot of that I owe to my father Michael and to the people that I've met through him or through Ballroom.

Michael uses the analogy of how clubs and balls are like our church. The commentators and DJ are like the minister of music and pastor; the call or response of it all is all there. There is definitely a spiritual aspect to it. I mean, I hold balls as a very sacred space, especially "ball balls" that we are throwing and not just these mock balls or exhibitions or collaborations with brands. And let's be clear—those are for the coin. No matter what folks are saying, they're doing it because there's a coin behind it, or there's access to people or things that they want for their professions. And all of that is okay because either-or thinking is rooted in white dominant culture—we can have both-and. There's a space for that. But I mean, our balls, house balls, the balls that people throw, are very sacred to me. They're a holy space. They're spaces where people literally discover who they are, express parts of themselves they never have before, reach deep down inside and pull out this performance that they may not even be able to do on a regular basis, on a day-to-day basis. All of that happens at balls. And so, it's a very, very sacred and spiritual place.

Here, Twiggy articulates the spirituality of a ball but also makes a stark distinction between the spiritual experience of going to balls thrown by people in the community and the lack thereof at balls thrown by people who perhaps are in the community but working in conjunction with brands or museums, etc.—professional, capitalistic ventures. Rightfully, she does not see those as sacred. I've been to some of those exhibitions, and I wholeheartedly concur. Karen forgive me, but there's something voyeuristic if not missing from a ball when it is composed of a certain ratio of white onlookers. It's like when I go to First Corinthian church up in Harlem with my aunt Sandie, and because I get there late, I end up having to sit up in the stratosphere section literally with a fresh tour-busload of Germans, or Swedes, or whomever, who are there to survey what an "authentic" African American gospel choir sounds like. I'm not even very religious (spiritual, yes), but for me, some of the sacredness is drained from the experience when you're watching an award-winning Black choir do the damn thing from up there in the nosebleeds with Björn and Lars. It's just off.

Still, commercial balls notwithstanding, the church analogy is forever emblazoned in my mind and spirit; the more I see ball culture through this religious lens, the more apt the metaphor becomes. Being Black and/ or Latinx and LGBTQ and finally finding a second family and sacred space like Ballroom is to be born again. It is kind of like finding the Holy Grail when you find folks like you who can *truly* put into context a moral philosophy and code that's not built around homophobia, transphobia, and a host of other judgments including shame around sex work, a job that is still for better or worse the one most readily available to trans women of color. Instead, like the disco track that could easily have been the offertory hymn of those early days of ball culture at the Paradise Garage—"Love Is the Message."

THE INTERVIEW
w/DJ, MikeQ

MikeQ is Ballroom's most preeminent DJ, producer, and audiophile, traveling all over the globe for gigs and collaborations as Ballroom's musical ambassador. I've been to a couple of balls where he's done live sets, and there's definitely a distinct sound coming from his pulpit that I can only describe as postmodern and voguer-friendly, a dovetailed mix of old and new sounds with an electronic kick that points to the future of a movement, to a genre we can't quite name yet. What stuck out to me in our conversation was Mike's childlike sense of discovery and enthusiasm for the sounds of Ballroom and, even greater than that, his adoration for the parts that make up the holy trinity of the Ballroom floor: DJs, voguers, and MCs.

RICKY TUCKER: So, tell me, how did you find Ballroom?

MIKEQ: I was in high school at the time and just started going out to the Village. I was coming into my own, having that awakening about being gay and stuff. This was in 2003.

I had always heard about this party that would happen at the Globe in downtown Newark[, New Jersey,] and always wanted to go. I was afraid at first for some reason . . . but I finally went in October of that year. I had never really been out to parties or anything like that prior to this. It was a cool party. They played a lot of hip-hop and stuff, but at the end of the night, the DJ started playing this different type of music. . . . All the drag queens that were there just started doing this crazy dance, what to me at first was throwing themselves on the ground [laughs], and I loved it so much, the combination of the music *and* the voguing. So, now I'm there every Friday just to get that same experience. Looking for more of that music!

AOL at the time was a big thing, so I'm on there with my little dial-up connections. You know, they used to have the little chat rooms and stuff, like the gay chat rooms. My screen name on there was MikeQ7000, and that's where I get my DJ name from, my AOL screen name. The Q has no significance; I just really liked Infiniti cars at the time, and they always named their cars Q and a number, so that's where that came from. Just being in the chat rooms, I was asking people, trying to find another place like the Globe where this music and this dancing would be at. That led me to the Club House in Harlem on 3rd and 122nd.

I started going there by myself. That first night I went up to the DJ booth trying to buy their CDs; still, there wasn't much to buy. There were two DJs: DJ Angel X and Tony Cortez. The Club House at least had an actual "Ballroom Experience," actual mini balls at the end of the night, whereas the Globe had voguing maybe the last few minutes of the night. So that's where I think I got a really good first experience of Ballroom.

RICKY: Who was around then?

MIKEQ: The LaBeijas were around, which was my first house, like around 2005, and I was maybe with them for like a year or two. You had your Jack Mizrahis and Selvins on the mic, a young Dashaun, Deasja, Leiomy, Roxy, Alloura, Kassandra, Caliente, Tia, Dawn, Lola, Champagne, Gina Gospel, Sequoia, Charles and Juan, Stephanie Milan, Jennifer Evisu. Houses that was around at that time was Ebony, Prodigy, Karan, Givenchy (now Mizrahi), Balenciaga, Blahnik, to name a few.

RICKY: Did you walk in a house or do DJs have a house too?

MIKEQ: I never walked in or out of a house. Walking balls is not my thing, but most of us DJs are in houses and some do walk. I am currently in the House of Ebony (previously Evisu, Valentino, and LaBeija) but have no requirements to walk. Like with you and writing, my contribution to the culture is DJing and making music.

After looking for more of that Ballroom music, I still felt like I couldn't find what I'd been hearing. There was this kid that went to the Globe who introduced me to FruityLoops (FL Studio) and Sony ACID Pro, which are the programs I use to make music to this day. I started playing around with them, making music. I think it was like 2004 when I made my first beats, and so I started posting my music online on walkformewednesdays.com (The Shade Board), and I eventually became the resident DJ at both the Club House and the Globe.

RICKY: What about the sound appealed to you, and what tracks drew you in?

MIKEQ: I was hearing songs like "Din Da Da," "Satisfaction," "Make These Bitches Gag" by DJ Vjuan Allure. I didn't know who Vjuan was at the time, and the track actually said his name in it. I didn't even know what they were saying; it seemed like some other kind of language to me. I'd never heard a name like that, Vjuan, only to find out how special he'd be to me and the entire community.

But there was something about the music and the dancing. . . . I think both of them combined is what really grasped me. Maybe the voguing alone could have gotten me, but in that moment, it was the collaboration of the two, and honestly, I wasn't into DJing or anything before—Ballroom brought that talent out of me.

I did love music though. I used to be home recording cassette tapes. I'd be there making my *own* radio shows [laughs]. I was the DJ and the radio host. I'd "come in" and do a quick interview with myself as the celebrity. So, I did that, but I didn't know that it would become this.

RICKY: Tell me more about the connection between voguing, MCing, and DJing.

MIKEQ: So, during a battle at a ball, you have me playing the music, you have your MC who's on the mic, and then you have your voguer. And the three work together. As I'm there DJing, I'm listening to the MC—I can DJ kind of blind now—but also, if I have the view,

I can watch the voguer, take what I'm hearing and what I'm seeing and mimic that moment, or do something special for that moment that compliments what you're seeing. That is, if you can catch it and know what to expect out of your voguer. The same goes for the MC; they're on the microphone but they're also watching the person who's voguing, and they get energy and inspiration from them as well as listening to me and riding the beat I am playing. And different people give you a different output. While you're voguing, you're listening to the MC as well as me. Those moments are created specifically for that time on the floor, which I think is cool—the vogue trinity.

RICKY: Michael [Roberson] talks a lot about the dance floor being a sacred space. He often compares the DJ and the MCs to the pastors, sometimes doing a call-and-response, and that could be at a disco or a ball. So, what MCs and voguers do you like to work with for that synchronicity?

MIKEQ: As far as MCs go, my absolute favorite is Selvin, aka MC Debra. It's always something different, always creative. Something could happen in the moment at the ball that night, and out of nowhere she'll make a chant from that moment. That's always surprising and fun to me. Gregg Evisu, Kevin JZ Prodigy, Precious [Old Navy], Jack [Mizrahi]—I love a lot of the MCs. But you also have your very obnoxious ones, who I won't name. . . .

RICKY: Ha! Well, then tell me what makes them obnoxious.

MIKEQ: It's mainly a lot of the younger people . . . a lot of the newer kids, which to be fair, they aren't *really* MCs all the time. It's especially bad when you have two MCs on the mic and they aren't together or in sync, and they got like two different chants happening at the same time? People talking over people; it just gets so confusing. It's like, you should be able to hear that and get it together.

And then with voguing, it could really be anybody. You have your good ones; you have your bad ones. Like Leiomy, love her. I'm pretty good with catching her dips and stuff. And there are a lot of other people: Inxi Prodigy, Divo Ebony, Tinkerbell Amazon, Honey Balenciaga, Makayla Lanvin, Paul Mugler. So many over the years. I can't even begin to name the amount of people that *I* get life from.

RICKY: Could it be a voguer that you've never even DJ'd for before that you could create that same good experience from?

MIKEQ: Totally. It could be a kid walking virgin vogue, someone we've never even seen before, and they come out and do things that are just like, wow. So, yeah, from top to bottom, new to old, that's part of the fun of the experience. The surprise of it.

RICKY: So, all these things evolve musically. You start with disco, then comes house. In what direction are we going? Like, have you heard more of a trap element in the music at balls lately?

MIKEQ: I'm trying to think of this moment. Well, with Ballroom, we sample so much from the current music, like with house, to hip-hop and trap or whatever. It's whatever the creator is feeling or wants to remix at the moment, and a lot of that stuff can be hip-hop or R&B, pop, viral videos, TV themes, movie lines, gospel, anything that someone wants to sample and then bring those elements into Ballroom. So, yeah, there's a lot more hip-hop and trap sampled music lately. I don't know if you know about Jersey club music, like their take on music, which is just flipping hip-hop songs into these more danceable versions, which is basically what is done in Ballroom.

RICKY: Is that essentially what you do with your production company, Qween Beat?

MIKEQ: Yeah, so, if it's something that I'm putting out professionally, I try to keep that less sampled, especially with hip-hop tracks. Don't want to get in trouble with copyright stuff. But I make music for Ballroom first; that's why it's called Qween Beat, because it's beats for the queens, and that's just music I think is fit for a ball. I have been tapped to create a few remixes of various genres, and so for me I always take a Ballroom approach to that—everything I flip, I'm gonna bring it back to Ballroom, and my main thought on that is, *How would it work in the club or on the Ballroom floor?*

RICKY: Do you ever work on a track with voguing in mind or like have someone test out one of your tracks by voguing to it?

MIKEQ: I don't have anyone in particular in mind, but I am thinking about voguing when I produce. I'm trying to think if I ever see a person . . . I do see a person, but it's just a silhouette in my head. So, all that is in mind, but once I get a good layout to the track, I do take it out to the club, like to House of Vogue [at House of Yes, Brooklyn] when that was happening, or at different vogue nights early on, to see what people like, see how they react, because, you know, some stuff is good, but not everything. Sometimes you need to go back and edit elements, take something away, do something different, if I didn't get what I wanted out of it from playing it in the club.

RICKY: So, you're traveling a lot for work these days?

MIKEQ: Not at the moment, because of COVID. My last gig was back on March 13 [2020] for the *Legendary* (HBO) after-party when we were wrapping. Prior to that I had been moving about the globe nonstop since 2011.

RICKY: That's funny, my last day in the office at the New School was Friday, March 13. That seems to be the day everyone was packing it up.

MIKEQ: Yep.

RICKY: What was that like working on the set of *Legendary*?

MIKEQ: It was a nice experience! I'm super glad that I was asked to be a part of it, and super excited to be there. They send cars to me, drive me an hour to Connecticut to the studio, chill, eat, and get ready. In terms of what it meant for Ballroom, being on set was amazing to me just to have made it to this point where we have TV shows and things about us, and it's a really great feeling after so many years of just being a part of this culture with no expectations. Watching back, I realized I had so much more fun on set, because there's so much you don't see on the show that happens behind the scenes, during twelve-plus-hour days across a month and a half, but it was fun.

RICKY: The theme song is a track you created. What was that process like?

MIKEQ: That opportunity came up before I even appeared on the show. The music director hit me up and said they needed a track for the show, and I had worked with him prior to that when he was doing the music for the Ballroom show, *My House*. He was the music director for that show as well. He wanted my original music but also stuff from Qween Beat, things to have for the show for the contestants to choose from for their battles. I sent him that, and within a few days, he wanted to know if I wanted to make a few appearances on the show and connected me with the producers.

I got on the phone with them and they quickly told me about the show and asked if I wanted to be a part of that. Then, James

Blake contacted me and said he wanted to work on some music. He told me that he was doing music for the show as well, so I believe they had contacted him to do the theme song first, but he felt he couldn't do that himself without respectfully having someone [from the community] who does the music themselves to come in. We linked up on that, and I scrambled to put something together. We laid it out, I took it to the studio with him, asked my artist and friend Ash B. to hop on the track, and she basically came up with the lyrics, and James Blake did the keys on the song. We recorded it at Electric Lady Studios, which is Jimi Hendrix's studio in New York, and so much has been recorded there, which was an amazing experience in and of itself. They [HBO] didn't give me an outline or anything. I just had the show name, *Legendary*, and basically, they used what I handed in. The rest was history, and that song is one of my favorites in my catalogue.

GOSPEL

Just before winter break at the New School, faculty and admin used to post to the wall-length windows of the Lang Courtyard multicolored fly-ers detailing the courses being offered in the spring. I can only describe the scene as a stained-glass theory chapel made of "sexy," relevant, and progressive titles reflecting the issues our university was so known for tackling. They read like headlines from a range of periodicals, from the *New York Times* to *Us Weekly*. Courses like "Occupy Wall Street" to "Be-ing Andy Warhol" to "The Politics of Xenophobia" to "RuPaul's Drag Race and Its Impact."

Dreading the day our Vogue'ology family would disperse, my class-mate, friend, and Queer Cosmos astrologer Colin Bedell and I deter-mined, before the fall 2011 semester's end, that in order to stave off the inevitable sadness, together we'd just have to follow our instructor Rob-ert Sember from class to class until we graduated in 2014. So, when I walked into the Lang Courtyard in winter 2011, exhausted from finals yet already scanning the stained-glass course wall for registration ideas, and saw "What Is the Sound of Freedom," taught by Robert Sember, I knew it would be the first class in that run of stave-offs.

"What Is the Sound of Freedom" was excellent. It fulfilled its purpose in terms of preserving some of our Vogue'ology fam; there were at least five of us from that course in there. But independent of that, it was great because it was like a super meditative getaway in a frenetic city many of us were still recently new to. Often our lessons were to simply listen. Listen to the sounds in our neighborhood. Listen to each other's recordings of what we thought the sound of freedom might actually be, which ranged from pop playlists, to children playing on a playground, to leaving our apartments in the morning. We listened to former New School faculty member John Cage's 4'33", a four-minute-and-thirty-three-second composition that instructs any musician playing it to play nothing at all, thereby "composing silence," which by way of place—contextual noises like doors opening, people coughing, airducts filling up, etc.—is actually impossible to do. It sounds very Emperor's New Clothes, but through that composition, what we ended up learning was that outside of a vacuum, true silence is, in fact, impossible.

But the course also recontextualized Robert as an avid listener, not just to our academic inquiries and personal woes but to *everything*. Actually, we learned that he, Michael, and a group of artists, activists, and thinkers from around the world were part of a sound-art collective called Ultra-Red (way cool), which, "in the worlds of sound art and modern electronic music, pursue a fragile but dynamic exchange between art and political organizing."[2] Their projects spanned the gamut of art installations and interventions, including the "What Is the Sound of Freedom" protocols our class helped facilitate at the 2012 Whitney Biennial as part of our final, along with protocols led by the mind-shattering philosopher Fred Moten, Michael, and many folks from Ballroom and the Vogue'ology collectives.

Did our class ever figure out the sound of freedom? No, because freedom is such a broad and subjective idea, one person's often usurping another's, and it's ephemeral, a moving target that still must always be aimed for, and what a silly question for you to even ask. But I *did* get a greater sense, personally, of what I thought the sound of freedom might be. Back then, and honestly, at this very moment, everything came back to our Vogue'ology class. In terms of pinning down the sound of freedom, what immediately came to mind was a PDF, poster, and track list Robert had given us at some point in our first few weeks of class called "What Is the Sound of Ballroom? Dance Tracks 1973–1997 (from the Ballroom Archive & Oral History Project interviews)." It is a list of twenty-seven songs that have been played, cherished, and vogued to at balls that Robert and his friend and colleague Mother Arbert Santana Latex Evisu put together while talking to a range of folks from the community. I kept the poster on my wall for all of my undergrad years and took it with me to London for my master's as well. It's since crumbled, but the PDF remains on my desktop and the songs in my periphery. All twenty-seven tracks in one way or another bolster Michael's balls-church metaphor and are truly a substantial portion of the soundtrack to Ballroom, if you can pin down an evolving sound long enough to print a poster. I won't go over the whole list—you can easily find the PDF through your search engine (the URL is in the endnotes)—but the following five of the twenty-seven tracks stand out to me personally as such acts of providence that they are each at least *a* sound of freedom.[3]

Loose Joints: *Is It All Over My Face?* / Female Vocal (6:56)
Is It All Over My Face? (12"). New York, NY: West End Records, 1980. Arthur Russell and Steve D'Aquisto—Producers and Writers. Ballroom Category: Butch Queen Face and Fem Queen Face. Contributor: Dashaun Williams Evisu; Felix Milan; Mink Xtravaganza; Monica Xtravaganza.

A track that I found prior to knowing folks in Ballroom, but seeing it on this list let me know that meeting them was fate. This song employs defiant female vocals and repetitions buoyant enough to keep vogue fem walkers afloat all night. It speeds and opens up during the climax, along with almost brutish male vocals at the end, which is key to having the girls lift their heads and hands up in praise.

Kevin Aviance: *Din Da Da* (4:08)
Din Da Da (12"). New York, NY: Wave Music, 1997. Kevin Aviance—Performer; Gomi—Producer; George Kranz—Writer; remake of George Kranz, "Din Daa Daa" (1983). Ballroom category: Vogue Fem Performance and Arms Control. Contributor: Blue Michael L'Amour; Jon Gabriel Richards Masai; Felix Milan.

This song is the Namu Myōhō Renge Kyō of ball culture. For me, not only is it the "Din da da" engine that keeps it going comparable to that of a mantra but the insane scatting bits in between often remind me of when ladies in Baptist churches get to shouting and speaking in tongues, and it's just all raw emotion. There's a transcendent element here due to the jazz of it all.

Masters At Work: *The Ha Dance/Ken/Lou Mixx* (5:56); *The Ha Dance/Pumpin' Dubb* (5:01)

Blood Vibes / Jump On It / The Ha Dance (12"). New York, NY: Cutting Records, 1991. Kenny "Dope" Gonzalez and "Little Louie" Vega—Producers and Writers. Vocal sample taken from the film *Trading Places* (1983). Ballroom category: Fem Queen Performance. Contributor: Pony Zion Garçon; Felix Milan; Andre Mizrahi.

This song is scripture because it is literally the sound of a voguer spinning and dipping, beats 1-3 of every measure equaling a spin, cranking up to fall into a dip on 4. You'll hear and see this often at a ball along with the audience throwing their hands down with the voguer to accentuate the dip—oh! Though community members maintain that dips are not called a death drop, I will submit the notion that to spin and fall into a dip—not an easy task—over and over again is the embodiment of a resurrection, and if this is apt, then "The Ha Dance" is the sound of being born again.

Jaydee: *Plastic Dreams* (3:03)

Plastic Dreams (12"). Ghent, Belgium: R & S Records, 1992. Robin "Jaydee" Albers—Producer and Writer. Ballroom category: European Runway, Models Effect, Pose, Pose and More Pose. Contributor: Arbert Santana Evisu.

This song was a new find for me when given this poster, but I think I connected with it immediately because, written in '92, it had the familiar house sound I grew up with, that "tat, tat, ta-ta-ta, tat" syncopation that is the mecca of house, grime, EDM, and on and on. When this song hits, your sweet pulpit has gone savage.

Rageous Projecting Kevin Aviance: *Cunty (The Feeling)/Emma Peele [sic] Dub* (5:36)

Cunty (The Feeling) (12"). New York, NY: Strictly Rhythm, 1996. Kevin Aviance—Performer; Jerel Black—Producer and Writer. Ballroom category: Butch Queen Vogue Fem (Soft and Cunt). Contributor: Blue Michael L'Amour.

All I'm going to say is that the name of the song is "Cunty" and you vogue to it. This is evidence that god is a woman and/or fem. Amen.

THE INTERVIEW

w/Lee Soulja, Part 2

Except for being Black, brilliant, and from the Bronx, Lee Soulja is kinda like the Forrest Gump of NYC nightlife—he was there for *all* of it: the birth of hip-hop, the night Keith Haring body-painted Grace Jones at the Paradise Garage, and the days voguing was ripped from the pages of fashion mags and brought to life on the dance floor. Hell, he was even in the Philippines for the deposal of Imelda and Ferdinand Marcos!

For this second interview with Lee, on July 18, 2020, we met via Zoom, a way of still connecting in spite of COVID-19's seemingly end-less constraints. Robert Sember and Michael Roberson were meant to meet us that day to talk about the House system as a needed response to displaced LGBTQ youth, but our two friends both had last-minute engagements, which ended up being kind of fortuitous. Instead, Lee and I got the chance to catch up, and after asking him my preliminary "How'd you find Ballroom?" question, and then listening to his epic response, I realized that this interview wasn't going to be solely for the chapter on "the Children" but also an in-depth illumination of the spiritual awak-ening that comes from that holy trinity of Ballroom, the dance floor, and NYC. Throughout our conversation, Lee confirmed several times the sacredness of the dance floor as a transformative space of worship, declaring how just being there indelibly changed his life. I needed to ask or say very little in this interview. In fact, I wouldn't even call it an inter-view. It was more like spending an afternoon with a legend.

As told by Lee Soulja:

I was raised on hip-hop and had been part of nightlife since I was about fourteen, doing clubs and stuff. So, when I first came into Ballroom, or recognized that there was this subculture even happening, it was by accident, by chance.

I grew up in the Bronx. Literally, where rap started was in my neighborhood, and I was there. P.S. 100 Park was across the street. Afrika Bambaataa, all of them, used to come out, plug into Monroe projects, like into the light pole, or they'd run the cable into somebody's apartment, and the next thing we knew, we'd be partying. We'd call them "jams." At that time, all of the buildings up there had community rooms, so everybody would throw little parties and charge a dollar or two. That's how everybody made their money. And we all had crews, so it was like Cold Crush Crew versus another crew. That was how hip-hop started.

So, I was a dancer as a young kid, and a couple of guys would see me dance where they'd have these roped-off sections, and they'd say, "Okay, you two be out in the front," and we'd dance or whatever. From there I got my first set of club gigs and stuff when I was fourteen, fifteen, sixteen, and it just went on from there.

Now, at the time there was this friend of mine—to be honest, I knew he was gay, but I didn't really care because he was my friend. I wasn't out at the time. We used to dance and stuff, and we would perform at certain functions. His name was Jude, but everybody called him Judee. His mother was Black, and his father was Jewish, so that's where the name Jude came from. He was maybe four years older than me; I was like fourteen and he was eighteen. This. Brotha. Could. Dance.

One night, he invited me to come Downtown with him. He was like, "C'mon, we're going to go make some *real* money." I had been doing hip-hop clubs up in the Bronx, like T-Connection and all the little places up there. You know, I was making cute lil money or whatever. So, that night we decided we were going to go to Studio 54.

We got dressed up! We went and bought these matching disco T-shirts that said "Disco, Disco, Disco . . ." and we had on Sergio Valente jeans. I don't know if you know that kinda thing, but designer jeans was the *thing* at that time. And we had on British Walker shoes. That was my first little bout with doing club stuff, so I had this big, *big* Afro, and I had bought these really fancy sunglasses. Like we were done up for disco days. We were done—we were ready.

So we get down there where Studio 54 was, and the street was blocked off—it was a *lot* of people! We were pushing our way through the crowd like "Excuse me, excuse me, ba-ba-ba . . ." And when get to the front of the line—true story—there was a security guard standing there and he was like, "Okay, calm down, calm down." So Judee says to the guy, "We got to get in! Check the list for our names. We're on the list." The guy was like, "You're on the list—whose list you on?"

Judee was like, "Listen, we're on the list of the two guys who run Studio 54 [Steve Rubell and Ian Schrager]." Now, mind you, the guard was like, "Really?" So, Jude points at me, and tells the guy that I'm Michael Jackson's "other" little brother, and we gotta get in there. I had these big sunglasses on and the whole thing. He goes, "We are meeting Michael in the club upstairs, and you holding us up. There's gonna be a scene—you gonna lose your job!" Jude was serious, honey.

Mind you, Studio 54 had like a little lobby by the entrance right under the awning, and one of the guys that ran the place [Steve Rubell] had been standing there and watching us the whole time. . . .

So, I was standing there like I was a celebrity with my glasses on, making sure nobody was touching me—I mean, I was giving *performance*! And Judee was carrying on like, "That's Michael's brother—we gotta get in there!" The owner came over to us and says, "You know what, just for your performance alone, I'm letting you in." And he let us in.

We followed him in, and he took us to where the cashier and the security guard were, and [the security guard] told him to take us up to where the VIP [section] was. Literally. So, we went up there to the VIP and guess who was up there? Michael [Jackson] was up there; Diana Ross was up there; there was a whole bunch of people up there, and this was my first time out—we had the time of our lives.

It must have been about one or two o'clock in the morning, and we were mingling, drinking, and watching everybody and how they were acting. There was a couple of guys who were coming on to us, asking us if we wanted to go downstairs . . . not to the main floor but *downstairs*. I didn't even know that Studio 54 had a basement level where other stuff was going on . . . so, that was the tea. We went down there, and I never used drugs; in fact, I was really naïve about drugs. You could have told me you was giving me Cloud 9, and I would have thought it was a new drink. I didn't know nothing about what anything was. I kept looking at Judee and being like, "Let's go see what the other floors got. Maybe there's more music or something." But Judee already knew. He was like, "Uh-uh. You're staying right here. We're having a good time."

Finally, this other guy came and said, "Well, we're going to the after-party at the Paradise Garage when we leave here."

Studio 54 closed around 4 a.m., and everyone was headed down to the Village to go to "the Garage," so we just followed the crowd, jumped in a car, and we went down there too.

It was the longest-ass line I'd ever seen in my life, but we got into the club, and I'm telling you, it *changed my life*. I had the best time in the world. Everybody went to the after-party there because we knew that

Grace Jones was performing that night. That night was my first time seeing her perform, and it changed my life. After that, every week it was like—guess where I'm going?

We did try to go back to Studio 54 a couple times, but I'm gonna tell you, Studio 54 had racial issues. People don't really talk about that, but they actually had racial issues, and I think if you really study the history, you'll hear some celebrities tell you about how they couldn't get in because sometimes security just looked at them as being Black.

Real truth and story—you know Chic, Nile Rodgers, and all of them? *Legendary*. Grace Jones had invited them to come to Studio 54, and they couldn't get in. The DJ was playing *their records* in the club, and they couldn't even get in! In Nile Rodgers's book, he says how they wouldn't even let him in, so he went home, and that's how he wrote the song "Freak Out" ["Le Freak (Freak Out)"]. At first it was supposed to be "Fuck You!" That's really what the song was gonna be, because that's how mad he was, but then they changed it to "freak out," and it became a hit. So I'm telling you that they had racial issues. I guess they were trying to create this ambiance of like gay culture, but it was really white people that had wanted to come there. They wanted to have this "perfect" mixture of people, but it wasn't . . . I mean, I'm not gonna say I didn't have a good time there . . . but *babyyy*, when I went to the Garage—it was everything. I could be myself; nobody really cared. It had a movie theater in the club; they had a sculpture room; the big main floor had an upstairs where you could go to the little rooftop area and everything. I'd never been to any place that was like that. Coming from urban clubs up in the Bronx, like hip-hop stuff, this was like paradise—that's why they called it Paradise Garage!

Now, there used to be another club back in the day when hip-hop first started called the Garage, which was up on Jerome Avenue. So when people used to talk about the Garage, I would get it mixed up with the hip-hop club, which is where DJ Theodore used to perform. He was the one that invented scratching, and the Hip-Hop Garage is the club he used to spin at. When I was a kid, I used to go there too. So when they used to say "the Garage," I used to think they were talking about that one until I went to the Paradise Garage, and was like, "Okay, *this* is the Garage."

So, when I went to the Paradise Garage, that's when I met all of the Children for the first time. I saw a lot of the kids there, dancing and voguing and all of that stuff. I didn't really know what it was, but I enjoyed watching everybody do their own thing, and it really wasn't a big deal. Guys, girls, drag—everything was going on there! I really appreciated that I was in a space where I could relax, be myself, dance, not dance, chill, go do this, go do that, and everybody paid it.

Through another friend of mine, I actually met Keith Haring at the Garage. Keith had heard that I was an artist and a dancer and asked me to come in the back of the club. He said he might need me to dance onstage with somebody, but it didn't pan out, because the person that was supposed to dance never showed up. He was gonna use me as a backup to get up there and just freestyle. At the time, little did I know, the person he was body-painting that night who was standing behind this partition thing—I couldn't see them—was actually Grace Jones, who was getting ready to perform. That was my first time going there, first time seeing the kids, and everything. The Paradise Garage is where I got in tune with a lot of gay culture.

After that, I began to dance more, and Judee and I started exploring a lot more clubs and the nightlife downtown. We started getting real bookings—real money, compared to the little pittance we used to make up at the little hip-hop clubs. I'm not knocking it, because you know, hip-hop was my roots as a kid. That's what I grew up on. I watched it change through all of its stages to being the hip-hop we know now. I knew a lot of those guys, from the birth of the genre, and I can tell you, I don't out people, but gay people were always a part of *every* subculture. Gay people were involved in hip-hop back then. A lot of it's coming out now, but I'm looking at people like, "Gimme a break, like y'all didn't know." At like twelve or thirteen, I knew! You can feel it around somebody. That look and the whole thing. But when the money runs out, that's when they wanna start outing people and being mad and angry and stuff.

Anyway, at that time, living in the Bronx, everything was happening right there in our neighborhood. It's not like we had to go far. Monroe Projects, Kips Bay, Castle Hill—we lived where all of this stuff was happening. J-Lo grew up in the area; Darrin Henson, famous choreographer from *Soul Food* and all of that was my next-door neighbor, and we used to dance and stuff. I knew all of those people.

I was a smart kid, went to high school and took college courses at the same time, so I was really trying to do something involving business. My parents separated, so I was always trying to make money to help my mom. Ultimately, everything was about helping my mom, to help take care of bills and stuff. My mom was very strict, but the thing about my mom was, as long as it did not impact my grades or work at home, she was okay with it. And she was watching all the work I was doing at clubs and everything, so the minute I came home, and my grades weren't where she thought they should be—it was a wrap. So I never let that impact me. I'm fifty-five now, but back then, it didn't take a lot to study. I had a photographic memory, so I was extremely capable in that area.

I started hanging out with a lot of downtown nightlife kids and stuff, and everybody had these glamorous names. I wasn't quite sure what Ballroom really was at that point, but it was part of nightlife, and I went to balls to watch my friends walk. I would get invited to perform, and I got booked to go overseas, tour some cities over in Asia, and that included going to Japan to do some stuff. And that's where I first met Willi Ninja. . . . I will eternally be grateful for my friendship with Willi, because after that I traveled all over.

In 1987, I wanted to audition for Michael Jackson's "Bad" video, and I was waiting to hear back if I got it or not, and in the meantime, I got a call. I ended up going to the Philippines, because Willi was supposed to be coming there to do a gig at the Playboy Club. *Playboy* was a big magazine at that time, and they had all these hotels around the world. At the top of the Playboy Hotel in the Philippines was this club. They booked Willi to perform, and so Willi was booking me to perform with him. He was like, "Hey, let's do the same thing we did in Tokyo," which was a little urban set for them, because they love Black American culture over there. He was like, "You do your lil hip-hop piece, I'll do my voguing piece, and we're gonna turn it out."

When I got to the Philippines, again, true story, Imelda Marcos was there—that's when the Corazon Aquino stuff was happening—and they issued martial law. I got trapped in the country. Nobody could go in or out, and I got stuck there for about a month. This is another instance where Willi looked out for me. I went there to go perform, and I still wasn't getting paid what I should have as a professional dancer in those kinds of nightlife gigs, and because he still couldn't get into the country, Willi told me to perform anyway—you know, the show must go on. He said, "This is how much the booking is paying me, and that's how much *you* should be paid." When he told me how much, I was like, are you sure—say it again? And that started a whole other conversation. . . .

When I finally got back to New York, I realized he and I were running in the same nightlife circles. I'm going from club to club. I go into this club—boom—there go Willi, saying, "What are you doing here?! Shouldn't you be home this late?" I told him I was about making that money. We had that little brotherhood. He took care of me. And *everybody* knew him. At that time, he had shut his House down and was traveling doing music videos and all of that. Of course, he was filming *Paris Is Burning* and stuff at that time too.

In *Paris Is Burning*, he said he wanted to travel the world and take voguing all these places, but by the time *Paris Is Burning* came out, he had already done that. In '89, he had been doing the stuff with Malcolm McLaren, who did the record "Buffalo Gals," and also did the first vogue record, "Deep in Vogue." That was *before* Madonna's "Vogue," plus Willi had danced with Janet—he'd really done a lot of stuff by that time.

There was also a huge ball called the Love Ball, which happened in '89; it's actually the last scene in *Paris Is Burning*. Everybody was at the Love Ball, Madonna and all of these people. This is how Madonna got to see a lot of the Xtravaganza kids. She used to come to the clubs like Sound Factory and see the kids and watch them vogue, and be like, "What is that? What are they doing?" So that's how she got it, and she ended up doing this little track called "Vogue," which wasn't even supposed to be a major track. It was supposed to be like a b-track, and it ended up becoming one of her biggest hits. Then she took the Xtrava kids with her on tour and everything.

But the Love Ball was maybe my third ball I'd ever been to, and all the celebrities were there. I ended meeting a lot more people. Now it was the late '80s, early '90s, and I had a whole bunch of friends from Ballroom, and I loved to go to balls and watch and be a spectator and everything, but I was still doing nightlife then. Never really being a part of a house but going there to support my friends and stuff. It's that whole network of family that first attracted me. Then Willi died in 2006. Like I said, I had a whole network of folks I worked with from the Ballroom community, and it took me a long time to join.

When I was twenty-one, twenty-two, I ended up getting *married* [to a woman], um, so it took me a long time to even accept my own sexuality. Even though guys were coming on to me—I was working in both gay and straight clubs—I took it as a compliment. I started dancing at the Palladium because this guy that I would always see on the train was flirting with me and gave me his card and said he worked for MTV. It was new in the '80s. Then my friend and I called him as a joke, and it ended up being a thing for real. They were filming *Club MTV* with Downtown Julie Brown—they used to film that at the Palladium on Fourteenth Street. So, we ended up going down there to dance and audition and the whole thing. I will say that I flirted back with the guy as a benefit. Instead of dancing like down there, I ended up dancing up on the speaker. I was like, "Thank you very much. I want to be where people can *see* me do my thing." But people in Ballroom never let anyone cross the line with me—and people would try.

Anyway, Willi died, and a lot of his kids came to me, and I became their father. The Xtravaganza kids were part of nightlife. When Willi was alive, Hector Xtravaganza—may he rest in peace—was Willi's father, so he then became my father. He was like, "You're Willi's brother, so you're my son!" And just like that, I had a gay dad. I'm thankful for it. RR Chanel, one of the pioneers of Ballroom, was also one of my fathers.

People in the Ballroom community were the ones that helped me really center myself and figure out who I was, my sexuality, and deal with the fact that I was molested as a kid when I was like eight years old. I was able to have those kinds of conversations without feeling judged. Because I blamed myself a lot for that. I suppressed a lot of that stuff, so being able to talk to people who have had all of these traumatic experiences and being able to find a way to have those conversations was my first look at understanding what the Ballroom family was really all about. These were conversations they could not have at home, not with their biological parents, brothers and sisters. They relied on their House family for that.

KIA LABEIJA

AKA: Kia Benow
HOUSE: Royal House of LaBeija
CATEGORY: Old Way
SUPERPOWER: Hand Performance
FAMOUS BATTLE: Kia LaBeija vs. Chise Ninja
NOTABLE QUOTABLE: "I'm definitely badass—I'm ready to push harder and push forward."

L ike turning already life-giving water into wine, Kia Labeija's approach to Old Way is an intoxicating flow, a much-needed elegant release distilled down from a dance form classically composed of steel-rod-firm hieroglyphics. Still ingenious Egyptian innovation, Kia's chosen style of vogue is a standout feminine iteration and therefore transformative, a much-needed response to decades of trudging through the great Sahara of masculine right angles—Kia is queen of the winding Nile.

But that in no way means she is all soft. No. Like vogue itself, her dance baseline is New York City, the irresistible treble of jazz-hand hi-hats and trilling fingertips on top of a subwoofer blasting concrete 808s. Dovetailing flowing cape-like arms with the staunch golden ratios of handmade face frames. Both male *and* female representation, classic dichotomies in Ballroom performance; yet, on today's call sheet, fem is the headliner and runner of the show—and this lady is gunning for a trophy.

But mainly, Kia's is the dance of audacity: the audacity of a trained Alvin Ailey dancer to walk a ball, the audacity of a cis woman in Ballroom to dare elevate the dance and infiltrate the discourse, the audacity of a non-gallery-represented artist to grace the cover of *Art Forum International*, the audacity of Southeast Asia and African America to reside in the same body, and the fucking audacity of an HIV+ kid to not just live and lean into her dreams—but to fucking thrive doing it.

CHAPTER 6

REALNESS

w/Gia Love

Walking categories, trans lives, and the unexpected prevalence
of gender norms within the Ballroom scene

WALKING REALNESS

Butch queens dressed like soldiers, saluting, the epitome of ants march-ing. A gorgeous trans women drenched in cream cashmere, a broad-brimmed hat, Madison Ave. on her mind. A queer B-boy in an Adidas track suit, smoking a blunt, strutting across the Ballroom floor like he just snuck out his girlfriend's bedroom window. About thirteen minutes into *Paris Is Burning*, an early spot in the film connoting its importance, these method actors run across the screen as Dorian Corey introduces us to the category of *realness*, or as Mother Corey puts it, the art of being "able to blend." All this flanked by Cheryl Lynn's queer-centric track "To Be Real." It's enthralling.

Realness is an aspirational category. It allows you, within the safe and brave space of a ball, to finally inherit your human right to leap from one end of the identity spectrum to the other, from male to female, butch to fem, gay to straight, basic to sharp, servant to Cinderella, and on and on. The person walking realness is like an immigrant (or the more compa-rably pejorative "illegal alien") finally being welcomed with open arms into the fold. It is indeed the chance to "blend" into the pool of the ac-cepted—yes, partially as a means of escaping "reality," but in some cases, like those of trans folks, it can be a rare space for self-actualization in the world *and* preservation from it. Both can be true, and that's what makes realness compelling. It is both in defiance of what bell hooks maintains to be society's greatest threat—the imperialist, capitalist, white supremacist patriarchy, and an assimilation into it.[1]

But beyond the four walls of a ball, in the outside world, the ability to blend and not be clocked is an utter necessity, again especially in the case of Black trans women who navigate day-to-day life in the brutal streets of all four carnal, cardinal corners of the United States. For them, being noticeably trans in public has always been answered with violence, sometimes verbal, often physical, always psychological. While at a Ballroom function, you might win a trophy, scoring tens across the board for convincingly resembling a soldier, a pampered housewife, or a young hunk, whereas in the streets of Harlem, the Bronx, Brownsville, or any other urban center, being or not being "clocked" as trans means the difference between peace and trauma or death. "You can pass the untrained eye . . . and not give away that you're gay," Corey says. "That's when it's real."[2]

This risk of not being "real" can be felt throughout *Paris Is Burning*, from the looming violence and catcalls at the trans girls walking down the street in Harlem, to the danger (and eventual death) of Venus Xtravaganza engaging johns on the piers, and even the tension of folks walking their particular category of realness, hoping their straight façade or what have you doesn't crumble before the judges' eyes. I remember watching with delight as Corey and Pepper LaBeija languidly narrated the evolution of the spectrum of categories that fall under the rubric of realness, taking turns defining the different iterations as Livingston framed them with corresponding visual examples. You get a sense that there could be as many categories as there are desirable identity types, which is totally subjective—and rapidly changing. That point is really driven home by Corey's "Back in my day . . ." and "Kids these days" kind of vibe she leads with when talking about the evolution of realness, but there's still an electric charge to her delivery that hints at the sheer possibilities of it all. Hearing about the realness categories is pretty exciting; some that stuck out to me are these:

1. **Fem/face**—This is an evolving category that dictates the standard of fem beauty for the times. Around the time of *Paris Is Burning*, circa 1990, fem realness meant a natural look, little to no makeup, fresh-faced, young and thin with like a modest B-cup. *Pose*'s India Moore is a prime example. Today, the needle of

realness has moved more toward Haitian carnival queen, women with all curves, sequins, and face fillers and augmentations. It's a notable shift and an idea I talk about later in the chapter about "body," particularly those of trans women in Ballroom.

2. **Executive**—Suits, aviators, and briefcases on Wall Street. Dorian Corey explains how outside a ball, because of your lot in life, you may be dejected, jobless, or even homeless, but "in a Ballroom, you can be anything that you want. You're telling the straight world that, 'If I had the opportunity to be an executive, I would be one.'"

   Side note: A couple of years ago while doing research at a ball in Toronto, I watched executive realness be walked by mostly Black men who were all sharply dressed and doing the damn thing, followed by a white guy in a similar getup (which in my humble opinion is a lil on the nose for executive "realness," but whatever . . .). He walked up to the front of the stage, asked for the mic, got it, opened his briefcase and started handing out papers to the judges and audience members surrounding the stage. He then returned back to the mic and explained how he is an attorney representing the Black Lives Matter movement and that the document he handed out was a case demanding reparations from the federal government. The audience gagged at the clever way he attempted to circumvent the disqualifying level of closeness he had to his category as a white man walking executive realness, *and* at his outright pandering to the judges. It was a fascinating turn of events—sociopolitically very complex—and might have won him the category based on gall alone. However, Dominique Jackson was a judge that night, and if you've ever seen her on *Pose* or *Legendary*, or speak publicly, or just gotten a good look at her face, you'd know bish was not here for that particular brand of white nonsense. She immediately got to the mic and stated *her* case for complete and utter bullshit. Her calmly stated counter was basically, This is our shit—get your own. The judges concurred.

3. **Butch queen, first time in drag at a ball**—A shady-ass category and meta satire if ever there were such a thing. In *Paris Is Burning*, the eponymous Paris Dupree walks this category, all fraggled and snatching off her wig, makeup a hot mess, essentially saying to the room and the world: "You know them poor butch queens

that never adjusted a wig properly in their lives yet show up to a function trying to walk fem realness in Payless pumps while knuckle-dragging their way down the catwalk? Well, that's this category."

4. **Banjee Boy/Girl**—Looking like the boy who probably robbed you on your way to the ball or the girl standing on the corner who witnessed the whole thing.

5. **Schoolboy**—Think Frank Ocean in a sweater vest, loafers, and glasses. Essentially, Poindexter realness.

6. **High-Fashion Eveningwear**—It's self-explanatory, but I'll let the genius master of ceremonies in *Paris Is Burning*, Junior LaBeija, put it in his biting signature way. He narrates as a woman in all fur everything struts down the catwalk looking completely fierce—minus the fact that she's carrying no handbag . . . "Come on now, it is a known fact that a woman do carry an evening bag at dinner time," he says, dead serious and artfully leaning into the mic. "There's no getting around that! You see it on Channel 7 in between *All My Children* and *Jeopardy*, *Another World*, *Dallas*, and the whole bit. You have to carry something—no lady is sure at night!"

   That last bit always kills me.

7. **Town and Country (my favorite)**—The Hamptons, Westchester, country clubs, tennis whites, cocktails in the parlor at 5 p.m. The town and country category is standout. Perhaps because it attempts to stretch our imaginations to their capacity, the very idea that LGBTQ POCs, often at the very bottom of social standing, could ascend if only momentarily (and aesthetically) to the top of the upper echelon in a country built on capitalist fervor. And that whiteness could *even* be erased from this role.

I remember watching the town and country section of *Paris Is Burning* with my (white) boyfriend at the time. I remember how both our eyes were wide as saucers, mine with excitement for what at the same time felt familiar and explosive to every norm I'd ever conformed to; his with . . . pity? Once the scene was over, he turned to me.

"It's kinda sad, isn't it?"

"What is?" I wanted to know.

"That they, like . . . aspire to be white."

"I dunno, maybe . . ." I started. ". . . or are they just trying out being on top—and why is rich automatically white to you?"

I don't remember much about the rest of the conversation, but I'm pretty sure he just rolled his eyes and kept watching the movie with his mouth gaped open. That particular boyfriend was super smart but said a lot of stupid shit. Still, I came away asking myself if there was actually something to his assessment. At one point in *Paris Is Burning*, Venus Xtravaganza literally, tragically but understandably, confirms that what she wants more than anything in the world is to be a kept white woman. Within her, the line between the transformative magic of a ball and real-life desire starts to dissolve. In terms of intent, then, maybe folks at balls should be reimagining wealth instead of emulating white people? Although, as Pony Zion and Benji Hart have postulated about such opulent categories, you can file them under the umbrella of the subjectivity of the artists' intent—they only have so much control over how the central theme of their art is received by their audience. By unabashedly leaning into it, are you defiantly commenting on the trappings of capitalism, are you simply being the most fabulous version of yourself—or are you just trying to be some fancy white lady?

My ex's comment also made me think about how tired I was of the lack of tolerance white people had for the cognitive dissonance that grips them when they see either typically white class territories usurped by another race or the construct of whiteness being dismantled—because that shit's totally made up. Over the years I've come to the conclusion that whiteness is basically a feather atop a saltine atop a haphazardly stacked house of cards atop a precariously arranged Jenga set atop a house built upon sand on a windy-ass day. It's fragile.

But I get it. Whether it's in the confines of a ball, a country club, a Beyoncé video, or a shopping mall, any ode to capitalism—which is intrinsically linked to whiteness—is kind of gross. That is, when it's not entirely elating. Yet, I submit to you that walking town and country or any sort of opulent category is less a "sad" mode of identifying with the oppressor and more a way of obliterating the terms by which the oppressor obtains their opulence, maintains said opulence, and defines this archetype of which you are shut out. Ultimately, I'd say being an LGBTQ BIPOC at a ball and portraying an affluent, straight, white, cis female or a horse jockey as opposed to a lawn jockey is a powerful performative act of defiance. It proves it's all just pretend.

But that doesn't mean that walking realness at a ball is some way of playing dress-up. In fact, if for no other reason than the lengths to which folks have to go in order to "achieve" it, walking realness can have *very* real consequences that affect one's very real life.

Fem queen realness is a great example. Over the years, being a convincing fem queen has evolved as much as our cultural definition of beauty. Back in the days of drag pageants, which were essentially pre-house-system balls, the competition came down to one category: fem realness. As we've seen in the case of Crystal vs. Harlow, in 1967, being a real woman meant looking lithe, pale, and almost prepubescent. White Warhol darlings like Edie Sedgwick and Twiggy were the looks du jour, and I'm almost certain there were folks starving and powdering themselves into oblivion in order to meet such a mandate. Also, in order to dazzle during these competitions, which were a nod to old-school beauty pageants, many of the contestants had to become seamstresses or at least fully exploit their innate talents. This is why sewing-adept women like Dorian Corey thrived in this arena, but for others who were less proficient at tailoring, such a deficiency in skill also dictated how their time was spent in terms of creating costumes, who they spent their time with in terms of enlisting help with this effort, and even their occupations, many taking up stints at department stores, dry-cleaners, etc., as a means of procuring trophy-winning garbs.

Post the drag-ball circuit and during the advent of the House system in the 1970s and '80s, realness morphed into meaning you were the epitome of high-fashion. *Vogue,* not the dance but the magazine and its aesthetic, including the women, ads, and apparel in its pages, became the standard of realness. The models within were "natural beauties," tall, minimally made-up angels with full eyebrows and a just-woke-up-dewy morning glow that was also reflected in the more honest if not rustic pornography of the time. This made way for a less-adorned look than its predecessors, and often, as in the realness subcategory of "face," called for girls to simply walk up to the judges' table, their hair slicked back and out of the way, clothing understated, faces pointed up to the sky to find the light, as if they were on a career-changing go-see for the role of 1987's next Revlon girl. This era of fem was walked at balls by women like Tracey Africa Norman and Octavia St. Laurent, whose culturally acceptable level of femininity translated outside Ballroom walls and eventually led them to real professional modeling careers due to their automatic congruence with trends at the time. Tracey Africa's realness, in particular, set her up for a groundbreaking stint in the fashion industry that ended devastatingly once she was found out as trans on a fashion shoot. Realness in this instance moved her up the ladder of socioeconomic hierarchy, yet the patriarchy's need to vilify trans women as sexual deviants concealing the truth clipped her ascension, ending her career then and there.

Also, in this era, the standard of beauty was less bodacious, so the level of femininity that a modest regimen of estrogen could afford you, bustiness not being a convention, was enough to score tens across the board. However, toward the end of this era, moving into the 1990s, opulent femininity became the brass ring, and the means through which Ballroom folks achieved this look varied in degrees of consequence, the opening scene of FX's *Pose* being an extreme example rooted in very real events. In it, House mother Elektra Abundance, played by Dominique "Tyra" Jackson, in an attempt to sweep the category of "royalty," leads her children (to the sound of the Mary Jane Girls' "In My House") into a "Royal Court" exhibit at the Brooklyn Museum. There, they proceed to boost (steal) the scepters, capes, corsets, and crushed velvet necessary to take home the winning trophy for their category, which they eventually do. While this is a hyperbolic execution of what goes on, if folks aren't working their fingers to the bone to earn enough money to magpie together such magnificent garments, many an LGBTQ BIPOC person has been put in legal and therefore lethal danger boosting the ingredients needed for a win (and thunderous acclaim) at a ball.

Enter the glamazon. In the 1990s and into the early 2000s, the era of the supermodel and the majestic house mother reigned supreme. Like Naomi Campbell, Tyra Banks, Claudia Schiffer, and the like, the women of Ballroom were now expected to be badass, buxom, and bodacious bosses. When as before, sure, surgical enhancements were at their disposal and often utilized, now more than ever, it seemed fillers, implants, lip and butt injections, and other curve enhancements were the lay of the land, and in an urban, lower economic, non-risk-averse community familiar with the idea that from struggle comes progress, and in a country where access to gender transitional services was almost nonexistent, the financial and physical costs of such enhancements were high if not fatal. All minimally invasive surgeries run the risk of being hazardous, but back then and still today, sketchy butt injections done in the basement of a complex in the Bronx are what cautionary nightmares are made of.

And today, the standard for realness seems to be matriarchal carnival queen, curvy, mature, bedazzled, and full of royal pomp and circumstance—in a way, the "Queen Mother" type Gia referred to previously. This should change any day.

On and on, achieving realness doesn't mean just meeting some conceptual threshold; it's a real way of life with fantastical to dire implications, and the more trans lives are acknowledged and accepted in society, and the more folks have access to the tools needed to achieve it, the more the line between real life and realness dissolves.

I recently read an article that anticipates the obliteration of realness as a category instead of interrogating the very real social chasms that capitalism, transphobia, and the construct of whiteness create that make realness even necessary. I find this problematic. In his *New York Times* article "Has the Ballroom Scene Outgrown 'Realness'?," House of Xtravaganza member and trans-male vogue advocate Sidney Baloue poses what I think is a simple question about a very complex topic.

Baloue's rare critique from within the community on the waning need and pertinence of realness is necessary, especially coming from him, a trans man in a subculture started by trans women and largely populated by gay men. Baloue rightfully attempts to poke holes in the fact that up until this point, for better or worse, Ballroom has necessarily been an answer to the heteronormative white patriarchy and its persecution of the masses. It's always been a two-partner dance. Baloue's take is that realness is a "competition based on passing,"[3] and that in the current age of destigmatizing HIV/AIDS and the advent of shows like *Drag Race* and *Pose*—and Billy Porter winning an Emmy for the latter— LGBTQ folks have hit a level of visibility that makes such necessary but culturally questionable categories as realness archaic and moot, if not just sad.

There's so much here to unpack, but my primary inquiry is this: Does visibility equal integration? Is it even real representation? A lot of the time, gained "visibility" skews closer to a picture presented for the sake of optics. If I, a gay Black man (or some other, like superficial version of me), am seen by the masses, even a hundred times over or in equal amounts to my straight white counterparts, does quantity, the number of hits, suddenly replace quality in terms of importance in public opinion?

The image accompanying Baloue's article actually is of Billy Porter tearfully accepting his 2019 Emmy for lead acting in *Pose*. This is a nod to the current climate of what could mistakenly be seen as trans acceptance, a time of what Baloue would refer to as "accelerated visibility" in a society that has "become more inclusive." Meanwhile, Porter isn't trans; he's just on a show where some people are. Yes, trans lives are more visible these days due to said show, but outside of Tuesdays at 10 p.m. on FX, the bulk of the increased public awareness of trans and gay folks focuses on the latest tragic AIDS transmission, murder of a trans woman, or protests fighting the end of either. I doubt *Pose*, *America's Best Dance Crew*, *Legendary*, or any television show will fully clean up years of negative imagery and, more importantly, the huge disparities between queer trans lives and those of their cis straight counterparts. Plus, these chasms are the places from which realness stems.

Now, I love Billy Porter, and I would never suggest that he and his brilliance don't represent the queer experience—just not all of it, or enough to dismantle inequities between sexualities or the need for realness as a category. Actually, I really don't see the direct link between him and the latter. Porter does however give me life regularly, be it through his acting or even when he's just pontificating in an interview. And I am a fan of *Pose*, but as we've seen through the brutalized and forgotten lives of trans legends like Marsha P. Johnson and Sylvia Rivera, a win for gay men like Porter does not necessarily mean a win for trans women, especially those of color (often the ones walking realness). Billy himself has said as much on many occasions in reference to his own win and multiple Emmy nominations for his work on *Pose*, and the contrasting lack of any nods for his Black and Latinx trans castmates. Sure, I could delve into the fact that Porter is the longest-running and most accomplished actor in the main cast, but the crux of the matter is that his visibility doesn't necessarily mean theirs. Even if it did, one moment of visibility equals social equality as much as the '90s show *A Different World* could create a Black 1 percent or Obama could ensure a still living and breathing George Floyd. Realness is a razor-sharp performative commentary on these harsh realities.

I think part of my issue with Baloue's *NYT* article is the lack of context and gravity he gives the act of walking realness, how it is an embodiment, not a parlor trick. I namely contest his semantics, though that's not at all as trifling a matter as it sounds. As I write this book, it is my understanding that to call ball culture a "scene" is to knowingly or unwittingly trivialize the lives and work of arguably the largest art collective and most marginalized folks on earth. Sure, we all slip up. I'm doing a control+ F search for the word "scene" right now—just to cover my tracks. However, that in tandem with the headline "Has the Ballroom Scene Outgrown 'Realness'?" is a slipup that runs the risk of trivializing not just Ballroom but Baloue's very own article by calling it a scene from the outset. It impressionistically paints a nuanced matter like realness as something that could be on the verge of a trend.

Similarly, when the article refers to walking the category of realness as " a competition based on passing," I think this is a bit reductive a definition of realness, though the space between realness and passing is a Venn diagram on the brink of being a circle, like the life of Venus Xtravaganza. I would estimate, though, that the difference is that passing is what one has to do in the streets, in the greater culture, in order to dodge the persecution of being othered and/or to reap the benefits of reading as one of the people in power, like that young biracial girl in the film *Imitation of Life* who has a Black mother but "passes" as white in her life outside the home, at times pretending she doesn't even know her own mother. It connotes tragedy, a betrayal. Walking realness on the other hand is an embodiment in the context of ball culture and ball functions that reclaims from mass culture who is allowed to be "real." Basically, it redefines whose lives matter. All of this distinction-making is to point out that, as it is within the Black community, the idea of "passing" has a stigma, is frowned upon. If you choose to do so, you're essentially a sellout, throwing your culture aside for the white-hetero gaze. From this perspective, it feels to me that Baloue, a seemingly adept and thoughtful writer, used the language of passing intentionally, a choice equating walking realness with trying to pass as cis/straight, to deceive—to pass as the oppressor.

However, the *New York Times* is for a thinking yet broad audience, and maybe using the term "walking realness" wouldn't have translated as easily as "passing" to their mostly straight white neoliberal audience. As a writer, I know firsthand the awkward balance of generating progressive editorial content versus having to pedantically lay out in every other paragraph what ball culture even is, and sometimes you just have to conflate the two by engaging in rhetoric that reaches down to the masses in order to bring them up to speed. Ironically, even such a small lexical concession could be viewed as a type of "passing." We all get by how we can, I suppose.

Also, Baloue, an Asian American trans man, innocently reframing a category like realness as "passing" has mildly derogatory, gender-hierarchical implications because the category is most often walked by Black trans women. Even though ball culture, like any subculture, is as much a microcosm of the world as it is an escape from it, it is never exempt from playing out the gender binaries and colorist tendencies set up by the mainstream. Humans are humans, and no matter where we are, there we are.

Yes, both trans men and women face the effects of inequality, and both walk realness or can pass as the opposite gender, along with gay or fem men walking butch and straight categories. But there is still a huge disparity between the way trans men and trans women are treated by the patriarchy and everyone else for that matter. Trans men are often seen as a non-threat for many messed-up reasons, including the latent notion that it's understandable to want to be a man because everyone should want to identify as the people in power. Trans women are seen as, among other things, weak and tragic for ever giving up that assumed power. Meanwhile, male toxicity is rampant and deadly enough for all of us to want to hang up our jockstraps, but that's neither here nor there.

They're not exactly apples-to-apples, but this discrepancy in perspectives reminds me of a moment I caught during one of the talks bell hooks did as scholar in residence at the New School.[4] She was talking to Laverne Cox, and when Cox rhetorically asked the question, "Am I feeding into the patriarchal gaze with my blonde wig?," hooks immediately answered for her, saying, "Yes." Like I said, not exactly the same as a trans man calling realness passing, but hooks's answering for Cox and not exploring the nuances and power of a Black trans woman defiantly wearing a blonde bombshell aesthetic, and the audacity in exercising any such choice, feels similar to dismissing realness. Cox later explained, "This is where I feel empowered, ironically, and comfortable. I think it's important to note that not all trans women are embracing this, but this trans woman does. And this trans woman feels empowered by this." Though maybe correct in regard to how close in proximity Cox's look is to that of her straight white oppressor, hooks's reaction felt like a type of swift judgment of a female experience that simply wasn't her own. While our brothers and, in this case, sisters in identity can often be our fiercest and most apt critics, anyone with an experience outside of our own is going to have some blind spots in their critique of, empathy for, and understanding of us, and like veering into the fast lane without a side mirror, ignoring these differences can be hazardous. Allies often unknowingly enact this kind of violence on one another.

Anyway, the idea that realness is a form of passing and no longer necessary is a complicated matter. At its root, the suggestion feels like it should come from someone who walked the category, or maybe a woman, or maybe the most marginalized of the group that walks the category, like a trans woman? Someone who can pinpoint why realness is even a thing? I dunno. I had this in mind recently when I was having a conversation with Gia Love, a model, an activist, a young woman of trans experience, and a friend. She's gorgeous, kind, and fun, and to see her growth as a political force over the last ten years has instilled in me a dedication to uplift Black trans women as they come into themselves—because the results are positively staggering. And the community at large subsequently becomes a better place for everyone. Gia has walked a little of everything, but her mainstay categories are realness and runway with a dash of vogue. She stands out in the world as a tall and bodacious, self-possessed glamazon, but if I had to personally assess her curves, soft features, sharp mind but sweet demeanor, and proclivity for bangin' wigs within the rubric of realness, as Mother Dorian Corey puts it, she "blends."

I explained to Gia Baloue's status as a member of the ball community and his general thesis that realness might just be on its way out as a category, and I asked for her opinion. She immediately said, "I don't agree with that—is he white?" I chuckled and told her no; I believe he's Asian American. She continued:

> Maybe that's why. When you think about white, Asian, or Latinx queerness versus Black queerness, we have a long way to go. They just have more space to *be*. I find that Black circles are truer to the [gender] binary, and other circles are more open because they have that space. For example, I live in East New York, Brooklyn and cannot walk down these streets looking like a man with a dress on. You know what I mean? That's where realness comes from. It is a performance of something that can be oppressive but ultimately, at the end of the day, challenges the gender binary—whether or not you look "real." Yes, heteronormativity is black and white, and realness as a category performs and upholds that binary—but it is also a critique of it.

So, as long as there are economic disparities, racial disparities, realness will be a thing, because that's how we, in proximity to cis-ness, keep a sense of safety and security, to be able to exist in this world. So, no I don't agree with that.

In her response, Gia confirmed my inkling that realness is a means of filling the prevalent gaps in social disparities and a way of avoiding dangerous encounters with transphobic men, but in doing so, it also married for me, in a way that Baloue had suggested, the acts of passing and of walking realness. They aren't the same, but they are inextricably linked. Gia and Baloue came together in that sense but were still on diametrical ends of the core matter, "Is realness on its way out?" I had a feeling that as a trans woman and trans man respectively, Gia and Baloue had given answers that were colored by their own experiences. We broadened the conversation a bit to take a look at gender binaries and how they might paint points of view in ball culture. Gia said:

Ballroom has become a very patriarchal space. . . . A lot of these men believe in the binary, and they believe in heteronormativity, and they uphold that. Ballroom can be healing in that it allows people to be themselves. But what it doesn't do is deal with that trauma, that generational trauma, cyclical trauma, that still exists. That's why in the Ballroom community there's health disparities in terms of HIV, drug use, et cetera, because although we have the space to perform and to be, people are still dealing with their demons. Junior LaBeija says it best— he's the most eloquent speaker and I can't quote him exactly—but he's just like, "We've been beaten, abused, robbed, raped, tortured, used-up, fucked-up, screwed-up, and then we still have the resilience to come to the ball and get it done."

As Gia suggests, these prevalent systemic issues sparked ball culture and continue to fuel its necessity. So as long are there are race and class disparities, and transphobia and homophobia, there will always be the need to redefine "real." Billy Porter's visibility might elevate his own social standing but does not equally or necessarily elevate that of Dominique Jackson. These dire, intricate issues go beyond Baloue's trendy assessment of the matter, so that when he writes that "there is no longer a novelty in seeing openly gay men in business suits or seeing trans women look like glamorous movie stars—they have now landed in the mainstream. Some spectators and category walkers claim that the category itself can now be boring to watch and to participate in, because it no longer feels subversive as it once did," like Gia, I patently disagree. No matter how boring a non-spectacle realness might be to outsiders or even community members at any given moment, it is so beside the point. The desire to transcend one's gender and/or class status and the courage it takes to then actually do it are equal parts a response to suffering and a love of our God-given gift to create—two wellsprings that will never run dry.

PONY ZION

AKA: Devon Webster
HOUSE: Zion
CATEGORY: Butch Queen Vogue Fem
SUPERPOWER: Lucid lines
FAMOUS BATTLE: Pony Zion vs. Marquise Revlon
NOTABLE QUOTABLE: "You author what vogue is—it's your penmanship. It's your script."

L ike light refracted off cold-blue steel pistons, Pony Zion is all clean lines, bright lights, and polished chrome—the vogue fem prototype of precision. With decades of innovative, category-elevating performances and trophies under his belt, Zion has achieved a titanic superiority over his peers in vogue fueled by years of professional and classical training in hip-hop, pop, ballet, and other dance forms. If you came to his ball even thinking you were prepared to walk vogue fem, girl, think again.

With hand motions that pop like crisp linen in the sun, and right and acute angles so sharp you won't just get chopped—you'll get cut, Pony defies any contemporary convention that would even suggest that fem hand performance is a throwaway element, fifth in line in importance to its more inflammatory vogue counterparts like the spin and dip—though he slays those too.

Like dancing jazz, whether improvised or painstakingly choreographed, his accuracy in voguing is meticulous—almost military. Perhaps this is the reason why when watching Zion, one is hit hard with the déjà vu of seeing *Rhythm Nations*, *Thrillers*, and *Screams* of lives past. A sprinkle of moonwalk preambling a dip. Matrix-level hand formations firing like fem machine guns. It's Zion's IRL forays into our collective unconscious, sparkling "yes, ands" framed and reimagined in a modern context, that both stops you in your tracks, awestruck with the promise of something new, and like an old friend, makes you Remember the Time.

That unparalleled accessibility is what makes this new father of King Maverick (Pony's son) and the founding father of the House of Zion a rare force of influence in the Ballroom community—and one of the most effective teachers of vogue on the globe. From choreographing moves for Chaka Khan, Mariah Carey, and Ashanti, to creating and investigating new subcategories of vogue—vogue theory, vogue fitness—to teaching young people around the world to use vogue as a blueprint for their own freedom.

CHAPTER 7

BODY

w/Luna Luis Ortiz, LaLa Zannell, and Gia Love

Black trans bodies, body sponsorship,
and resolving the trauma in our bodies

When you're receptive to information, like really ready to make room for it, the sky opens up and data rains down. The case of discovering Marlon Riggs's *Tongues Untied* is one example. It was also the case in finding Resmaa Menakem's book *My Grandmother's Hands*, which, no lie, was recommended to me three times in one day while I was writing this book.

The first recommendation was from Robert Sember during a meeting for 400 Years of Inequality, an initiative founded by our friend, the brilliant public health advocate and scholar Mindy Fullilove, MD. The 400 Years coalition commemorates through solemn observances the first arrival of slave ships in America in 1619—the start of our ecology of inequality. Robert, Michael Roberson, and I sit on 400YOI's organizing committee, along with an impressive group of bright and hardworking activist-scholars from all over the map. On one of our Wednesdays together at 4 p.m., I'm sure either before or after we talked about pie, which for some delightful reason is our default topic after dismantling inequality, Robert quoted *My Grandmother's Hands*, a book essentially about how dire it is that Americans—specifically, Blacks, whites, and blues (police force)—metabolize centuries of race-related trauma or what Menakem calls, the "white body supremacy" with which we've been saddled.[1] Not remembering its specific context, I fully remember the quote Robert selected to read to our group, because Menakem's apt and agile use of the word "phantasm" haunted me for several minutes afterward. He read:

> The concept of "the Negro" was created to help white Americans deal with the hatred and brutality that they and their ancestors had themselves experienced for many generations at the hands of more powerful white bodies. *The phantasm of race was conjured* to help white people manage their fear and hatred of other white people.[2]

"The phantasm of race was conjured" lyrically sums up for me the construct, the innate farce of the whole thing. What I think Robert was getting at with this quote was that, in our efforts as an organizing committee dedicated to raising awareness about inequality in a historical context, working under the premise that the arrival of slave ships on our shores was one of America's earliest and most defining engagements with inequality, it was important for us to know the event's laddering up to that defining moment, how violence begot violence, and how these traumas still live out in the bodies of every American—instigators, enforcers, and victims alike. I believe Robert was proposing that after observing and contemplating the four hundredth anniversary of Jamestown—1619 to 2019—we should look toward healing. That maybe for the next iteration of our initiative, we may want to focus on collective recovery. And according to Resmaa Menakem's quote in *My Grandmother's Hands*, that should all but certainly start in our bodies.

Side note: Rereading that quote just now, I would edit it by saying, "the phantasm of race was also conjured to help white people manage their fear and hatred of *themselves*"—not just one another, which may already be implied, and if redundant, still bears repeating because it doesn't necessarily go without saying. To be clear, I'm rock-hard solid on the fact that the very idea of Blackness, the construct of the Negro, is just white people violently running from their own shadows.

That was my first encounter with the book. The second was through Amanda Furches, one of my oldest friends whom I've known for nearly thirty years, and at the time I'm writing this, we're not yet even forty years old. Same day as Robert, this dancer turned Pilates instructor turned holistic physical therapist friend of mine posted to Instagram the following quote from *My Grandmother's Hands*:

> Few skills are more essential than the ability to settle your body. If you can settle your body, you are more likely to be calm, alert, and fully present, no matter what is going on around you. A settled body enables you to harmonize and connect with other bodies around you, while encouraging those bodies to settle as well. Gather together a large group of unsettled bodies—or assemble a group of bodies and then unsettle them—and you get a mob or a riot. But bring a large group of settled bodies together and you have a potential movement—and a potential force for tremendous good in the world.[3]

Amanda and I grew up in North Carolina together and met in our fifth-grade class for gifted kids, and though she's academically sharp as a whip, her excellence has often manifested most obviously in her attention to, care for, and use of her body. As preteens, hanging out with her always meant walking to Peter's Creek, or bike riding to Reynolda Gardens, or cutting flips on the foam gymnastics gear the sports teams left out at Hanes Park. Our set of friends *was* a kid collective of settled bodies, Black and white kids together enacting the progress we wanted to see with our active bodies twenty-five years after the civil rights movement and in the rural South.

Anyhow, my point is, Amanda knows the body, and for her to vouch for this book on the same day as Robert, and with such a phenomenal quote, was a sign I should get it. What was central to this second endorsement was that it expanded on Robert's earlier inference that a group of body-aware and secure individuals can collectively recover from trauma, and it raised the stakes by suggesting that by acting together in the name of a movement, they could be an ideological and physical force with which to be reckoned.

That assertion formed by the seemingly happenstantial relationship of these two quotes was profound to me, especially in my thoughts around Ballroom and how voguing is a form of expression, and even more, as Pony and Benji suggested in chapter 1 and many folks confirm on the regular, it can be seen as a means to freedom. Jonovia also said as much, though more intimately, when she said that voguing is often her needed boost of morale. Here, voguing was the esteem heightener

Jonovia needed to know she's "that girl," and she did it while in the mirror, where we are perhaps most aware of ourselves situated within these bodies.

Ballroom competitions, along with the breakdance battles of the '80s, and rap crews spitting sixteen bars for glory and validation, have often been compared to the world's most safe and constructive gangs, and the idea that a lot of this is done through the body, in the context of this second quote by Menakem, substantiates them as "potential movements [and] forces for tremendous good in the world."

The third recommendation of *My Grandmother's Hands*—that *same* day—came from the author himself, Resmaa Menakem, on *10% Happier*, a podcast I listen to that's hosted by ABC News anchor Dan Harris about the positive effects of meditation and mindfulness practices on our everyday lives. Along with therapy and actual meditation, through interviews with contemplative masters, 10% helped me personally process the familial and systemic trauma residing within my own body. That day, the same that Robert and Amanda contacted me, Menakem came on the show and explained in such well-corroborated detail the thesis of his book, the metaphor of how his grandmother was a sharecropper at four years old and how her hands were therefore never supple, how such hardships are passed on hereditarily through epigens. To that point, he said the reason he chooses to use the term "white-body supremacy," as opposed to "white supremacy," is because the effects show up in our DNA and are most manifested in our bodies.

So, I conceded and bought the book later that day. As everyone suggested, it ended up for me being a crucial way to understand surviving, acknowledging, and metabolizing racial trauma in this very moment in time in America—through the body. It lays out a path of not avoiding but feeling and processing the damages of racial inequality, allowing it space so that its darkness doesn't envelop us. How the body isn't just *a* tool for trauma recovery but rather the first and most essential place, even more than the mind. Whether you're interested or not, I suggest you pick up a copy of *My Grandmother's Hands*, and actually, if you're not interested, you probably need to read it the most. Personally, it helped recalibrate my framework for this body section of the book.

Yes, "body (yadi-yadi)" is a category walked by mostly fem queens and others at a ball, those most bodacious (in all aspects of the word) dominating the category and walking the runway like they're proud of it. Judges might cop a feel. Tight or revealing clothing is welcome. I've seen the girls and butch queens show up body oiled. As with realness, the body category might also mean a certain level of commitment and access to augmentation, as bangin' bosoms, curves, and hips are all classic accoutrements to the category and tend to spark tens across the board. This category is liberating because, unlike high-fashion categories like town and country or Madison Avenue, it actually reinforces and celebrates non-white standards of beauty, albeit often at the hazard of folks who go to great lengths to achieve these features. But again, this is the ongoing balancing act of real vs. realness, the line of which is thankfully drawn subjectively.

And that's all interesting, but this idea of how we can individually and collectively reenact or instead metabolize and recover from trauma in our bodies is most intriguing. How being a trans woman successfully walking body after your hormonal and/or physical transition, finally being heralded for your femininity by your peers after being physically threatened, endangered, and brutalized by the outside world for not blending in, might just be a type of bodily recovery from a lifetime of such trauma. My friend the journalist Channing Gerard Joseph writes about William Dorsey Swann, or "Queen," a former enslaved person from the nineteenth century—and likely the first drag queen, who threw then illegal drag parties (basically balls), physical gatherings or movements of bodies settling together in defiance, often considered by police and newspapers at the time as riffraffs or a mob of undesirables.[4] Perhaps predating a more apt nomenclature, in today's context, would Swann and his cohort actually be seen as trans women? If so, was it healing, an act of relief, a form of collective recovery and personal reclamation for her to put on those parties, where she and others could wear dresses and be who they truly were? Was this Jim Crow–era sanctuary an even riskier preamble to walking realness at a ball today? If nothing else, theirs was one of the first LGBTQ movements devoted to recovering from the persecutions of generational trauma, namely enslavement and gender discrimination.

We often talk about the lineage of voguing. How a spin and dip on the four beat, the hands of everyone in the room hitting the floor simultaneously, everyone shouting "Oh!," is the sight and sound of your inheritance, reverberating off your bones and echoing off the ceiling so loud the ancestors must have felt it. If we can hear them, then in theory, they *must* hear us. Or how vogue is what ancient Egyptians planted in us, hieroglyphic stories of peace, war, victory, and failure that blossom up from us in flourishes of revolutionary dance. How voguing then becomes a living archive within us and how, based on this foundation, voguing is also a way to tell our own modern stories, the passing of a baton in an epic, historical relay race charting the Black and brown experience. How we are also voguing narratives of our enslaved ancestors, and because their stories, their names, their families and culture were ripped from them in the transatlantic trade, voguing is their unerasable inscription, because only print can be redacted, not spiritual movement. In this context, vogue is a defiant, bodily act of collective recovery from ills that are the spoils of the capitalist war. We know that, at their best, Black and brown queer bodies voguing at a ball is an act of capitalist abolishment—but to what magnitude? Does it heal the past? Recourse the future? Create an alternate universe? Transcend time? The answer is yes.

During my time considering Ballroom and the body as an archive, a vessel for self-expression and self-actualization, trauma and recovery, I've also been thinking about the role capitalism plays in the community, and this doesn't always come out as clearly delineated as, say, ball culture is a triumphant answer to the corrupt question of capitalism. Like Ballroom, like everything, the nature of its role is much more nuanced than that. I think that, in many ways, like the high-fashion categories in which folks wear Dior, putting on airs in order to equalize who can be considered high-end, capitalism and Ballroom are more intrinsically and implicitly linked than a simple question and answer: not Q&A but more like A(+q) or Q(+a). The cheese doesn't stand alone, or rather, it has yet to, and what kind of breakthrough would ball culture even represent if it existed in such a vacuum?

Which brings me to what I've only been able to refer to as the "sponsored body," a concept I've been kicking around that I don't want to place any moral emphasis on in any direction per se, but instead would like to approach with a multifaceted curiosity when it comes to my friends and family in ball culture. It's basically the idea that we are all inextricable from the capitalist machine, our bodies and their anciently inherited and contemporarily accruing traumas being "sponsored" by corporate entities, and with that being maintained, exacerbated, or even resolved by that sponsorship. In the case of bodies from New York's

Ballroom community, because of the network of recurring corporate and not-for-profit sponsors that support and service the culture, these dynamics occur in very specific ways with a range of individual and collective outcomes.

∞

The double doors to the Ballroom opened up, and it was clear that Jokers were both out and wild, two of them maniacally striding up the runway, purple spandex and lapel corsages sealing the authenticity of their looks. As the voguers dueled, Poison Ivy, Two-Face, several other Gotham villains and a crowd of kids kiki'ed along to the hijinks, while a house track layered with Jack Nicholson's haunting Tim Burton-esque laughter piped through the speakers. I knew this would be a ball to remember.

Inspired by the comic-book insane asylum Batman almost always ends up sending villains to (until they inevitably break free again), I figured the "Escape from Arkham" kiki ball would be a perfect pop-referential starter ball to bring my two little teenage cousins, Eniyaah and D'yavion, to. They were visiting from Charlotte on their spring break, and it was my goal to tire them out with events and inordinate amounts of walking to and from them, which I knew they'd end up complaining about. Almost everyone who visits from home does. It would be a ball during the day, and like most balls, all ages, so again, perfect for the kids. I'd also invited one of my best friends, Kareem, to come along and capture some of the ball's more kinetic moments, as he was going to be my main photographer for this book. And I'd called up and invited Christian, a friend and MFA student in her early twenties whom I'd met during one of my guest lectures at another friend's class at the Pratt Institute. She'd come up to me after I'd read an essay on the art of the interview and the specific level of intimacy you get when interviewing other Black artists, and she asked, "How do you stay yourself in a room full of white people?" She'd asked it in all earnestness it seemed, because she was one of only two Black students in her graphic design program at Pratt and had found that difficult coming from Hampton University in her undergrad, which is historically Black. Christian was also from Virginia and going to school in New York City, which I'm sure only exacerbated her alienation. My answer to her question was that she had to know her own voice, keep an unshakeable internal monologue and sense of her own identity in any room, but outside of that, I was honestly still trying to figure it out myself. We became fast friends after that, and so I figured going to a mostly Black ball with an all-Black crew was just the ticket to help us both get closer to there.

I'd prepped Kareem and the kids beforehand with a seriously worded conversation about the importance of respecting everyone's space at the ball, as it was sacred and not ours, even though we were all Black, and in the case of Kareem and me, queer. We could watch, even participate, I told them—but we were *not* to get in the way. *Comprende?* Everybody comprende'd, but perhaps I need not have worried, because when we walked into the living comic-book fantasy of the insane-asylum-themed ball, which was appropriately held in the multipurpose room of Monte-fiore Medical Center in the Bronx, Kareem and the kids all stopped cold in the doorway, their eyes big as dinner plates.

As at most balls, folks were both sitting and standing, everyone going apeshit and forming a T-shaped runway, a wide vertical catwalk leading up to the horizontal row of judges backdropped by trophies. In front of them a twisted-looking white-faced, green-wigged Joker MC was carrying on, wearing a green polo and form-fitting purple jeans, and giving us a play-by-play of the duel between the two voguing Jokers. "Cat, cat, da-da-da, dat! Judges scores . . . tens across the board!" As he shouted into the mic, a bright smile developed across Christian's face. Eniyaah's jaw was on the floor. "Go ahead," I told them. "You can go up to the runway, but remember what I said about respecting people's space. Here, I'll find a place for your stuff." They handed me their things. Being two Black, southern, young ladies (sixteen and twenty-two respectively), Eniyaah and Christian had gotten along like a house on fire on the long train ride up to the Bronx from Crown Heights. They both nodded in my direction and ran up to the crowd just as a patent-leather-wrapped Catwoman came high-kicking her way down the catwalk.

I turned to give Kareem direction, but being the consummate pho-tographer, he'd already run up to the crowd, beaming and excitedly flick-ing his camera, all six-foot-two of him doing his best to crouch down and out of the way while getting his shots. Perfect. I turned to D'yavion, who was looking kinda averse to the whole spectacle, uncomfortable even. To be fair, he was a fourteen-year-old straight boy from North Carolina who was in New York for the first time and at a ball in the Bronx to boot. I'm sure he felt out of place, because he literally was, but even being able to sympathize with that feeling, I'd hoped his reaction would have had a quarter of the enthusiasm his big sister's did. Still, I got it. "D, why don't you grab that seat over there and keep an eye on our things. I'll be over in a bit." I handed him the pile of jackets and purses and watched as he ambled across the floor. Ugh, teens. Time to werk.

I took a step back and quickly scanned the room. It was brighter in there than at any ball I'd ever been to, probably because of the time of day, I thought, before realizing that even though it was roughly 6 p.m., there weren't even any windows to see the time of day. So, it must have been the fluorescent hospital lighting that made it brighter than normal. And I wasn't mad, per se. I'm severely nearsighted, so the light brought a level of lucidity to the stage that was clarifying enough for me to notice the other photographer, a long-gray-haired lady flicking away, she and Kareem circling the Ballroom like two differently calendared planets in orbit around the stage's solar flare. Her presence triggered a little competitive heart murmur in my chest followed by a tap on my shoulder. "Hi!" I turned to my right to find a young white hipstery lady in her late twenties standing there smiling.

"Are you from Vice?" she asked.

"Uh, no," I chuckled, not flattered but not exactly insulted either. "Why, do I look like I'm from Vice?"

"Oh, no . . . I mean, maybe?" she wavered. "I'm from the *New York Times*. Someone from Vice is supposed to be meeting me here."

Ah, I thought. "No, no. I'm working on a book about ball culture, so this is basically research."

Her eyes brightened. "Oh, cool."

She handed me her card and explained that the woman competing against Kareem for Pulitzer Prize–winning realness was also from the *Times*, her photographer. Curious. I thanked her for the card, found a chair in the back, and continued surveying the room.

A proud and sexy bat girl with green-streaked hair and petite green wings sauntered in from the hallway and directly onto the runway, twirling and spinning in like a Halloween hurricane. Kareem was still running all around the room, shooting and blissfully hooting and hollering with encouragement for the walkers. Christian and Eniyaah were still awestruck, D still a bit sullen but watching the show, nonetheless.

To the right of me, stood three young cis women—two white, one Asian American—who were practicing their vogue fem moves, almost showing off, which I suppose is the whole point. I could tell they felt separate from the main event, likely because they were, both in proximity to the stage and in demographics. It felt like they were here to prove themselves and that having their own show in the back was an appropriate act of defiance, their cis fem bodies voguing an act of resistance. I thought to ask them a ques— another tap on the shoulder.

"Hi!" said a hipstery-looking white guy in his early twenties.

"Hello," I said.

"Do you identify as queer, and are you sexually active?"

"Yes, and in theory."

"Awesome. Would you mind filling out a survey? I'm from the NYDH, and we're collecting information on sexual practices amongst young men of color."

"Uh, yeah, sure."

He handed me the form and a pen, and I began filling it out. The questions were your run-of-the-mill invasive but quantitative sexual-history probes: how many partners you've had in the last blah blah months; race; whether you used protection; if not, with how many people didn't you; and so on. This was normal, especially for a kiki ball, because as in the early days of the main scene, the New York State Health Department helps to fund balls in exchange for data. I finished and handed Kevin my completed survey and noticed at that moment off to the left just before the runway, was the corresponding obligatory table of pre-stuffed condom and lube packs, diaphragms, and literature on the merits of getting tested for HIV and other STIs and how to go about doing so. Again, normal. I'd known since Robert and Michael's class that the efforts to gather data on sexual behavior and to get sex health information out to folks in Ballroom, a demographic stricken with AIDS since the crisis began in the '80s, are now the status quo. Not-for-profit and government-based organizations like the NYDH and the Gay Men's Health Crisis have done this work for decades, partnering with the community for events like the aptly named Latex Ball, the largest and longest-running sexual-health awareness ball held annually by GMHC for the past thirty years. The relationship between GMHC and the Ballroom community in particular is symbiotic, many young LGBTQ people benefiting from their services at balls and through other services provided around the city. The connection is so sympatico that GMHC even owns the trademark to the Paradise Garage, the now-defunct club that was once a safe haven for folks in the Ballroom community.[5]

Even though they aren't exactly corporate entities—"not-for-profit" being the operative part of their nomenclatures—and even though I know it's a well-meaning status quo dynamic between GMHC and ball culture, it occurred to me that these organizations indeed utilize a sort of "body sponsorship" pipeline that young folks in the community go through from their teens through adulthood—though one *far* better than any pipeline our education, Social Security, or justice systems could implement on their best days. But the level of branding going on that day in that space during the "Escape from Arkham Ball"—DC Comics being the main engine but also the STI info table piled with packets stuffed full of a range of condom brands, the New York Department of Health, the *New York Times*, Montefiore Medical Center, the girls attending who were from a slew of houses ranging from Old Navy to Juicy to Chanel, Vice (evidently), even this very book that I'm writing—suddenly stood out to me.

I had a lot of questions. When the bodies of LGBTQ BIPOCs are sponsored by organizations that are part of what I later learned could be termed the "nonindustrial complex" or, to be more precise, the "not-for-profit industrial complex," how is that different from when, say, MTV, Madonna, FX, and HBO do it? How are they the same? Is the complicated as layered and paradoxical as everything in Ballroom (and the world)?

When I last spoke with Jonovia Chase, she'd hinted at this complex mix of sponsorship pros and cons from her standpoint as a woman who has done incredible work as a ball community organizer, trailblazing her way through NYC's not-for-profit pipeline, starting with Harvey Milk High School and the Hetrick-Martin Institute as a Ballroom kid successfully groomed for leadership, all the way up to her integral role working for the organization, House Lives Matter. She said:

> I went to Hetrick-Martin. That's family; that's like home. They provided us with a place to focus our passions. We were so radical and so excited about bringing about change and being more liberated. HMI provided us space to holistically grow . . . and have tension and understand how to address certain circumstances—even how to take on different systems, including HMI, because HMI is still, of course, as we know, affected by these nonindustrial complex behaviors, and young people are not shy to call those things out when they feel like they're doing harm. But still, it's a very sacred space for sure.

Just shy of providing details on their shortcomings, Jonovia commented on organizations like HMI that train young folks like herself to be progressively brazen, so much to the point that they may even welcome from their young clients a critique on their leadership-building process. Having visited there during the time that Jonovia attended, I can tell you that one reason HMI might welcome such critical thinking from clientele is that the institute is run by folks who are critical thinkers themselves, often queer people of color who work in public health and are independent scholars or scholars from ball culture, who themselves hold a healthy appreciation for radical movements and an ample suspicion of institutions, bureaucracy, and their motives. That's why they're there, to teach the children to navigate them in the name of change.

Unfortunately, the brilliance, care, and thoughtfulness of its staff doesn't always exempt organizations like HMI and GMHC from having to answer to the governmental powers that be and to major donors that are capitalist in nature and dole out programming mandates based on seemingly unpredictable capitalist trends. Often the staff's hands are tied when it comes to creating initiatives for their community that will be given the proper funding.

The vibrant Luna Luis Ortiz is another person from Ballroom who discovered Harvey Milk High in their teens, then later became a compelling and effective spokesperson, storyteller, and HIV activist at HMI; then worked as a photographer for the HIV/AIDS art archive Visual AIDS, and currently is GMHC's community health coordinator. In a conversation we had about his incredible trajectory, Luna explained in a little more detail the role funding plays not only in the initiatives launched by not-for-profits but also in the lives of people who participate in them.

RICKY TUCKER: How'd you start the work of telling your story about HIV? And what inspires you to continue that work?

LUNA LUIS ORTIZ: Being at Hetrick-Martin, you meet people who will become your mentors, and back when I was there, they sort of looked at me like a poster boy for my HIV story. I used to just imagine them talking about me at the all-staff meeting, like, "This kid has a story. We need to use this one a little bit more." And eventually, they did come to me and was like, "Oh, we're going to do this thing so that we can get funding, so we're going to cast you to do a story about gay youth." Or "The *London Observer* is interested in writing a story on the school, but we want to put your AIDS story in the article."

And so, being intrigued by the attention of media triggered me into being more open, more out there; it's almost like AIDS was giving me an advantage in a way. And if I was going to die, which is what they told me would happen at age sixteen, seventeen, eighteen, back in the '80s, then I was going to do something about it. I saw it as an opportunity to educate and to be seen. Because, before I died, I wanted to leave a legacy, which is also why I started doing photography and art, because all of that was supposed to stay when I died. I didn't want to be forgotten.

RICKY: Has that changed now that you've lived like forty years longer than they said you would?

LUNA: Well, when you're told at fourteen that you're going to die, it kind of stays with you. It's like this thing. Somebody asked me if I think of death every day, and I kind of do. Here I am alive, and nobody ever said anything to me about *living*. It became this thing for me. And still today, I'm almost fifty, I'm thinking about death. It doesn't leave you. It's traumatic to a point, but it's also been my drive to live more. Then, as all of my friends died, I was more intrigued with life, because then I wanted to live for them.

RICKY: I'm reading a book right now about processing trauma through the body. How do you process that trauma of living with death every day?

LUNA: I do that through my job, by trying to guide people through their own grief. Because, yeah, that unresolved trauma is why in Ballroom and gay culture we have people doing crystal meth, and that's why people don't care enough about their bodies, and don't care about being infected and all of this stuff—it's these layers of shit we've been dealing with as a community, from loss to murder. Look at all of our trans women. Those murders affect you in some sort of way. I read those articles about their murders and I'm left with this thing, this feeling. Then in the midst of all of that, you throw in COVID, and the fact that people don't have homes? It's layers of shit that we're really not doing anything about.

RICKY: Has your work with agencies changed now that HIV/AIDS isn't necessarily chronic?

LUNA: Not a lot has changed. When you're connected to an agency, Hetrick-Martin, GMHC, Harlem United—all the jobs and projects I was a part of—they always want you to do things their way, but I always end up doing them my way. I'm usually hired because they like what I was doing. So, why would I change? My messaging and my way of being is just what it is.

But of course, the work has changed some because everything is changing, people are living longer. All of our work is possible because of funding, and funding sources change through time. So, for example, if we're living longer, they're saying we don't really need to do [HIV] prevention work anymore because there's PrEP [pre-exposure prophylaxis]; everyone is taking PrEP, so a lot of places are pushing it. And unfortunately, because many agencies need the money to pay staff and provide services, they have to go in that direction in order to stay open. That's why it's really important that when agencies do fundraising, that you support them in some way, because it's money that's gonna help fund other projects that the CDC or whatever don't mandate. Help agencies fundraise in a different way, because fundraised money is money agencies can use freely.

RICKY: Is the Latex Ball an example of that different kind of fundraising?

LUNA: Latex Ball doesn't count; it's not a fundraiser because it's free to get in. There's a reason it's free—because it's healthcare almost; it's a community event and information. How are we gonna charge for important messaging and free STI testing? Plus, at Latex there's like twenty-five other agencies there providing services. It's not just GMHC. How will you be exposed to them if you can't afford it? The promise was that it was always gonna be a free event for educating folks. In 2006, our funding ended, and we had to get more funding, and that's why we reached out to people like Rihanna, Madonna, Beyoncé, and of course, none of them did anything, but we did find other funding. It's true [laughs], we tried. And I mean, they live off of us, and we're not asking for much, like twenty thousand dollars, [which] for them is absolutely nothing. That's a Birkin [bag], girl—that's nothing.

There were several takeaways from this portion of my conversation with Luna that did indeed point to the symbiosis between not-for-profits and capitalism, a dynamic often tying the hands of program facilitators, guiding their direction and dictating various levels of sponsorship of the bodies of young folks in Ballroom. It seems, though, according to Luna, that this is qualitatively a mixed bag. Oh, and before I forget, I just want to say: Beyoncé, Madonna, and Rihanna—support the fucking Latex Ball! It's the least you can do.

Though the mentors at Hetrick-Martin picked Luna as a spokesperson for the program based on how much funding he might garner as a bright and affable teen with HIV, he felt like ultimately this need-based choice wasn't just symbiotic but mutually advantageous—it gave him a sense of purpose, which at age sixteen, is a precious vantage point that many grown-ass folks never even reach before the end of their average lifespans.

His sense of purpose intact, the trauma of being in constant proximity to death stayed with him, and as a way of metabolizing that trauma, Luna devotes a substantial part of his life to instilling those reasons to live in others—and is a riot to be around in the process.

If you ever meet Luna, or see him speak in the media, you'll see that being in the spotlight and engaging with young folks is where he shines. Even for our interview, he had me meet him at The Center, the famous LGBTQ community organization that caters to all types of needs, including STI testing, counseling, and professional development. From there, we walked down to the piers where the children usually are, voguing and such, and we just sat there shooting the shit for an hour or so about the ins and outs of his life in Ballroom. We laughed a lot. Luna still has the sunny innocence of a teen unbothered by death, which according to him isn't the case, and if so, only speaks to the lengths to which he must go to shine so effortlessly all the time. I felt like he thoughtfully carved out a unique teaching moment for me, but also like I was one of thousands of young queer folks to receive this hands-on treasure of an experience from Luna. In the end, if these mentor dates, like the one we had, were catalyzed years ago by the strategic marketing of "not-for-profit" staff who instigated them because of their need for funding, that specific type of sponsorship of young folks' bodies seems invaluable if not crucial to the future of the Ballroom community, as well as this book. So good or bad, the thought occurs, what if HMI weren't at the whims of public funding? Would there be a world-famous but globally effective ambassador to LGBTQ youth like Luna? Would Luna be something else professionally that's just as impactful? A teacher? A baker? Would other, less gregarious students have been made front and center spokespeople for HMI?

And while the person-to-person human resources of HMI turned out to be exemplary in spite of having to be powered by a need for funding, Luna also pointed to the problematic nature of the public programming and services offered by not-for-profits being dictated as such. He talks about a federally mandated push for education about and access to PrEP, a drug that helps prevent HIV infection and transmission during sexual intercourse but does not prevent other STI infections that are typically dodged by the use of a condom. And while PrEP is in many ways a godsend to the gay community, it also feels like part of the trendy false sense of invincibility money-grubbing Big Pharma tends to distill into a pill and hand out to the masses for life-long consumption. At their root, these kinds of lifestyle drugs, such as PrEP and "the Pill," which is used every day, whether or not people take it before sex, and also marketed as a skincare supplement, are functional but unabashed forms of body branding. One prevents life; the other, death.

This part of my talk with Luna reminded me of a conversation I had several years prior for the *Paris Review* with philosopher Paul Preciado about his book *Testo Junkie: Sex, Drugs, and Biopolitics in the Pharmacopornographic Era*. In it, Preciado talks about the pharmacology industry's goal and practice of inserting pills into our everyday lives with the hopes we use them for our entire lives. To Luna's point, Preciado told me: "What is happening with AIDS research is that they are also thinking of consumers who can become lifetime consumers. This is how the pharmacopornographic regime works. . . . They would say, No, no, you can fuck as much as you want, but be sure you take your pill. The management of subjectivity and identity is not so related to the body and the movements of the body, but much more to the very materiality of the body. The level of control has been downgraded to a molecular level."[6]

PrEP is a kind of body sponsorship and controls the actions of the body on a molecular level. Through this lens we can see that in order to reach their capitalist ends, Big Pharma produces drugs to be taken— and paid for—by bodies for a lifetime. Using funding as leverage, government agencies mandate that not-for-profits focus their attention on programming that ensures their clients consume the drugs Big Pharma pushes not in addition to but in lieu of services covering a range of modes of prevention, like condom use and other sexual-health practices. It's a government-sanctioned monopoly on brand identity on a molecular level.

And it gets even more complicated. As much as not-for-profits can be forcibly sucked into the capitalist machine, the capitalist machine can at times sponsor bodies in a way that creates isolated incidents of altruism and community development. Gasp. I know.

One obvious example of poignant body sponsorship that Luna and I actually discussed that day on the pier was that of Pedro Zamora, the twenty-something AIDS activist who passed away from AIDS-related complications before our nation's very eyes during the third season of MTV's *The Real World* in San Francisco. We talked about how Pedro's presence as a roommate on the show, his fierce storytelling and HIV advocacy throughout that season, his loving and rich relationship with his partner at the time, Sean Sasser, and his subsequent untimely death hit us both hard, me being an impressionable thirteen-year-old *Real World* fanatic who that same year (1995) had lost my aunt to AIDS-related complications. Luna being a contemporary of Pedro's, an activist with HIV doing the good work of prevention through storytelling. We both got chills even broaching the topic of Pedro Zamora, and Luna had this to say about him:

> It's almost like he made being gay a beautiful thing, and he made living with AIDS an educational, beautiful thing too. It was perfect timing for that. We needed that at the time. That was supposed to happen, even though I wish it hadn't happened like that. . . . Pedro did something for us.

Because I felt the same way as Luna did about Pedro, I've talked to so many folks over the years about him, and almost invariably, they agreed that the broadcasting of his storyline was some of the most socially and emotionally moving use of personal narrative in the history of television as a medium. It almost elevated reality television to a virtue.

Now, it's obvious that capitalism is the devil, and if you glean nothing else from this book, please know that I condemn it and can't wait for the day when together as a conscious society we finally get a collective clue and dismantle the beast with our bare fucking hands. That being said, I do wonder, as with well-meaning not-for-profits with their hands tied, having to operate under for-profit constraints at the behest of funders, and as with the singular-feeling case of MTV and Pedro, if body sponsorship by a straight-up capitalist brand can, in fact, address certain traumas, or rather undo those caused by capitalist greed? I know, I know. Sounds far-fetched, but just stay with me for a minute.

MTV may have "gotten it right" with its sponsorship of Pedro Zamora and his queer HIV/AIDS story, though I'm sure at least part of the reason they cast a young HIV+ Latino gay man on the *Real World* stemmed less from any sense of social obligation and more from a basic desire to shock six unsuspecting twenty-year-old strangers—some of them politically conservative—with a poz roommate at the height of stigmatization, ignorance, and paranoia surrounding how one might contract HIV, never in a million years imagining that Pedro would pass away in front of the world or anticipating how much that passing would cause a seismic shift in the hearts of millions of people. No. I think MTV inadvertently provided a service and based on the at-times vapid content in the seasons prior to and following his San Fran cast, Pedro's profound storyline was an act of social providence produced by something much greater than Bunim/Murray Productions. Still, one for team MTV, I suppose.

But as we discussed in chapter 1, MTV, pardon the pun, dropped the *ball* when it came to sponsoring bodies in Ballroom by way of their flat and cruel portrayal of the kids from Vogue Evolution on *America's Best Dance Crew* and then screwed up even more acutely on the same show with its maltreatment of Ballroom legend Leiomy Maldonado, completely botching almost every chance to positively represent a woman of trans experience on television in the early days of doing so. When I'd finished writing chapter 1, I was ready to leave the Leiomy through line behind, not necessarily looking for some sort of act of redemptive sponsorship for her, and while her acting turns on *Pose* and further expansion into the world of choreography were notable professional addendums, I didn't at all see the value in using them as a response that might dignify MTV's shitty behavior a decade earlier. Then of course, that changed, because what do I know.

∞

In February 2020, my photographer friend Kareem and I were fortunate enough to attend a leadership retreat in the Catskills with a program called H.E.A.T. (Health and Educational Alternatives for Teens), like HMI, an organization funded by the City of New York and offered to young LGBTQ BIPOC folks, many of whom are members of the Ballroom community. Michael Roberson invited Kareem and me to the retreat for book research, and I will forever be grateful. The trip was made up of a number of those workshops Michael is famous for: a mash-up of pop culture, discussions of theological and sexual health, and YouTube tutorials, flanked by personal context and life-changing conversations on the history of ball culture, realness, the politicization of Black fem bodies, trauma, etc.—all meant to spark in this group of young people a sense self-worth, history, and community pride.

Kareem and I were a little standout in that we were there on research and *way* older than the kids there, who were primarily in their early twenties, but after watching an array of videos of ball legends, some a refresher from my Vogue'ology days eight years prior and participating in almost therapeutic levels of discourse around systemic oppression, we were welcomed into the fold. We were gratefully able to transition from being outsiders to guests to family by the time the weekend was over. But this is how Ballroom has always worked: it's an exclusive club that welcomes every outsider.

Toward the end of the last day of the retreat, Michael showed us a series of brutal videos showing the marginalization of LGBTQ folks, the second to last of which was a horrifying incident where two men in Newark took turns beating up a Black trans women as she apologized profusely for simply existing, and instead of intervening, passersby recorded the scene, saying things like, "It's a man." By that point, I was emotionally drained. I'd cried a lot of the weekend, tears of joy and outrage, but I guess by now you know that making me cry isn't that hard a task, though I swear it's a result of aging! Like unsightly grays randomly springing up all over my head, the older I get, the more I'm unexpectedly endeared to babies and dogs and triggered by the plight of others. The worst. Anyhow, what I really wasn't ready for was the very last video Michael showed us.

Leiomy Maldonado hits the screen.

Time freezes.

Long, lean, polished, and fierce, she's seen teaching a voguing class in the city, the team of Black and brown bodies behind her catwalking their way across the floor like the world's most elegant answer to fascism and other patriarchal bullshit. She sails across a dance studio. Struts down a city street. She runs like the winning athlete she is. She spins in slow motion under the soft disco lights of a ball, the category, vogue fem. Leiomy's voice blends in sweetly as the images roll across the screen:

Hey Lei, what did you do to make a mark on this world?
What mountains did you climb?
Which angels gave you their wings?
Which skies have you flown,
And when you reached the heavens,
who was there to catch you when you fell?
And did they tell you that you saved them too?
Like you saved me?
That they're mending their wings and holding them up to the sun?
Just to step back, and watch you fly.
So, go head, Lei
Fly.

The final slide reads:

Every Athlete can leave a mark on this world.

Then:

Equality

Then the Nike "Swoosh":

Nike.com/equality

Watching that clip was rapturous, and it turned me into a blubbering mess. I yelled out, "When was that?!" in spite of myself. The kids told me the Nike commercial was for Pride 2018. "Omg," I said, wiping away tears. "You all need to slow down with this making-me-cry shit."

Why was I crying? Well, even though this commercial was done starkly in the name of capitalism, I was touched by the completeness of Leiomy's narrative, how this Nike ad was a plain case of what MLK had said, that "the arc of the moral universe is long, but it bends toward justice," even if I knew that Nike might have only been leveraging the televised redemption of folks like Leiomy, or Serena Williams, or Colin Kaepernick to sell shoes, it still felt like justice. I hope I get the chance one day to ask Leiomy whether, outside of whatever Nike paid her, or maybe actually including it, if that's what it felt like, justice. I'm certain there was a discrepancy between the two bodily feelings of her MTV . . . *Dance Crew* performance of fierce voguing being met with Lil Mama telling her to "Act like a lady," versus the grace of starring in her own commercial, doing her own dances, on her own terms, and in the end, to a backdrop of her own words. I'm sure of it.

Sometimes justice is pricey, political, poetic, or murky. Sometimes it is so crystal clear, and in those moments, despite how shitty MTV, Nike, and we all are, even if only momentarily, America becomes an enlightened witness. And maybe that's the point.

Americans cannot be extracted from capitalism until it is dismantled. If the very foundation of American capitalism is the historic disenfranchisement of Black bodies, specifically through the trauma of enslavement and the riches it afforded the white class over centuries of enforced free labor; and if all such traumas in the name of capital reside in the body and can only be metabolized thoughtfully through the body, then it stands to reason that the branding and sponsorship of Black and brown bodies, whether industrial or nonindustrial, run the risk of compounding those traumas but also, perhaps, even holds the potential to undo some of them. And from what I can deduce through this writing process, having talked to so many folks in the Ballroom community, the difference between further harm done and a path to healing is the intention and awareness of the individual being sponsored. Like Luna and everyone else I've interviewed. "Getting it right" when it comes to these Ballroom partnerships with corporate entities isn't just saying no to them; it's saying yes, being an enlightened witness—and then doing it your way. That seems to be the path to ownership, a world of entertainment and culture performed *and* owned by Ballroom.

Twiggy Pucci Garçon explains how *Pose*, the show that she works on, starts to do it right by having actual Ballroom bodies influencing every aspect of the production, unlike in the past when resources were just taken from the community:

> I mean, getting it right is involving Ballroom meaningfully at the crux of the production, but what does that look like, and what does that mean? One example is having production crew from the actual community in the writers' room, choreographers from the Ballroom scene coaching the movement, and some of the makeup artists, hairstylists, and the production assistants working on set. All of that, to me, is getting it right. To say that, in season one, we had the largest cast of LGBTQ people ever on a TV show is getting it right—and to continue now to be in season three, where one of Ballroom's greatest icons, in my opinion, Jack Mizrahi, now Gucci, is a staff writer. So that's getting it right for this particular show. Saying you are committed to meaningfully involving Ballroom at as many levels as possible—that's a different conversation. And getting it right on the next Ballroom-focused project will look totally different, and hopefully expand.
>
> I would like to see Ballroom not go through this cycling in and out of mainstream over the years, as if it can just be tossed around. Ballroom is here and has been here. Ballroom is meaningful. It is real. It's not a joke. It's not a game. It's not here just to entertain people. It deserves as many resources, as much attention, and as much people power as every other thing that is remotely similar to it.
>
> I often compare [Ballroom] to sports. We have international leagues for basketball, football, swimming. Why don't we have that for Ballroom? Why aren't these same brands and corporations treating us the same? If y'all want to give us a coin, give us a coin to create the sort of infrastructure that people can sustain themselves around. Growing up, I always heard you couldn't put Ballroom on a resume. Well, I have made it part of my life's mission to disprove that notion. I was like, "Why can't you?" And so, I don't want to be an anomaly. I don't think it should only be me. I think it should be any and everyone who wants to make Ballroom their career. There should be a path to do that. I'm tired of this, "Oh, *Paris Is Burning*. Oh, *Vogue*. Oh, Vogue Evolution. Oh . . . these things just come up and then just go away for a while." But I say, No, kiki happened. No, *Pose* happened. Now, *Legendary* happened. We just need to keep going.

BLACK FEM TRANS STORIES

THE INTERVIEW

w/LaLa Zannell

The House of the Lord. The House of LaBeija. The House of Representatives. Lala B. Holston-Zannell has an epic trajectory, having been a product of and having worked in a range of American systems—including the prison-industrial complex. But after each and every one of those "sponsorships," she gathered and retained the pertinent knowledge needed to be of critical service to the many communities she's been a part of. Today, as the American Civil Liberties Union's trans justice campaign manager, she is uniquely positioned to help the LGBTQ community dismantle structural oppression, in particular, working to ensure that Black women of trans experience rebuild and recover from systemic trauma. LaLa's insight and tenacity are only outdone by her warmth, which she infused into the following odyssean story of her journey from overwhelmed house mother and sex worker to holding the highest position of any Black trans woman in the ACLU's one-hundred-year history. My hope is that hearing, entirely in her own words, her story, which took her from incarceration to domestic violence to negotiating a job offer, will help folks in Ballroom, other trans women of color—and everybody for that matter—nimbly navigate such extraordinary spaces and know the power of being an enlightened witness who is backed by the right organization.

LALA: When I moved to New York, I was done with Ballroom. I had been incarcerated in Atlanta for doing sex work, just got caught up in this bad scene. Previous to that, there had been a trans woman killed on the stroll, and so the neighbors, the white folks, were tired of us anyway, because the stroll was in the white neighborhoods— downtown Atlanta. They were tired of us on their property and clients on their streets and stuff. So, City Hall did this real overhaul; they started being tough on sex work. They pulled all the benches up. They cut the trees in all our little cuts, so you couldn't do anything. I was arrested and ended up going to jail, and the judge ended up giving me the hardest sentence ever because at that time I still had a Michigan ID, so he was like, "Oh, you're coming down here to do sex work?!" I had the money to bond out, but I refused to, and the judge was mad about that, too, but I was like, "If you're going to get me for something, it's going to be soliciting. You're going to get me for doing what I did. You will *never* get me for soliciting no rides. I live around the corner—how am I soliciting for a ride?"

That experience was . . . I think that's where God wanted me to be. My mind was too busy at the time. Like, every day I was living to survive. Surviving—not thriving. I wasn't thinking about what tomorrow looked like, or the next five days or whatever. I was balancing so many other people's lives.

I transitioned when I was fifteen. Now I'm forty-two, and over my lifespan, I've had *so* many chosen children. And, like a parent, I put my life on the back burner when I was still a child myself. I was living life not realizing I was missing out on my own life. So, I think when I went to jail and had all that time, it made me really rethink that. I couldn't do it anymore; I needed to refocus. What was I gonna do when I got out of there? My spirit was telling me, *You have to leave Atlanta, because if you don't, nothing's going to change.*

I'll never forget. I got out on Mother's Day, and I got out to nothing. All those chosen kids I had, all those brothers and sisters I had, couldn't hold down a $750/month apartment. Everybody had moved and scattered. I didn't know where my shit was. I was like, you know, *What?* This is a reality check for me, that these folks are broken and in trauma—it's transactional, respectfully so, and they're kids. I'd put my faith in them to handle things they could not handle. At that moment, I had to break away, and do what's best for me and live my life.

One of my girlfriends was like, "Oh girl, come to New York. They have opportunities, they have this, they have that." I was like, okay, I'll come or whatever. I went out one last night, and honey, it was Pride Weekend in Atlanta. After that I went and gathered all that I could, gave my stuff away. My sons and them were like, "You really moving to New York?" I was like, "I swear, I'm on a flight tomorrow. I'm outta here." They were like, "Wow. Where you gonna stay?" I was like, "I'll figure it out."

My sister and them were staying in a shelter in New York at that time, but my ego was there. I was like, "I ain't goin' to no shelter, boo. That's not where it's at." So I did what we typically do, flip through a Rolodex, and we find things—oh, my ex lives in New York! So, I went back down memory lane, moved in with him, and that wasn't a good thing. It ended up being a toxic, domestic-abuse relationship, *very* violent. I'd never been a victim of domestic abuse in my life, and in that situation, I was like, *Who is this person?* I think it stemmed from his sister, who was living with him at the time. She was a bitter, cisgendered woman who was very upset and couldn't understand how happy I was and how he could love me. She was a lonely and bitter person.

While I was there, I met a woman who's now my chosen sister, Christina Herrera, and we went to The Center for something, and she told me to come to the back where they were doing this trans support group. We went, and they introduced me to all these amazing trans women, and at the end of that group, when it was time to go home—I didn't want to go. But I also didn't know where I was gonna go. They did an intake for me and called the New York City Anti-Violence Project, where I later ended up working. They got me into a shelter and even in *that* moment, I was like, "I am not going to no shelter . . ." But I still trusted the process and was just like, *Fuck it, it's better than going back home to my ex.* At that moment, I left everything there—I mean everything, clothes, everything. I mean, he didn't even know I left, and I had to get an order of protection so that he wouldn't try to find me.

I remember when I got to the shelter and [was] sitting in intake and seeing all of these cisgendered women and just feeling like I was in prison again, like, *God, I'm at rock bottom again—what's going on?* But what I learned in that experience of being in a shelter was that God put me there so that I could get my priorities right by putting me in a place that wasn't easy, where I was not going to get comfortable. God also put me in that space because prior to that, I could not *stand* cisgendered women. Like, if you were not related to me, I was not engaging with you. Don't play with me, don't kiki with me, don't laugh, you stay on your side of the street—I'll stay on my side. I learned in that experience that there were so many women who were broken. So many women had lost their children, because shit happens. But through that process, they were so empowered by me and my confidence and me being me. I helped pretty much all the women who I was in the shelter with. They're all out now, and

I helped one of them get her kids back; I helped another one who was battling addiction. And they would really just defend me. I used to get into fights in the neighborhood, and they were like, "No girl. You not gonna go to jail—I'll whup their ass for you!" I was always reminding them that they were beautiful, that they're smart and that that was just a situation that they were in. It didn't mean they were gonna be stuck there.

Just seeing how people discredit and treat homeless people, like they're lazy . . . and then how people in shelters think that they've fucked up in life. I heard their stories and what they went through, people with mental conditions who the system just throws into homeless shelters, and how their families just discard them and say, fuck them. All of that experience taught me so much and humbled me so much. So, from there, because the organization helped me out so much, I wanted to help other trans people get those same services. I ended up landing a job at the New York City Anti-Violence Project. I started working the front desk, then went to being an intern to becoming an organizer, and then became the lead organizer. I ended up working there for like ten years.

But I was so burnt out from direct service work—and I was doing work with *violence*. All of it was around violence against queer and trans folks all across the country. All the time—violence, violence, violence. I couldn't escape it. It was like I was reliving that trauma all the time, putting my living experiences in the closet, locking it up, and not allowing myself those feelings, so that I eventually crashed and burned. I was mentally in a place that was just not sustainable.

Some dear friends kept sending me this job description for a position at the ACLU, and I kept being like, "That's the ACLU; they don't want me, honey. I'm not gonna make it over there—they're so corporate!" And they just kept telling me to apply, just apply, just apply. I didn't apply. [Laughs] They called wanting to know why I didn't apply, and I told them I just didn't think I was a fit, and that I'd missed the deadline. They still said apply. So, I did my resume and applied. Oh, and I want to point out that I would have never applied to the ACLU if it weren't for Jonovia; that is my sister. We went to lunch before I applied, and she was saying all the reasons I should do it, and I was like, *Gosh, you're right.* I just went for it.

The lady who ended up being my boss called me and asked if I could do an interview that day at 4 p.m., and I was currently working and couldn't leave, so she said I could do it over the phone. I had to leave, sneak into the conference room like I'm just on the phone when really, I'm doing a job interview. I thought I sucked at the interview because people were knocking and stuff the whole time. I'm literally still working, like "Shhh. I'm on a call!" I felt like I'd bombed it so bad, but they ended up actually wanting me to come in and do a second interview and present to them what my vision for trans justice was. So, I did this presentation with a bunch of people standing around.

In that moment, I wanted it. In that moment, I was like, *This feels right.* It felt comfortable. My spirit was like—go for it. I did a third interview, and it was months before I heard from them, so I thought, girl, I didn't get the job. Then I got the email saying they wanted to give me an offer. They sent it to me, and I was like, *Well this is different* . . . I sent the letter over to my friend to look it over for me, because I thought it sounded good and I was ready to go, and my friend was like, "No, girl. Look at the offer—and negotiate. They're gonna like that." So, I negotiated to not start working for two months, because after the Anti-Violence Project, I needed a break. I was going to lose my vacation and other time, and so the ACLU also compensated me for that. They bought out my 401(k). I negotiated my travel needs. I asked them, "What does it mean for you to hire me, and what does it mean for a white woman who has never supervised a Black trans woman to do so?" I negotiated so that she had to train with a professional developer who was a Black woman from Vision Change Win.

Now, is it perfect working there? No. The ACLU has been around for over one hundred years, and all those old ways are embedded within, *but* they are more open to having those hard discussions than in any other workspace that I've seen or been in. I remember on my first day working there, I was in a staff meeting, and my eyes were so big about the way that people were talking. I was like, *I would be fired if I said some shit like that,* because they were so vocal! I was like, *Wait, this is a weird environment—they really just say what they want!* My boss told me they believe in the civil liberty of freedom of speech. It's different than working at a queer organization, because at the ACLU we're maybe like 2 percent of the staff and we're a staff of like five hundred. Trying to get your work seen and your issues seen is hard. You'll get overlooked if you're not like, "Hello!" And I work on a national level, so you have to work with states to change trans issues based on their laws. There are a lot of white trans men and women, but on a national level, I'm the only *out* Black trans woman.

Right now, we're working on trying to decriminalize sex work, and because of how COVID-19 has affected mass incarceration, I've been trying to get DAs around the country to decline to prosecute sex offenses, talking about how they're really lower in offense level. Now Pennsylvania's not really been prosecuting them during the pandemic, and I've got something coming up in Missouri, and I have to go back into PA because now they're using other ways to criminalize sex work—"We didn't arrest them for prostitution, but we got them for loitering," they say. Or they get folks for attempting to buy or attempt to sell. So, I'm having a lot of conversations about how those are still lower offenses and how we just shouldn't be arresting *anybody* right now—even with the trans murders that are happening.

It's sad, but we expect Black men not to kill us; we expect them to understand when we live under hyper toxic masculinity where Black men's masculinity is so fragile, in an administration [Trump] that says you can kill us, beat us up. You're not supposed to hire us, and can't get healthcare; you can't befriend us, but then you tell Black men not to harm us or hit us. You can't do both. We have to have a median where we're dismantling what is happening. That's what's missing. And then we want to put people in jail, and I'm not for putting *anybody* in jail. Even those who cause harm.

I remember I was working with Islan Nettle's mother, Delores, and I supported *her* decision, because she was her mother, and if she wanted justice and wanted him to go to jail, I'm supporting her. But my personal values? He's not going to learn anything. He's gonna go to jail, be in the system, and then he's going to be praised for killing a trans person! Where's the lesson learned? People want you to go to prison and pay your debt to society, but when you're Black, the debt is never paid. If we as Black people don't forgive and let them live, then the white man is gonna come along and put more obstacles in their way to send him back to prison, because they're making money on us in prison. As Black people, we have to forgive, or we'll never heal.

But we have to heal within the trans community first. I walked realness for a while back when I was walking balls, but then I just left it alone, because for me, it was so . . . harsh. Because you have gay men, who don't even like women, judging it. Their idea of real was like Mary J. Blige and these high-glam figures and all of that. But a girl who's just regular degular with some sneakers or a jumpsuit on wasn't a look that was "real," like oh, okay . . . she's cute . . . then sometimes it's like, "Oh, look at her big ole feet," and stuff. We have to stop picking individuals apart, because you don't know that person's internal struggle. Sometimes it goes too far, and people internalize those things when it's coming from their peers. So, how they used to compete just wasn't me. I couldn't do it. Voguing—that's competition. There's elements to it, you're dancing. Runway, you're going up and down in a certain way. Realness, that's a different kind of critique. So, before we want our cisgender counterparts to love us and care for us, we have to do that ourselves. I say that coming from Detroit where it was very . . . binary. It was like, this is what a man is, this is what a fem queen is. Internalized transphobia can hurt someone, make them suicidal, cause trauma, or someone could cuss you out and whup your ass. [Laughs] Let's keep it real.

However, I can see how for some people, it might be gratifying to hear those comments. It teaches them how to prepare for those comments in the real world, because you gotta do what you gotta do to "blend." So, I will say, that I learned a lot from realness and the realness girls about contouring and what to wear to get the confidence to walk through the hood, because this is the first time I have never not lived in the hood in my entire life, so I understand. Realness can help you navigate living in your hood and hold your head up.

After that, we can call in other folks. Everyone wants to sit together and build and be allies—I don't need no allies. Allyship is a word, it's like a badge that you put on to think you've done something. You ever been to a Black Lives Matter rally and white people show up with a sign, five minutes later when it's over, they sit around and say, "Oh, hey nigger!" You *just* left the rally—what happened?! "Allyship" is only performative to them. I need you to really be in authentic engagement, in authentic partnership. We're in this together, and it's not performative. I need you to be my coconspirator in this movement together. But I think we need to get together as trans folks and settle our differences first. Our internalized racism, colorism, anti-Blackness, transphobia, xenophobia—there's a lot of that—and then bring in our LGB counterparts, and when we have that, then we can say, okay now we'll bring in our hetero-cisgendered folks. Yes, we've evolved. We've made a lot of progress. I love it. But what we don't do is educate the folks that don't think like us along the way. We say, hey this is a new law, but don't say why this law has changed. This is the harm it's caused. This is what this means.

Generational trauma is so imbedded in us that you don't even know it's in your DNA. I've got so much stuff passed down to me, and I won't ever understand it unless I sit down and try to figure it out. They say it takes over five generations to get molestation out of your family bloodline. So many things happen systemically that get passed down to us from our grandparents.

I remember my mother always told me, don't agree with me because I'm your mother—now watch *how* you say it, but if you don't agree with me, say, Ma, I don't think that was fair or right. I'm not always perfect or right. Older people always used to pick up my little sister and kiss her, and she'd be like, "Nooo." My mama would be like, "Ask my child, 'Can I pick you up?'" They still have agency even though they're a child. That's where the predatory things happen. They need agency or consent to tell their auntie or uncle, "I'm tired of sitting on your lap. I don't want you kissing me." That child at an early age needs to know that they have agency over their body and what happens to their body. That is a cycle that my mom has broken in my family, and I see my sisters and brothers and them doing it, and now their friends are too. It's beautiful to see.

THE INTERVIEW

w/Gia Love

This portion of my July 26, 2020, interview with preeminent trans advocate, model, and icon Gia Love was pure joy for me on a lazy Sunday afternoon. She is a joy to be around, and accordingly, in the aftermath of a summer stricken with the murders of Black, trans, and Black trans people (which we discussed), I wanted to ask her about how she finds and leans into joy during these cruel times as a thinking and socially engaged person sitting at the intersection of those identities. Luckily, the concept of trans joy is central to her ethos, pathos, and logos. She also cast a spotlight on some of the limits of the not-for-profit industrial complex when servicing Black women of trans experience. Enjoy.

RICKY TUCKER: I saw you speak at the Black Trans Lives Matter protest at the Brooklyn Museum the other day, and you were talking about the murder of Islan Nettles and how you all shared a trans mother. Can you tell me a little about how her passing is affecting you?

GIA LOVE: Yeah, so I wouldn't consider her a friend, just to be very clear; but I would consider her a sister. We weren't really particularly close, but I did know her personally because she was a Juicy and because she was very close with Courtney, who is my trans mother.

And that's the thing. That's what a house is like. She was a Juicy, so I loved her, but I didn't have her number, type of thing. But I can speak to her death. I remember, because it was really at the beginning of my transition. I remember probably like two weeks after her death, this Black guy tried to talk to me in the street and I was absolutely terrified. I literally ran, because I was just like, "Excuse me?" I just didn't know . . . what the result of that would be. I never really know. . . . The situation that happened with Islan was the first in my transition, the first time that I was really able to see something like that. And maybe before, when I was identifying other ways, I was blind to the reality of a trans woman, and what we go through. It was like a wake-up call, in a sense.

Before that, I feel like the younger generation wasn't *really* having a conversation about the lived experiences of trans women. Oftentimes people romanticize it, like "This experience of being a trans woman is great because then you have this relationship with trade, which is a different type of relationship than if you were a gay man." But the violence that we're subjected to because of the fact that we're trans is not really romantic—at all.

If I can control my destiny, one thing that I will just never allow to happen is that I will not be a victim of transgender-based violence at the hands of some Black nigga who's really insecure about his sexuality and feels like he needs to take that out on me. So, I'm very intentional about how I engage men. I'd rather be lonely than be dead, and I'm not commenting on women who choose to navigate those spaces, because that's a choice that they make; but for me, I have decided that if you're not treating me like I feel like I should be treated, I'd rather be lonely and really lean on the support of the people that do, even though it's not intimate love in the sense that you're fucking me, but it's like I get love from my house family, from my personal family in the Ballroom community. And that love, for me, is everlasting.

RICKY: Well, you're such a huge inspiration, and a community figure. Losing you would take a toll on your family, but also the community at large.

GIA: Right. And I get it. I get that people want to be loved, but at what expense?

RICKY: Absolutely.

GIA: So, one of the ways that I deal with transphobia, toxic masculinity, fragile men that I've engaged with in the past, is by letting them know how fucking *low* they are and how *fab* I am. I had a conversation with this man the other week. I was like, "You know what? I'm not going to take that course this time. I'm not going to go there, because I feel like that's really revealing some things about myself that I'm working through." I don't have to big myself up. They're not going to see me as the person I see myself as, no matter how I tell them that I'm the girl, that girl, the ultimate girl in the world. They won't believe that, so I won't be that to them.

So, I just explained to him how I've always gotten the short end of the stick in every relationship I've ever had with a man. A lot of these guys' sexual explorations or just *self*-explorations were done at my expense, with no care about how that would affect me. I told him, "As a trans woman, my gender identity and how that shows up in the world is very interwoven into every aspect of my life. But if *you* decide that you want to fucking freak out tomorrow and that you don't like trans women anymore, you can do that. That's a gift; that's a privilege. I live with this every day. The very reason you are attracted to me is the very same reason you fucking hate me—that's very problematic. I was like, "You need to do some healing and you need to do some work, because I choose not to allow men to explore on my time."

RICKY: *Amen.* Where do you see yourself going professionally or academically, because it seems to me like you can do so many different things.

GIA: I just want to finish school. I have so much working experience, so when people say, "What do you see yourself doing?," I don't really know, because I literally have so much working experience without having the degree, and I've had so much leadership experience in jobs. I'm actually about to transition out of my job now, and I'm going to be devoting more of my time to Black fem trans activism.

My objective is to really center our joy and not our pain. A lot of time we have resources out there, like GMHC [Gay Men's Health Crisis]. They give us PrEP, but that's not the whole entirety of my life. My life doesn't look like HIV prevention and condoms. It's like we're just running from this disease; that's what we're going to live for—to die? I want to provide resources for Black trans artists that address health from a holistic framework and also from a full-body, full-person framework. I'm not going to treat your identity; I'm going to treat your *personhood*. What do you need to thrive and be healthy? We aim to address the much-needed nuances of our identities, especially in our professional lives.

RICKY: That's really exciting. That's awesome. One thing I'd like to land on is if you want folks out there to focus more on the joy in trans lives than your suffering, tell me what brings you joy. What should we know about Gia in terms of her joy?

GIA: Well, I'm a tennis player. I love to play tennis; I love to watch tennis. Honestly, I feel that if I grew up in a household that was like, "Oh, try this, try this, go to dance classes, go to this," and they put me in tennis, I would be pro today. People don't know I play tennis, but I'm like *really* good. I love tennis—I love it.

And I love to just be in the community that I have created for myself and just really share love and receive love from the ones that I love and who love me for who I am. My happiness and my joy is just really about being around people, like-minded people, people that really care about my health and well-being, and protecting people like me and just really constructively moving forward: emotionally, in terms of our careers, really supporting each other. I have a really good core group of friends, Jonovia [Chase] being one of them, where we really work with each other. We're really respectful and intentional with the work that we do. That's the center of my joy at the moment.

RICKY: I have two things to say about that. One of them is that when you said you love playing tennis, it brings to mind to me your old love of being on the debate team. There's something about a back-and-forth that seems to engage you.

GIA: I do that. That's like my life. When I was in debate, I was in debate. When I was in tennis, I was in tennis. When I was in Ballroom—I was in Ballroom. I'm getting back into tennis now and trying to train so that I can play tournaments in the winter. Actually, one of the guys who used to train me was in the Ballroom—

RICKY: For real? Wow.

GIA: Yeah, Ryu Mizrahi. He's a legend for face. Basically, like ten years ago when I came into Ballroom, I found him there. I had my own friends, and he was with his own people, but then one of my fathers is his son, and that's how we built a relationship. He's been trying to get me to play tennis all these years, and one night I just hit him up like, "Yo, I'm ready to start playing." I sent him five hundred dollars, and I was just like, "Buy me all the things I need," and he did it, and now I'm playing. Do you live in New York?

RICKY: Yep, I'm in Crown Heights.

GIA: Okay, cute. I'm doing a cookout in August. It's going to be a celebration of Black trans resilience, well, Black trans women. I was at that Women's March, and I took issue with the fact that they're saying, like "If this is a Women's March and we're centering women, why are we saying 'Black trans'?"

RICKY: Ugh. Of course.

GIA: Because even in research sometimes, when they say "Black trans," it's a dog whistle for people, and what they think that means is they're making trans men invisible, when they're really just talking about trans women. Our experiences are very different. You know what I mean? And the reason why I will continue to center *Black* trans women is because it's a Black trans thing. Because in this country in particular, systemic racism is a thing. So, if you think that Black people are on the last rung of the ladder, and then you just want to say trans—no, Black trans women are on the fucking last rung of that ladder, and that's why we are counting twenty-five of us who have been murdered in a very specific and unique way. It's not like there's nuance to the murderers either. No. Every time, it's a Black cis man in some situation with a trans woman, and she's getting murdered by him, and his weapon of choice is a gun. So, it's a very specific narrative, right? I'm also not having it when they say, "All Black Lives Matter"—not doing that either. No. Black trans women matter. The thing is, saying that plays into that realness trope, how we're not supposed to speak about or uplift our trans-ness? No. I am a Black trans woman, and we are not going to be afraid to say that.

RICKY: That's so important. Unfortunately, there are all of these experience erasures that are happening at the moment. Maybe it's what happens when so many diverse groups form coalitions.

GIA: Right? Let's talk about it. Black trans women are disproportionately criminalized. The way that we navigate the criminal justice system is very different. There's just so much that is unique to being Black and trans. I'm not going to allow people to erase that.

RICKY: Well, I'm going to keep an eye out for the flyer, because that cookout sounds amazing.

GIA: Yeah, it's going to be great. This is everyone's opportunity to show up for Black trans women in a way that is really centered around joy, centering celebration. And hopefully it can be an annual thing.

RICKY: Do you have a name for it yet?

GIA: Yeah, it's "Gia Love in Collaboration with Friends: An Event Celebrating the Resilience of Black Trans Women." I'll be giving out roses and buttons to all the Black trans women who come.

RICKY: Love it.

MY TWO GAY DADS

w/Michael Roberson and Robert Sember

*The trappings of the not-for-profit industrial complex,
2020 vision, cosmology, astrology, and theology, the future
of Ballroom—and giving it up to the Universe*

M ichael and Robert have been emotionally and intellectually supportive of me for a decade now, and like visiting family members (on a
good day), every time we speak, I come away recharged.

They are both funny, socially engaged critical thinkers with a wealth of
knowledge on public health, philosophy, theology, the arts, pop culture,
and so much more, and accordingly, those multitudes color the pitch of
this final interview. Even in this excerpt, we cover a ton of ground. In it,
they confirm and expand upon many of the ideas we've charted throughout this book and more: not only the motives of the capitalist machine
but the trappings of the not-for-profit industrial complex, presumptions
on Blackness, the future of Ballroom and ownership of its narrative,
bodily trauma, the hidden opportunities within the COVID-19 crisis—
and how when you're in doubt, give it up to the Universe. After telling
you about them for so long, I hope M & R's warmth and brilliance come
across "in person," and like me, you finish this interview excited for the
future of ball culture, maybe even the world.

RICKY TUCKER: Thanks for doing this, you two.

MICHAEL ROBERSON: Absolutely. In March [2020], me and Dom-
inique/Tyra [Jackson] had to do this little talk over at Middle
Collegiate [Church] every year, and of course it had to be done

on Zoom. The theme was "revolutionary love." And Dr. Jackie Lewis, who is the minister there, an African American woman that graduated from Union, the very first Black and first female minister in its thirty-year history, she wanted to do this piece around what does Ballroom have to say in this moment, and me and Tyra did it. One of the things I wanted to say was, and I really believe this the more I think about it and sit with it, it began to play out: the universe is forcing us to take a cosmological pause, right? We're often always in motion. And so, asking us to take a cosmological pause. Nope. *Forcing* us to and asking us to ponder on three requests.

The first question is a philosophical question, which is, Who do you desire to be now? Not who are you? Who are you *going* to be? Who do you desire to be? You have the power to choose how you want to reflect yourself in the universe. Who do you desire to be?

The second one to me is a theological one, which is, How do you desire to love more expansively? We oftentimes hear Robert talk about James Baldwin's "ethic of love." This thing that we do has to be grounded in love, not only personal, right?, but in a collective way.

And the third one is a political one, which is, how do we begin to organize away from a political right not to die versus the right to *live*. Those are two separate things, and I just think as the year begins to unfold itself, to me, that's what's playing out— and it's not accidental. I remember coming into 2019, saying that 2020 was a year of perfect vision, because in order to have perfect vision, the old, that what you always saw, you have to begin to let that go. Let it die.

RICKY: Let it die—and see differently. But you can't see with those same eyes. The notion of being reborn is so necessary.

ROBERT SEMBER: "Crises" and "apocalypse" being the words, "crisis" meaning an opening, "apocalypse" meaning the sort of flowering of things. An apocalypse, as the sort of opening out of these profoundly troubling times. And the question is, are we going to seize the freedom that this moment, in a way, is offering us? And I have to say, I have very, very bad days, because as I look at the way in which I see people behaving, [it] is so destructive of the freedom that they're being offered: to be free of hatred, to be free of the four hundred years of history, to sort of really move into a new era of re-creation and of a kind of loving renewal. It's just . . . really devastating.

And it feels like these fires [in the forests of California] are representative of the force this energy of transformation can be in the direction of life or in the direction of really extraordinary death.

MICHAEL: But always life, because death is this sort of precursor for life. But to your point, Robert, folks don't know the notion of reseeing differently. Folks don't know that it's a moment of freedom—if you've always been abused, right? If you only knew that part of what you call love has always been traumatic and the dysfunction has become so functional, then when you're offered new sight, that's painful.

ROBERT: That is painful.

MICHAEL: And so, people self-medicate, all kinds of holding on to old structures.

RICKY: Michael, I have two questions. You've probably told me this before, but how did you find Ballroom? And what was Ballroom before AIDS and what was it after, with all of these sponsorships and sort of partnerships with nonprofit agencies? What did it look like before, and what did it look like right after?

MICHAEL: I'll talk about that piece first. I can't tell you with first-hand experience what Ballroom looked like pre-AIDS, because I was not in the House-ball community yet. I can tell you from a historical consciousness kind of way, but I didn't get involved in the Ballroom community until '94, '95, and didn't know about Ballroom until like 1990, '91, because Ballroom didn't come to Philadelphia till 1989, and to some degree, it was through *Paris Is Burning* that I found it. And then going to clubs and seeing people vogue, but I didn't know that was *Ballroom*, just knew that that was Black gay culture.

You'd be in the clubs and people would scream out house names, "Ferragaaaaamo!" and stuff like that. That's when I realized. But I *can* tell you what Ballroom was like before community interventions, before the nonprofit-industrial complex.

RICKY: Yes. That's the term I was searching for, "the nonprofit-industrial complex."

MICHAEL: There's a relationship between what Ballroom looks like today, with these community-based organizations, to what it did when I first got to Ballroom and prior to that. So that's number one, but number two, I got into Ballroom following my children. Then I worked at Kennedy High School [in Philadelphia] as a crisis counselor, and Damon Hume, who was one of my first children, winds up being the icon, Jay Blahnik. He went to Kennedy High School, and then it was Leeroy; he went to Pennsauken High School [in New Jersey]. And my son Jay Lee, who had gotten into the house-Ballroom community. Jay became an Ebony; Leeroy became a Cartier. And so, they gave me the courage to follow them, because I wanted to get involved. So, it's an interesting thing around how you can then be led by your children, which has nothing to do with one's age necessarily, or one's status in life, but it is dialogical in so many ways. And so, following them, I became a member of the House of Romeo Gigli in 1995, and then maybe a year and a half later left Romeo Gigli and followed Jay in '96 to the House of Ebony.

Then I moved to New York City in 1999. And then three, four months later, we left the House of Ebony and created a House of Manolo Blahnik, in 2000. And then in 2003, one of them decided to leave the House of Blahnik because it was becoming something that they necessarily didn't desire it to be. And I wanted us to begin to look at what I call internalized racism, where we're naming all of our houses after white designers.

My friend John Gabriel, who was an Xtravaganza, created this initiative, sort of this intersection between Ballroom and spirituality, the House of Saints, a collaboration with Unity Fellowship Church. He and I began to have a conversation around forming a house. And then I stole Dominique Jackson—Tyra—from the House of Allure, and we created House of Maasai, named after the African tribe, Maasai. But then I took Maasai and merged it into the House of Miyake-Mugler, and I became the New York father; Tyra, the New York mother. Then I left Mugler in 2008 and cofounded the House of Garçon with Shannon, Whitney, and Julian. Then I left Garçon, and became a Milan, left Milan, and now co-created a house with my two sons, Trey and Benny.

I think my biggest tragedies that impacted me and my consciousness were being teased every day when I was young for being extremely feminine, being called "faggot" and "sissy" all day, every day, probably is in relationship with me becoming big and going to the gym.

So that's one tragedy, then being molested between the ages of three and five. And then my father wasn't there, and so, feeling abandoned, which explains why I created my first house with my first child, Jay Blahnik. And this latest house I created with two of my other sons.

RICKY: Speaking of family, I've tried to remain conscious in the book of just saying people's names, saying their names out loud at the end of a thought about them. And there's so many folks that keep coming up as through lines throughout everyone's story. Hector [Xtravaganza] is one of them. Arbert Santana is another. So many people have talked about them in interviews. So, a question I have for you, Robert, is I've read the article you wrote for *Arts Everywhere*, this idea around the body as a living archive. Can you tell me more about that in the context of Ballroom?

ROBERT: At the moment I've become very captivated by the writing—

RICKY: *My Grandmother's Hands?*

ROBERT: Exactly, exactly. I've been teaching sort of the past two, three years, and in the spring, as COVID was happening, I was teaching for the third time, this course called "Enfleshment," and it really is sort of an attempt to try and pull through a lot of these ideas. So many of them originate with Michael and certainly with what I have been so blessed and grateful to have received by proxy, through him and his Union Theological Seminary education—

MICHAEL: Robert was like a student; Robert was a classmate by proxy.

ROBERT: I was! I really became that kind of leech in the whole thing, so that experience was really transformative for me as well. But this idea that we live through our bodies—the fancy way of saying it is the phenomenology of life—Ballroom has a phenomenology, very unique and specific conditions of lived experience. The work with the body in Ballroom is core to all of that.

This idea stems from how Ballroom emerges from the marginalized experiences of transgender women, particularly, that very intentional and very intense relationship to the questions of embodiment. That dialectic, that conjunction of everything that has been impressed onto me, the historical identity issues that have been impressed onto me from this culture. The inherent dignity of the body. So, this question of the truth of the body is so profound. And for me, one of the remarkable things about Ballroom is how that gets externalized and made available as a kind of collective embodiment and a collective consciousness.

I think this is how Ballroom is actually carrying through this profound ethic that you can trace back to African sociography and aesthetics—the aesthetics, not the artistry, the aesthetics, the central understanding of the world through the body and in relation to the body and to collectivity, that fundamental awareness of interdependence, that capitalism is intent on fragmenting in order to be able to alienate and commodify. In Ballroom, there is this deep sense of the performing body, the moving body, or what we could say in a certain sense is the *resurrected* body. This is so radical because it speaks to an anti-capitalist sociality.

As the interview you, Pony, Benji, and I did together talks about, there's a certain sort of violence that gets played out through this distinction between appropriation and commodification. I think the body knows all kinds of things. It gets layered; there's an archeology now we know through epigenetics, which is becoming so important, that there is a transgenerational transmission, not only of trauma. I mean, so much of the focus is on adverse childhood events, the negative stuff. But there is also a transmission of the things that we would call resilience, of those things that are about survival of the sort of traces of all that embodied awareness that enable you to make a way out of no way. These are the stories that I feel we get that are witnessed and told; this is what it means to hold the problematic. To be of history but not confined by history.

MICHAEL: It's where you come from.

ROBERT: To know you come from somewhere.

MICHAEL: Yeah.

ROBERT: But you are coming—you're becoming. And I think this is so extraordinary. I mean, the person who's working this is Resmaa Menakem in *My Grandmother's Hands*.

RICKY: Oh, it's such a good book.

ROBERT: Resmaa studied with a psychiatrist at Harvard who has for many decades now run a trauma lab. He's really brought this understanding of the critical central importance of the body, especially within trauma work, that you can't do meaningful trauma work through just talk therapy. And this is where in Ballroom I think there's also a therapeutics.

I mean, you've heard Michael tell the story a fair amount, how in an interview, Leiomy said, "I vogue in order to survive. I am an angry Black trans woman to carry all of this. I vogue in order to be able to live." I think that there is something to the excess of trauma, and of the sort of day-to-day work of survival, that Voguing is profoundly therapeutic for, collectively therapeutic.

MICHAEL: Robert, you are speaking something that Tyra and I were just discussing. You know that Dasia just passed about two weeks ago.

ROBERT: Yes. I read that.

MICHAEL: Remember I had to call Tyra [Dominique Jackson] and she broke down? She was doing a photo shoot, and she broke down, then she called me back. She made this connection that you just made, and she wasn't only talking about Dasia, but about all these other girls too. She said, "I got to do more. I got to do more. I really got to do more."

There are no spaces in New York City where these girls can have the hermeneutics to perform, and because there's no space to perform, they're dying. The hermeneutics of the body, you think of Princess Janae, even though she's riddled with cancer and pain, she was performing to save her life, to be able to survive, and now there's no space for that.

ROBERT: You know in my wrestling with the academy, I was just talking with my mother. She was saying to me that she feels just perpetually sad and ready to cry. I was saying to her, "I think feeling sad makes sense to me. I feel sad. I have some really bad days. I feel very sad. There's lots to be sad about." I mean, the work of letting go, when you cross over, the work of changing, there's a lot of suffering. Michael, you were talking about this. I mean, to be liberated to claim your freedom, this is hard work. All kinds of shit is going to be kicked up, and you're going to have to acknowledge the pain of letting go of certain things.

I told her that in the United States, we need to remember that violence and hatred is a particular form of intimacy. And the wound, the kind of deep wound that is the central wound of this crisis . . . I was saying to my mother, how one of the things that's so hard about being here is I feel that through COVID, what we need in these moments is to be able to be together in a trusting and loving and compassionate way. But the fact is, is that again, we're seeing that it is poor, working-class, or what the Poor People's Campaign refers to as low-wealth, those folks who are just always teetering on the edge, who are bearing the burden of this. It's a constant reminder that we are connecting again to the unaddressed wound. The wound of oppression, this wound of racism, this wound of inequality.

I said to my mother, we may be physically distanced, but we don't need to be socially distant. We can be socially very intimate with each other, and all of those sorts of things. I hate the war metaphors that get used in medicine, but we have to, like our ancestors, my grandparents, my mother's parents, came together during the Second World War, we have to do this. But one of the things in the United States that makes it so fucking hard to do this is that we *are* the war. The wound is the war. How do you heal in this? It's a really sort of devastating process.

RICKY: Well, your mother's a Pisces, right?

ROBERT: She's a Pisces. They really feel the deep, deep sadness of this moment. But at the same time, she's Pisces, so she is relentless. I mean, at the same time as we were talking, I was going, "I have no worries about you. You have so much life force that you'll be able to move through this." So, I do think that in the Ballroom scene, you see all of these things, you see this wound,

you see the working through of this wound. There's a lot more
to say.

MICHAEL: It's true. Robert, you were talking about epigenetics and
this notion of the transmission, we oftentimes think of a generation of pain and suffering but not this thing around resilience. I
think it's absolutely important. In Ballroom, it's not special, necessarily; it's just indicative of. So, one of the reasons why, when
I wanted to go into a PhD program, I wanted to view this work
through an African American studies lens versus a queer lens
was because it is just this assumption that Ballroom, ontologi-
cally, is Blackness. So, of course, there's really not an ontology of
Blackness, but it is what you talk about, Robert, the fact that Ne-
groes woke up, went to bed, woke up, went to bed for centuries
as slaves, somewhere in their ontology they must have known
that this wouldn't last forever. It's the economy of knowing that "I
know that I know what I know," and thinking you're right. What
if we lifted that up more today?

ROBERT: Which is why, Michael, this is the thing that I've been puz-
zling, sitting with. I've been learning a little bit, reading a little
bit about the "deaths of despair." It's been around for a few years
now in public health. "Why is the United States the only country in the developed world, the advanced, the wealthy nations,
where there is a declining life expectancy?" And it's not everybody. White people without college education, their life expectancy is declining significantly. A lot of that decline in the past
few years is owed to an incredible increase in opioid overdoses
and suicides. And often those are exactly the same thing. And
this is where Ruby Sales [social justice activist] goes, "We have to
ask the question, 'Where does it hurt?' And why do some white
people think that other white people are unredeemable?"

MICHAEL: There you go. That's so true.

ROBERT: Folks are calling this the "deaths of despair" because this
constituency, these white folks without college education, just
seem to have the sense that they're falling out of relevance. They
are in a way, a problem, indicative of a problem. That W. E. B. Du
Bois, "What does it feel like to be a problem?" Now the recent
research, and this is the point I want to make, is on this, and

among the issues that they survey are on levels of hopelessness and levels of stress.

Then they do this research across many different communities, including African American and Latinx communities, and match up the populations, the samples, same thing, education level, region, employment, or unemployment, whatever it might be. They try and control for all of those variables; white folk score unbelievably high on hopelessness and reported stress.

MICHAEL: And that's not funny, but it is. Because they should be. Yeah, sorry, go ahead.

ROBERT: African Americans are much more hopeful or report being much more hopeful. The speculation, the hypothesis . . . I mean, part of it is these white folks have much lower church membership and church attendance than other white folks and much lower rates of holding relationships together. There's much more social isolation.

Another really exquisite case study of this is Nick Kristof of the *New York Times*. He's a Pulitzer-winning columnist. He went back and he looked up what had happened to every student in his high school in the year that he graduated. Predominantly white. Almost every single one of them who stayed was dead. Drugs, murder, suicide, early cancer, smoking, whatever. Whereas the generation above them, their parents and their grandparents, robust, healthy, active, optimistic, but with this band of people in their fifties, despair, despair, despair.

RICKY: What do you think the demarcation between these generations is then? Is there a hypothesis of what happened?

ROBERT: Neoliberalism.

RICKY: Hmm. You can say that again.

ROBERT: Neoliberalism. The war on the poor. Just this complete sort of abandonment. But I think I'd add to that, what Ruby Sales says, "The realization," especially for that band of folks, "that white supremacy is swiftly losing its currency."

RICKY: And then the disparity between what they've been sold about being "supreme," because they're white, and the actual truth of the matter.

ROBERT: Exactly right.

MICHAEL: Do you remember, Robert, though, at Union, this is when I was living there in 2015 as a resident, they did this thing. I forgot what it was, but it was when Dr. [Eboni] Marshall Turman and Dr. [Sara] Azaransky were on this panel. I remember, Dr. Marshall Turman said that "white supremacy is on death row." It sounded like, oh she just wanted to sound like Cornel West or something like that, but I think it speaks to what you were talking about, this notion of currency.

ROBERT: I think so. It's going to take a long time to die, but I do think it's unsustainable. I mean, it's spiritual death. Capitalism is spiritual death.

MICHAEL: Absolutely.

ROBERT: And white supremacy is just the concentration of that in every aspect of one's life. And so, you can't stay spiritually dead and thrive. You are a zombie, and you start to take other folks down with you or you make more zombies—or you disappear.

MICHAEL: And Rob, to that last point about that study, around Black folk and their relationship to the church—and we give credence to church—but it is really the notion of theology; we just call it church.

ROBERT: Exactly. I mean, the other form of church is collective struggle. It's this thing that you were talking about, which is hundreds of years old: you go to sleep, you wake up, you go to sleep, you wake up, and you're enslaved, and you're brutalized, and your families get torn apart and everything. Something survives that, an inherent dignity, this notion "We will be free; that it is our destiny." And that our collectivity, our shared experience, is our wealth. We may be in misery, but we are immiserated in community.

RICKY: It's shared consciousness; it's a shared level of consciousness.

MICHAEL: You see oftentimes in white families this dialectical tension generationally between young folk whose parents are voting for Trump and young folks are like, "Ma, how the fuck could you?" That tension. That doesn't necessarily translate in Black communities politically, but it does translate through sexuality. You're having younger Black folks be like, "Ma how are you going to be homophobic? What's the problem?"

There's that same tension when Gabrielle Union and Dwyane Wade support their transgender daughter now, having other Black men say, "Dwyane Wade is my boy," then critique him on supporting his child. So, we have to be able to sit with this as well and understand that, you know what, Black homophobia is nothing but white supremacy we remixed with Missy Elliott on it. That's all it is.

RICKY: Ha!

ROBERT: It's true.

RICKY: No, it's true. I mean, it happens in my family all the time. My niece who is bisexual and dating a girl right now said to her little brother, my nephew, "You sound like a girl right now." Like, what?! And it's so hard to explain in real time to them why that's wrong. I could easily be correcting them all day. Anyway.

ROBERT: Yeah. The long work.

RICKY: When we talked with Pony and Benji, Robert, you mentioned becoming an aware witness in these exchanges with different corporations or different business ventures. So, I guess, my question is for Michael, do you feel like with *Pose* and *Legendary* and all this stuff, is the Ballroom community coming closer to ownership of these ventures?

MICHAEL: Well, ownership of what though?

RICKY: Well, like instead of someone facilitating the telling of their story, Ballroom folks owning them for themselves, financially, I guess?

MICHAEL: So, I'll say that in two ways. I think that some Ballroom folk think that that's what's happening, that they're already owning their stories. Folks in power desire for you to believe that you are now owning that space. That's number one, but let me back that up.

I remember, Robert, when we did the Whitney Biennial and that question was asked, and Dashaun said, "Vogue belongs to everyone." I remember Frank had a visceral response and said, "Kind of like a street." He said that vogue belonged to everybody. But that's how it translated into his life. And Dashaun is one of the most wonderful, nicest, warmest people that you know, very talented, but in some ways, he believes that. And I'm not saying he's wrong, but he believes that. And he's been able to capitalize off of that belief. That's number one.

The politics of being seen and recognized can be really salacious, real seductive. And it can make you believe because you're being *seen* that somehow there's some power that you own in that. To some degree, the press desires for you to believe that. The flip side of that is that it's true, because you're being seen by the boy in What-the-Fuck Kansas who can now say, "I don't have to kill myself."

There's this sort of messiness in it. So, I don't know. I do think it's interesting, these kinds of conversations that we're having, these tangents where you have some folk who believe they're extremely leftist and progressive with their, "How could you? You're selling yourself?" Blah, blah, blah, and then you've got other folks who are very much like, "Listen, this is my town. I can do the talk I want to do, and I want to make money off it. I need to capitalize off of it." And then there are those Joe Bidens in the middle, who try to balance it out. I just think that the dialogue is so important; the wrestling with it is very important, I think. And I don't know if it's necessary to reconcile that yet.

The *Pose* process is very different than the *Legendary* process. I think that *Pose* has done some things that *Legendary* has not done. If it weren't for Pose, Janet Mock would not have become the first Black trans woman to get a major production. And now she can tell these trans stories. But then some Ballroom people would say, "But she's not Ballroom. She grew up privileged." So, there's that class analysis too.

Then you have Benji Ninja [Benji Hart], who has this wonderful essay that gives a wonderful sort of race and class analysis around ownership. He asks, who does voguing belong to? It created tension in the house-ball community when they published it in one of the Ballroom forums. You had Jonovias and Gias of the world saying, "Absolutely, absolutely." You must respect Ballroom to own it.

ROBERT: Benji has a Black woman, Mariame Kaba, the prison abolitionist, as the person who sits him down and says, "You've got to think more dialectically about that." It's been a struggle for me too. I've had to sit myself down and say, "You've got to understand that the steps that are being taken, it's easy to critique. It's easy to say, 'Well, this is the failure of this particular venture. This is it's horizon. This is its limitations.'"

That's important, but you also need to be able to say, "What space has this venture opened up? What has it made possible now as the next step?" And so, you've got to think dialectically, strategically, [not] to get caught in the obsession of the critique, which is the academic temptation, where you're only able to elaborate on the failures of a particular television moment or a particular partnership. The critique is important, but it needs to be in the service of what's the next action. The critique is the foundation of the strategy.

Let's recognize that there are folks elsewhere in the world who are seeing the show and are seeing something to live for. That this makes it possible. But also, with each of these things, you say, "Well, the desire was to actually have a community speak its own story." How did this work? For *Pose*, it's a question I sit with, which is what has *Pose* accomplished? How has *Pose* fulfilled its promise? And then what is the work that remains to be done that *Pose* couldn't do? What is the work that *Pose* needs to be doing next?" And out of this is emerging a sense of the horizon of desire, which is deeply anti-capitalist. I've stopped engaging in the mundane question of, "What is art?" And I'm much more now in the movement question of, "What can art do?"

MICHAEL: What does art do?

ROBERT: That's what it is. What does it do? Not what is it? But what can it do? And let's start with that. And the question then goes, "What needs to be done in the world?"

MICHAEL: Well, you're going to find, I think, like during the AIDS epidemic, there's going to be a high demand for art next year [post-pandemic]. Art will be the theologian. It will be the theologian. Just like the pandemic.

When I went to Union, I remember being critiqued by professors, like Eboni Marshall Turman, who said I didn't lift up enough theologians. And I said, "You recommend some theologians on the imperfection of being Black and gay, then I'll lift them up."

And Robert and Ricky, both of you all, have you all heard—it's only about three minutes long—the little piece that Huey P. Newton spoke about in terms of the need for the Black Panther Party to join forces with the women's and gay liberation movement?

RICKY: Wow, no, I haven't.

ROBERT: I've heard that. It's amazing.

RICKY: I love him. *Love* him.

ROBERT: It's one of those moments where you go, "Oh my God, the world used to be so much more radical than it is now."

ACKNOWLEDGMENTS

This book would never have been possible without the loving cooperation, enthusiasm, and wisdom of the vogue, House, and Ballroom community of NYC, specifically Michael, Gia, Jonovia, J'Lin, Lee, Pony, Benji, Lala, MikeQ, Twiggy, Luna, and Robert, for whom I will be eternally grateful for their candor, their compelling stories, and their kindness for sharing them. To Roísín and Maya, thank you for allowing this process to stay new and exciting across several years, thereby making it easier and more rewarding than I ever could have imagined. A special thank you goes to Emrys Eller, Luna Luis Ortiz, and Kareem Worrell for contributing stunning images, at times, following me around from ball to ball to procure them. Thank you, Beacon Press, for upholding a long lineage of publishing smart, radical—and Black—authors until I could join the ranks. It's such an honor. I couldn't be happier. To Mindy Fullilove and the entire 400 Years of Inequality coalition, let's keep fighting, loving, and reimagining what can be. To Havanna, Trevor, Jacqueline, Toni, and the rest of the Vogue'ology crew, let's have a reunion soon! I'll be missing y'all till then.

Shout out to New York City, the only place this book could have been written. And to the New School and Goldsmiths, University of London, for laying a foundation of scholarly and professional rigor that made this intensive process seem like a breeze. To Ariel, Lindsay, Amanda, Audra, Ian, and the rest of the Byers clan, and Patrick, Elana, Jenny, K'teen, and all of Winston-Salem, NC, I am very much of y'all, ya buncha weirdos.

My infinite love and gratitude go to my five aunts, one in each borough: Gisette (Staten Island), Elsie (Manhattan), Sandy (the Bronx), Sylvia (Brooklyn), and Jackie (Queens), who throughout my education, fed me both literally and emotionally, ensuring that I could even make it to this point. Similarly, thank you, Uncle Leif! To dearest Caroline, Harrison, Andy and the McWhirter clan, Nico, Cherish, Theo, Belinda, Greg, Jack, Deepayan, Love-Jeet, Gurdeep, Mumtaz, Nicky, Vicky, and all the misfit toys of Dean House, thank you for making London my real second home. To Tony, your thoughtful encouragement has very much made this possible. An eternal thank-you goes to Leslie Goldman, along with Joanne, Rebecca, and Anne, for helping me learn that creativity can be both a profession and a family. And to Andrew, for showing me that I don't have to go missing from migration if I don't want to.

To Stephanie, Nicole, Colin, and Todd, this proves there are more 54 days to come. To the New School Five (Kate, Lila + Kai, Ted, and John), we're doing it, y'all. My undying love goes to Justin, Laura, Luis, John Reed, Lori Lynne, and everyone at the New School Creative Writing team for being a consummate safety net and a blast at parties. To Lynne Tillman, thank you for charismatically showing me the true meaning of the word "exacting." To my squirrel friends SJK, V + A, Moo + MC Mel-E-Mel, thank you for insisting that fun stay on my to-do list. Thank you to Writers House Pittsburgh (Maggie, Shuchi, and Rose), and Lambda Literary, for providing me time and space—and family. To Mr. Albert Thombs, thank you for seeing my mind at five years old, and for being a Black man and the best teacher I've ever had—and for being relentless about them both. To my godson, Archer Derven—check out what's possible.

To Neil and the spaceless timeless tether. Clocks are only a nuisance. Geography, a blue dot. Joy, an infinity promise.

Sarah, thank you for everything. I love you to the moon. Can I play my Nintendo now?

To my smart, gorgeous, kind, and hilarious Black family: Keller, David, Simone, Rana, Niyaah, D'yavion, Jonathan, Jilahn, Sincere, Selah, and Sage. I love you all more than anything. Every day we get to rewrite our story—let's seize the opportunity. And to Nana, Mimi, and Aunt Ronnie, I hope you like our edits.

Finally, to Diane. Thank you for that ride to the airport. It was worth at least ninety thousand words.

NOTES

PREFACE

1. Michael Roberson, email to Ricky Tucker and 400 Years of Inequality Organizing Committee, October 25, 2018.

2. Ricky Tucker, email to Michael Roberson and 400 Years of Inequality Organizing Committee, October 25, 2018.

3. Roberson, email to Ricky Tucker and 400 Years of Inequality Organizing Committee, October 25, 2018.

4. Tucker, email to Michael Roberson and 400 Years of Inequality Organizing Committee, October 25, 2018.

5. Roísín Davis, email to Ricky Tucker, November 6, 2018.

CHAPTER 1: WERK

1. *America's Best Dance Crew*, MTV, season 4, episode 1, August 9, 2009.

2. *Paris Is Burning*, directed by Jennie Livingston, performance by Dorian Corey, Miramax, August 1991.

3. *America's Best Dance Crew*, MTV, season 4, episode 2, August 16, 2009.

4. Sean Howe, "How Madonna Became Madonna: An Oral History," *Rolling Stone*, August 23, 2020, https://www.rollingstone.com/music/music-news/how-madonna-became-madonna-an-oral-history-94288.

5. Ryan Murphy, and Brian Falchuk, *Pose*, season 1, episode 2, FX, June 11, 2019.

6. Robert Sember, Pato Hebert, Pony Zion, and Ricky Tucker, "Now We Know We Can Reclaim the World We Want: A Conversation with Pony Zion and Benji Hart," *ArtsEverywhere*, March 31, 2020, https://artseverywhere.ca/2019/06/20/pony-benji.

7. Leocine, "bell hooks: Pt. 1: Cultural Criticism and Transformation," YouTube.com, December 10, 2006, https://www.youtube.com/watch?v=KLMVqnyTo_0.

8. *America's Best Dance Crew*, MTV, season 4, episode 4, August 30, 2009.

9. Another version of this conversation was edited by Robert Sember and appeared on *ArtsEverywhere*, June 6, 2019.

CHAPTER 2: MEMORY

1. A'Lelia Bundles, *On Her Own Ground: The Life and Times of Madam C. J. Walker* (New York: Scribner, 2001).

2. Chantal Regnault, "Introduction," in *Voguing and the House Ballroom Scene of New York, 1989–92*, ed. Stuart Baker (London: Soul Jazz Books, 2011), 4.

3. Langston Hughes, "Spectacles in Color," in *The Big Sea: An Autobiography* (New York: Thunder's Mouth Press, 1988), 273–74.

4. Hughes, *Big Sea*, 227.

5. "Hamilton Lodge Ball: An Unusual Spectacle," *New York Age*, March 6, 1926, queermusicheritage.com/nov2014hamilton.html.

6. "Hamilton Lodge Ball Is Scene of Splendor," *New York Age*, February 22, 1930, https://www.queermusicheritage.com/f-black-phil.html.

7. "Third Sex Hold Sway at Rockland When Hamilton Lodge holds 65th Masquerade Ball and Dance; Police Arrest Two," *New York Age*, March 4, 1933, https://www.queermusicheritage.com/f-black-phil.html.

8. Staples Duckett, "Double Feature," *New York Age*, March 13, 1937, https://www.queermusicheritage.com/f-black-phil.html.

9. "Celebrate Pride Month by Honoring These Black LGBTQ Trailblazers," NBC News.com, June 27, 2020, https://www.nbcnews.com/feature/nbc-out/celebrate-pride-month-honoring-these-black-lgbtq-trailblazers-n1232341.

10. "She's a He," *Jet*, August 5, 1954, https://www.queermusicheritage.com/f-black-phil.html.

11. *The Queen*, dir. Frank Simon, Evergreen (Grove Press), 1968.

12. Regnault, "Introduction," 1.

13. Mikelle Street, "Crystal Labeija: 5 Things to Know About the Ballroom & Drag Icon," Billboard.com, February 16, 2018, https://www.billboard.com/articles/news/pride/8114073/ballroom-icon-crystal-labeija-what-to-know.

14. Michelle Handelman, "Dorian, a Cinematic Perfume," Michellehandelman.com, https://www.michellehandelman.com/performance/dorian-a-cinematic-perfume, accessed January 13, 2021.

CHAPTER 3: VOGUE

1. Michael Roberson, email to Ricky Tucker and 400 Years of Inequality Organizing Committee, January 17, 2019.

2. Cristina Cacciopo, email to Ricky Tucker, February 2, 2019.

CHAPTER 4: THE CHILDREN

1. "Tongues Untied," Africanah.org, June 28, 2015, retrieved October 27, 2020, from https://africanah.org/tongues-untied.

2. *Tongues Untied*, directed by Marlon Riggs, Frameline/California Newsreel, 1989.

3. Robert Sember, "Live to Be Legend," *ArtsEverywhere*, June 20, 2020, https://artseverywhere.ca/2019/06/20/live-to-be-legend.

4. Ricky Tucker II, email to Ricky Tucker Senior, July 28, 2011.

5. Ricky Tucker Senior, email to Ricky Tucker II, July 28, 2011.

6. Ricky Tucker II, email to Ricky Tucker Senior, July 29, 2011.

CHAPTER 5: CHURCH

1. "Michael Jackson Studio 54 Interview," YouTube, posted January 6, 2010, https://www.youtube.com/watch?v=cQAFmYGjaU4, accessed March 22, 2021.

2. "Mission Statement," Ultra-Red, 2000, http://www.ultrared.org/mission.html.

3. Robert Sember and Arbert Santana, "What Is the Sound of Ballroom? Dance Tracks 1973–1997 (from the Ballroom Archive & Oral History Project interviews),"

graphic, 2009, http://directus.veralistcenter.org/media/files/f9facb03a64640006ab
593ddd39988f7.pdf.

CHAPTER 6: REALNESS
1. bell hooks, *Understanding Patriarchy*, Imagine No Borders, n.d., retrieved August 16, 2020, https://imaginenoborders.org/pdf/zines/UnderstandingPatriarchy.pdf.
2. Livingston, *Paris Is Burning.*
3. Sydney Baloue, "Has the Ballroom Scene Outgrown 'Realness?'" *New York Times*, October 22, 2019, https://www.nytimes.com/2019/10/22/opinion/ball
-culture.html.
4. "bell hooks and Laverne Cox in a Public Dialogue at The New School," October 13, 2014, https://www.youtube.com/watch?v=9oMmZIJijgY.

CHAPTER 7: BODY
1. Resmaa Menakem, *My Grandmother's Hands: Racialized Trauma and the Pathway to Mending Our Hearts and Bodies*, illustrated ed. (Las Vegas: Central Recovery Press, 2020).
2. Menakem, *My Grandmother's Hands*, 63.
3. Menakem, *My Grandmother's Hands*, 151.
4. Channing Gerard Joseph, "The First Drag Queen Was a Former Slave," *Nation*, January 30, 2020, https://www.thenation.com/article/society/drag-queen
-slave-ball.
5. Paradise Garage Trademark Details, JUSTIA Trademarks, October 8, 2010, https://trademarks.justia.com/777/96/paradise-garage-77796759.html.
6. Ricky Tucker, "An Interview with Paul Preciado," *The Paris Review Daily*, December 4, 2013, https://www.theparisreview.org/blog/2013/12/04/pharmaco
pornography-an-interview-with-beatriz-preciado.

INDEX